Collins
Revision

NEW GCSE

Biology

Foundation and Higher

for Edexcel

Revision Guide +
Exam Practice Workbook

Author: Gemma Young

Contents

Contents

Classification and naming species

Grouping living things

- We can classify (group) living organisms according to their shared characteristics.

- Some characteristics (such as feathers) are unique to a group, while others (such as a **backbone**) are common to several groups.

- Animals with backbones are called **vertebrates**. There are five vertebrate groups:
  - *Fish* exchange oxygen and carbon dioxide across gills, and lay eggs (**oviparous**) that are fertilised externally.
  - *Amphibians* exchange gases through their moist, permeable skin and lay externally fertilised eggs.
  - *Reptiles* and *birds* exchange gases via their lungs and lay internally fertilised eggs.
  - *Mammals* give birth to live young, which grow inside the body of the mother. Eggs are fertilised internally.

- Vertebrates are either cold-blooded (**poikilotherms**), which means they can't control their internal body temperature, or warm-blooded (**homeotherms**), which means they can.

- Fish, amphibians and reptiles are poikilotherms. Birds and mammals are homeotherms.

- All living things belong to one of five groups called **kingdoms**:
  - **Animalia** are **multicellular**; cells do not have chlorophyll or a cell wall; they feed heterotrophically (find food from their environment).
  - **Plantae** are multicellular; cells have chlorophyll and a cellulose cell wall; they obtain food autotrophically (make food by photosynthesis).
  - **Fungi** are multicellular; cells do not have chlorophyll and are surrounded by a cell wall not made of cellulose; they feed **saprophytically** (on dead organic matter).
  - **Protoctista** are **unicellular** (except seaweed), with a distinct nucleus.
  - **Prokaryotes** are unicellular, but without a distinct nucleus.

- Within each kingdom, living things are further divided into smaller and smaller groups: phylum; **class**; **order**; **family**; **genus**; **species**.

- An example of a shared characteristic among the phylum **chordata** is a rod that supports the body, such as the backbone in vertebrates.

> **Remember!**
> Not all living things fit neatly into categories based on anatomy and reproductive methods. Also, new organisms with unusual characteristics are always being discovered. This makes it difficult to place them into distinct groups.

- The more characteristics organisms have in common, the more closely they are related – they share a **common ancestor**.

- Viruses do not belong to a kingdom because scientists cannot decide whether they are living organisms.

What is a species?

- Most biologists define species as organisms that are capable of breeding together to produce **fertile** offspring. This means their offspring can reproduce.

- The offspring of two different species are called **hybrids** and they are usually infertile.

- However, there are complications with this definition of a species because:
  - not all hybrids are sterile (many plant hybrids are fertile)
  - not all organisms reproduce sexually (some produce asexually).

Binomial classification

- All organisms have a two-part (**binomial**) name. For example, the species name for human is *Homo sapiens*. *Homo* is our genus name, *sapiens* is our species name.

- The binomial naming system is used because it prevents confusion over having many different names for the same species.

- Binomial classification is important because it enables scientists to:
  - communicate information about the thousands of different species
  - recognise areas of great **biodiversity** that should be targets for conservation efforts.

⬤ Improve your grade

Naming new species

Higher: Scientists exploring an area of the South American rainforests discovered several species of frog. They gave each species a new binomial name.

Explain why classifying organisms in this way is important. *AO1* [3 marks]

Identification, variation and adaptation

Variation within a species

- If you come across a species but you don't know what it is, a **key** will help you to identify it.

- The descriptions in a key come as opposite statements.

- Choosing one statement that fits the species will lead you to the next.

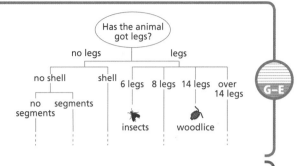

Using a key. You find an animal with eight legs. How do you identify what kind of animal it is?

- Members of the same species have different characteristics. For example, humans vary in their hair colour and blood groups. This is called **variation**.

- Variation can be either continuous or discontinuous:

  - In **continuous variation**, characteristics are spread over a range of values. Height in humans is an example – a few people are either very short or very tall, and there is a full range of 'in-betweens' (intermediates).

  - Tongue rolling is a characteristic that shows **discontinuous variation**. There are no intermediates, but rather distinctly different groups: people who can roll their tongue and people who cannot.

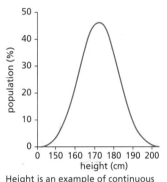

Height is an example of continuous variation.

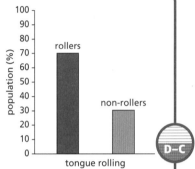

Tongue rolling is an example of discontinuous variation.

EXAM TIP

You may be shown graphs of variation data and asked to identify which type is being shown. Continuous variation is displayed as a line graph; discontinuous variation is displayed as a bar chart.

Variations complicate identification

- Variations such as those seen in hybrid ducks – which have characteristics of both parent species – can make classification complicated.

- **Ring species** refers to a chain of related species that are closely connected geographically.

- Species within the chain show variation, but they can still interbreed and produce hybrid offspring.

- However, the variations between the species at each end of the chain are so great that they cannot interbreed. They are distinct species.

Adaptations

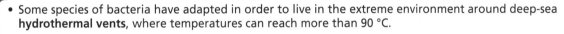

- **Adaptations** are the characteristics of an organism that enable it to survive in its environment.

  - The desert fox is adapted to survive in hot, dry conditions. It has large ears that lose heat and help to cool it. Its light-coloured fur reflects heat and provides camouflage.

  - The polar bear is adapted to survive in very cold conditions. Thick, white fur insulates and camouflages it.

- Animals living in cold regions are usually larger than those living in warmer environments.

- Large bodies have a smaller surface area relative to their mass than smaller ones. Heat is lost from the body at its surface, so if a body is larger, proportionately less heat is lost from it.

- Some species of bacteria have adapted in order to live in the extreme environment around deep-sea **hydrothermal vents**, where temperatures can reach more than 90 °C.

- Adaptations of these bacteria allow them to use a chemical produced by the vents (hydrogen sulfide) to produce energy.

Improve your grade

Polar bear adaptations

Foundation: Explain how the fur of the polar bear is a good adaptation for surviving in the Arctic.

AO2 [4 marks]

Evolution

Darwin and his theory

- Charles Darwin was the first person to propose how **evolution** takes place through **natural selection**.

- He described his ideas in a book titled *On the Origin of Species*, published in 1859.

- His theory was a great shock, as people at the time believed in the special place of humans in the natural world and in a benevolent creator or God.

- Darwin incorporated the ideas and observations of other people, including Alfred Russel Wallace, into his theory of natural selection.

Evolution in action

- These ideas are central to Darwin's theory:
  - There is variation in characteristics between individuals of the same species.
  - Overproduction means that organisms produce more offspring than will survive to adulthood.
  - There is a struggle for existence, or competition, between individuals for resources.
  - Individuals best suited to compete for resources (better **adapted**) will survive to reproduce and pass on the gene controlling their advantageous traits to their offspring.
  - It is possible that individuals less suited for competition may become extinct.

- The result of individuals becoming more suited to a particular way of life means that, over time, new species emerge.

- You can see this in the many different species of birds that developed from a common ancestor. The change is called evolution.

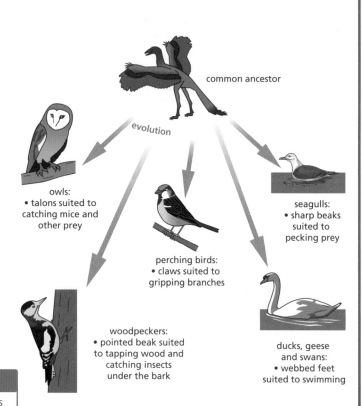

common ancestor

evolution

owls:
- talons suited to catching mice and other prey

perching birds:
- claws suited to gripping branches

seagulls:
- sharp beaks suited to pecking prey

woodpeckers:
- pointed beak suited to tapping wood and catching insects under the bark

ducks, geese and swans:
- webbed feet suited to swimming

The evolution of birds

EXAM TIP

You may be asked to explain how certain species evolved. Do this by applying the stages of natural selection: variation, overproduction, struggle for existence, survival and reproduction.

Speciation

- **Speciation** (the formation of new species) provides evidence for the natural selection of organisms.

- Geographical isolation is one way speciation occurs. For example, on one side of a newly formed mountain range the climate might be wetter and colder than on the other side.

- Over many generations, the part of the population living on the colder, wetter mountainside might change through natural selection to enable it to better withstand the harsher climate.

- Eventually, the difference in characteristics is so great that the population living in the harsher climate becomes a new species.

Improve your grade

Human evolution

Higher: Scientists believe that humans evolved from ape-like animals. Millions of years ago the Earth became drier and forests were replaced by grasslands. Before this change all apes walked on four feet. Afterwards, populations of apes emerged that walked upright on two feet and were able to see further across the grassland.

Use your knowledge of natural selection to explain why apes evolved in this way.   *AO1* [3 marks]

Genes and variation

Genetic variation

- There are two types of variation:
  - Environmental variations are **acquired characteristics** caused by environmental factors.
  - Genetic variations are inherited characteristics caused by **mutation** or reproduction.
- Inherited characteristics are controlled by **genes**, which are sections of **chromosomes**. Chromosome are long molecules of **DNA** tightly wound around proteins.
- Genes enable cells to make proteins, which result in characteristics such as eye colour and leg length.

Remember! Some characteristics can be caused by both inherited and environmental factors. For example, the genes that control tallness can be inherited, but a child will not reach their potential height without a healthy diet.

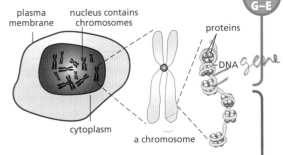

Chromosomes exist in the nucleus of most types of cell. Each gene is a section of a DNA molecule.

- Each sperm and egg contains only a half-set of chromosomes – in the case of humans this means 23 (human cells have 46 chromosomes).
- When the sperm and the egg fuse during **fertilisation**, the half-set of chromosomes from the male pairs up with the half-set of chromosomes from the female, to form a full set.
- Our parents pass on their genes to us (50% from each parent) during fertilisation. We therefore inherit their characteristics.
- Genetic variation between parents and offspring may also be caused by:
  - Crossing over: the exchange of bits of chromosomes and their genes between chromosome pairs.
  - Gene mutations: changes in the number of chromosomes or in the genes that chromosomes carry.

Supporting Darwin's theory

- There is a 99% similarity between human DNA and chimpanzee DNA, but only 88% between human and horse DNA. This illustrates how organisms have evolved over time, but share a common ancestry.
- Bacterial resistance to antibiotics is an example of evolution in action (see page 17 for how this happens).
- Darwin's *On the Origin of Species* is an example of how scientific knowledge was disseminated. Through correspondence and presentations, Darwin discussed his theory both before and after his book's publication.
- Today, the scientific community plays an important role in **validating** evidence:
  - Research results are checked anonymously by other scientists (**peer review**).
  - If validated, the work is published in **scientific journals** available to the wider community.
  - **Conferences** are held to communicate new ideas in a particular area of research.

Genetic terms

- Each chromosome in a pair carries the same genes in exactly the same place (**locus**). However, chromosome pairs may have different **alleles** on each chromosome.
- An allele is one form of a gene, e.g. the gene for eye colour has many different alleles, causing blue, green or brown eyes.

- If the alleles of a pair are the same, the individual is **homozygous** for the characteristic.
- If the alleles are different, the individual is **heterozygous**.
- An allele may be **dominant** or **recessive**. Dominant alleles mask the effects of a recessive allele.
- All of the characteristics that make up an individual are their **phenotype**.
- All of the genes are the individual's **genotype**.

Family pedigrees

- **Pedigree** charts show the way characteristics of related individuals pass from one generation to the next.
- They provide helpful information about the purity of **lineage** of plants and animals, which is important to farmers.

Improve your grade

Hair-colour inheritance

Foundation: Katy has red hair. Both her parents have brown hair.

Explain how Katy inherited red hair, even though her parents do not have it.

AO2 [3 marks]

Monohybrid inheritance

Mendel's experiments

- Gregor Mendel (1822–84) was a priest who studied how single characteristics were inherited in pea plants. This type of inheritance is called **monohybrid**.

- Mendel **cross-bred pure-breeding** short plants with pure-breeding tall plants.

- He collected and grew the plants' seeds and discovered that their offspring were always tall. The characteristic 'tallness' dominated the characteristic 'shortness'. Mendel called 'tallness' a **dominant characteristic**.

- He then bred the offspring together and found that some of these plants were tall and some were short. He called 'shortness' a **recessive characteristic**.

How characteristics are inherited

- From his experiments, Mendel drew the following conclusions:
  - Sexually reproduced offspring receive the same number of genes from each parent. The development of any particular characteristic, therefore, must be controlled by a pair of genes (one from each parent).
  - Alleles must split when **gametes** (sex cells) form.

- Mendel used letters to symbolise alleles. For example, he used 'T' to show the allele which controls 'tallness' in pea plants and 't' to show the allele which controls 'shortness'.

- The **Punnett squares** opposite summarise the results of Mendel's crosses between pure-breeding parent plants and first-generation plants.

Cross: TT × tt			Parent plants
Parental gametes	t	t	Pure-breeding recessive parent
Pure-breeding dominant parent T	Tt	Tt	First-generation plants
T	Tt	Tt	

Cross: Tt × Tt			First-generation plants
First-generation gametes	T	t	
T	TT	Tt	Second-generation plants
t	Tt	tt	

The results of Mendel's experiments.

EXAM TIP

You may be asked to create a Punnett square. The question may tell you which letters to use to represent the alleles. If not, use any upper-case letter for the dominant allele and its corresponding lower-case letter for the recessive allele. Be sure to choose letters that look different, e.g. Aa not Zz.

Probabilities

- Punnett squares are used to predict the probabilities of outcomes from crosses.

- First-generation plants each have two different alleles (heterozygous). However, all of the plants are tall because the T allele is dominant, and this masks the effect of the t allele, which is recessive.

- Not all of the second-generation plants have the same combination of alleles:
  - 50% are heterozygous (Tt)
  - 25% are pure-breeding tall (TT) (homozygous, dominant)
  - 25% are pure-breeding short (tt) (homozygous, recessive).

- The characteristic height of plants separates in the second generation in a ratio of three tall plants to one short plant.

- The phenotype 'tall' is expressed in either homozygous or heterozygous plants because the allele T is dominant.

- The phenotype 'short' is expressed only in homozygous plants because the allele t is recessive.

How science works

You should be able to:
- format data into diagrams such as Punnett squares and pedigree charts
- interpret the data and predict outcomes based on it.

Improve your grade

Mendel's experiments

Foundation: Mendel discovered that the colour of pea flowers was controlled by a single gene. The red allele (R) was dominant, and the white allele (r) was recessive. He crossed a pure-breeding red-flowered plant with a pure-breeding white-flowered plant. What would be the genotype and phenotype of the pea plants that were produced? Use a genetic diagram to help you. *AO2* [4 marks]

Genetic disorders

Gene mutations

- A change in a gene's DNA is called a **mutation**.
- As genes carry instructions for building a protein, a mutation may alter a type of protein, or cause no protein to be made at all.
- If sperm and eggs carry a mutation, then any offspring will inherit the mutated gene.
- **Genetic disorders** are the result of inheriting gene mutations.

G–E

When things go wrong

- **Cystic fibrosis** and **sickle cell disease** are examples of inherited recessive genetic disorders.
- Cystic fibrosis affects the movement of fluid in and out of cells, causing a thick, sticky **mucus** to form, particularly in the lungs and digestive tract.
- Symptoms of cystic fibrosis include:
  - mucus blocking the airways of the lungs, causing breathing difficulties
  - lung infections because of bacteria becoming trapped in the mucus
  - problems digesting food, which can lead to malnutrition
  - bone disease.
- Treatments for cystic fibrosis include physiotherapy and massage, medication, and a nourishing diet.
- Sickle cell disease is caused by a mutation that alters **haemoglobin** molecules and causes them to absorb less oxygen. This also results in the red blood cells becoming sickle-shaped.
- Symptoms of sickle cell disease include:
  - feeling weak and tired
  - sudden pain, known as a **sickle cell crisis**, caused by sickled red blood cells forming clumps in the bloodstream, blocking blood flow to organs and causing organ damage.
- Treatments for sickle cell disease include medication, lots of fluids and blood transfusions.

D–C

Inheriting genetic disorders

- If a mutated allele is dominant, or a person inherits two copies of a mutated recessive allele, then the individual in question will be affected if the mutated allele is the cause of a genetic disorder.
- The risk of someone inheriting a particular disorder can be predicted using pedigree analysis. This looks at a disorder's inheritance pattern and predicts the risk for future generations.
- In pedigree charts, generations are indicated from the top using Roman numerals, and members of each generation are numbered from the left.
- In the pedigree chart opposite I-1 and I-2 are carriers because II-3 (one of their children) has the disorder.
- II-4 and II-5 have a 1 in 4 probability of being a carrier.
- III-5 has a 1 in 4 probability of being a carrier because they have a sibling with the disorder.

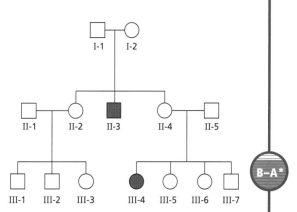

A sample pedigree analysis for cystic fibrosis.
The squares are males and the circles females.
A coloured shape indicates an affected individual.

B–A*

EXAM TIP

You may be asked to analyse the outcomes of genetic crosses using probabilities, ratios or percentages. In the example above, a child having cystic fibrosis is 1 in 4 (probability), 1:4 (ratio) or 25% (percentage).

⊙ Improve your grade

Sickle cell disease inheritance

Higher: Ben carries the mutated gene for sickle cell disease in his sperm. Janet is neither affected by the disease nor is she a carrier of it.

What is the probability of their children having sickle cell disease? Show how you worked out your answer.

AO2 [3 marks]

Homeostasis and body temperature

Constant conditions

G–E

- Living things keep their body's internal environment stable, or constant (no changes). This is called **homeostasis**.
- Regulating body water content and body temperature are examples of homeostasis.
- The process by which the body regulates water content is called **osmoregulation**.
  - Signals to the brain send information about the water content of the blood.
  - The brain sends signals – **hormones** – to the kidneys, to regulate the amount of water they remove in urine.

D–C

- All examples of homeostasis are self-regulating – that is, the body adjusts automatically to keep the internal environment stable.
- The triggers for these responses are called stimuli.
- For example, we need to keep our body temperature at 37 °C. The stimuli that trigger responses are the body becoming either too warm or too cold.

> **Remember!**
> Human body temperature needs to remain at around 37 °C because the **enzymes** that control the chemical activity of our cells work best at this temperature.

Thermoregulation

G–E

- The body regulates its temperature through **thermoregulation**.
- Responses to *increased* body temperature include:
  - Increased blood flow through the blood vessels in the skin, making you look flushed. More blood causes more heat to be lost from the skin's surface.
  - Sweat is produced. Heat from the body evaporates the water in sweat, transferring heat away from the skin.
  - Body hair lies flat against the skin, preventing air becoming trapped next to it. Air is a poor heat conductor, so the absence of an air layer allows more heat to escape.
- Responses to *decreased* body temperature include:
  - Less blood flows through the blood vessels, which means less heat is lost from the skin's surface.
  - Shivering is caused by tiny muscles under the skin contracting and relaxing very quickly. This causes the muscle cells to release heat.
  - Body hair rises away from the skin, trapping a layer of air next to it to insulate the body.

D–C

- Body temperature is monitored by the thermoregulatory centre, in the part of the brain called the **hypothalamus**.
- The thermoregulatory centre detects the temperature of the blood, processes the information and sends nerve impulses to sweat glands and hair erector muscles, which control shivering and blood flow through the skin.

Vasoconstriction and vasodilation

B–A*

- **Feedback** is the information about changes in a self-regulating mechanism that allows it to adjust, maintaining a constant internal environment.
- Because the information reverses any change away from normal back to normal, we call it negative feedback.
- **Vasoconstriction** refers to the narrowing of blood vessels in the skin. Blood flow through the skin is reduced, therefore heat loss is decreased and body temperature rises.
- **Vasodilation** refers to the widening of blood vessels. Blood flow is increased and more heat is lost through the skin.
- Nerve impulses pass along the nerves from the thermoregulatory centre to the muscles in the walls of blood cells, stimulating contraction and causing them to narrow. When the muscles relax the blood vessels widen.

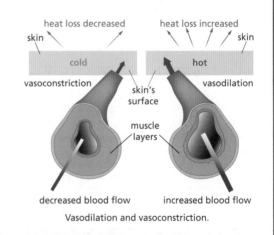

Vasodilation and vasoconstriction.

Improve your grade

Cooling down

Foundation: Sandeep is running a marathon. When he gets too hot he begins to sweat. Explain how sweating cools the body down.

AO2 [2 marks]

Senses and the nervous system

Nerve cells and the nervous system

- A **neurone** is a nerve cell that consists of a cell body with thin fibres stretching out from it. The fibres carry electrical impulses.

- Bundles of neurones form nerves and these nerves form the nervous system:
  - The central nervous system (CNS) consists of the brain and spinal cord.
  - The peripheral nervous system consists of the nerves connecting the sense organs with the central nervous system.

- Nerves consist of different types of neurone, which send electrical impulses in particular directions:
  - Sensory neurones send impulses from **receptors** in the sense organs to the central nervous system.
  - Motor neurones send impulses from the central nervous system to muscles and glands.

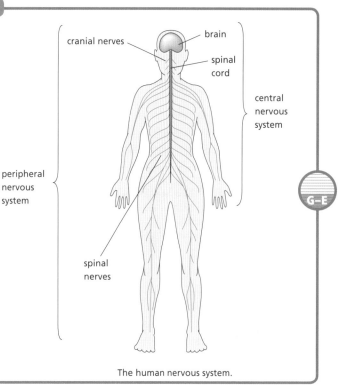

The human nervous system.

G–E

Receptors

- Receptors in the sensory neurone fibres detect stimuli. They convert them into electrical impulses (**nerve impulses**) and send them along neurones to muscles and glands.

- Different types of receptor detect different types of stimuli:
  - photoreceptors detect light
  - thermoreceptors detect changes in body temperature.

- Some types of receptor can be found all over the body. For example, thermoreceptors are in the skin.

- Other types of receptor are concentrated in sense organs. For example, photoreceptors form a layer of cells in the eye called the **retina**.

- Sensitivity to touch depends on:
  - the force bearing down on an area of skin
  - the number of touch receptors in the area.

- Fingertips are very sensitive to touch because they contain many touch receptors.

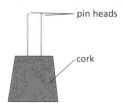

A simple touch-tester using a cork and pins.

D–C

EXAM TIP

You can test skin sensitivity by using a touch-tester. If your blindfolded volunteer can feel two pins, the chosen area has many touch receptors and shows high sensitivity. If they can only feel one pin, the area is less sensitive.

Dendrons and axons

- Sensory and motor neurones have similarities and differences.

- They both have a cell body and fine branches called **dendrites**.

- The fibre that carries electrical impulses from the cell body to the dendrites is called the **axon**. Motor neurones have very long axons, whereas sensory neurones have short ones.

- The fibre that carries electrical impulses to the cell body is called the **dendron**.

B–A*

Improve your grade

Paralysis

Foundation: An injury that results in a broken spine may cause a person to be paralysed. Explain why.

AO1 [3 marks]

Responses and coordination

Responding to stimuli

G–E

- **Involuntary responses** are those we do without thinking – they are automatic (for example, pulling your foot away after treading on a sharp pin). We have them to protect our bodies from damage.

- **Voluntary responses** are those we think about (for example, checking your mobile phone before answering it).

- Different parts of the central nervous system coordinate different **responses**:
  - The brain coordinates voluntary responses.
  - The spinal cord coordinates involuntary responses.

Stimuli and response pathway

D–C

- Stimuli (plural of **stimulus**) are changes in the environment – such as stepping on the pin – which cause an action in a living thing.

- Responses are the actions taken, such as jerking the foot away from the pin's point.

- Stimuli and responses are linked by the nervous system in the following pathway:

  stimulus → receptor → sensory neurone →
  CNS → motor neurone → effector → response

- Nerve impulses are sent to the effectors. Muscles are effectors and the impulses cause them to contract (shorten).

- Receptors are linked to effectors by a chain of neurones.

- The fibres at the end of one neurone are separated from the beginning of the next neurone by tiny gaps called **synapses**.

- **Neurotransmitters** are chemical messengers that carry information across the synapse.

- The myelin sheath is a fatty substance surrounding dendrons and axons that speeds up the nerve impulses along neurons.

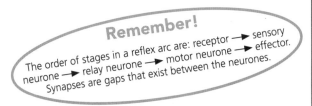

① neurotransmitter stored here is released by the arrival of nerve impulses

③ neurotransmitter stimulates the next neurone in the chain, triggering new nerve impulses

ending of the neurone

beginning of the next neurone in the chain

② neurotransmitter is released into the gap of the synapse. It passes across the synapse

→ direction of nerve impulses

How a nerve impulse travels across a synapse.

The reflex arc

B–A*

- The involuntary behaviour of the person pulling their foot away after stepping on a pin is known as a **reflex response**.

- Reflex responses are automatic and usually fast. They help to protect the body from damage.

- A reflex response is brought about by a chain of nerves called a **reflex arc**.

- The diagram below shows how the reflex arc works. The numbers indicate the path of the nerve impulses.

Remember!

The order of stages in a reflex arc are: receptor → sensory neurone → relay neurone → motor neurone → effector. Synapses are gaps that exist between the neurones.

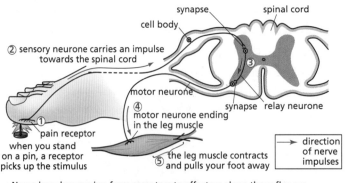

synapse   spinal cord

cell body

② sensory neurone carries an impulse towards the spinal cord

③

motor neurone

synapse   relay neurone

④ motor neurone ending in the leg muscle

① pain receptor

when you stand on a pin, a receptor picks up the stimulus

⑤ the leg muscle contracts and pulls your foot away

→ direction of nerve impulses

Nerve impulses passing from receptors to effectors along the reflex arc.

Improve your grade

Synapses
Higher: Explain how an impulse travels over a synapse.

AO1 [3 marks]

Hormones and diabetes

Hormones

- **Hormones** are chemicals produced by **endocrine glands** in the body and released into the blood. They circulate in the bloodstream and affect different tissues and organs.
- Hormones help to regulate the body's activities and maintain **homeostasis**.
- The pancreas is an organ that produces two hormones: **insulin** and **glucagon**. These help regulate blood glucose levels.

Regulating blood glucose

- Blood glucose level is normally about 90 mg per 100 cm³ of blood, but it rises or falls depending on circumstances:
  - It rises following a meal, as digested food is absorbed from the intestine into the bloodstream.
  - It falls during exercise, as vigorously contracting muscles use extra glucose for energy.

- The pancreas monitors the level of blood glucose and triggers a response to return the levels to normal if they change:
  - Insulin is released from the pancreas when the level of blood glucose is high. It helps convert glucose into another type of carbohydrate called **glycogen**, which is stored in liver and muscle tissue.
  - Glucagon is released from the pancreas when the level of blood glucose is low. It promotes the conversion of glycogen into glucose, which is released into the bloodstream.
- Hormones are **specific** to their **target tissue** – they can only bind to the membrane of their target tissue's cells and not to any others.

Diabetes

- **Diabetes** is a condition in which the body cannot properly regulate its blood glucose level so it becomes dangerously high, increasing the risk of serious health problems.
- There are two types of diabetes:
  - Type 1 occurs when the pancreas does not produce enough insulin.
  - Type 2 occurs when the pancreas still produces insulin but the target tissues – liver and muscles – become **insensitive** to it.
- Type 1 diabetes usually occurs in younger people. Type 2 diabetes can develop as people get older.

- People with Type 1 diabetes usually need daily injections of insulin, into the body's **subcutaneous fat** (such as the thigh), to reduce blood glucose levels.
- The amount of insulin required for Type 1 diabetes depends on factors such as diet and the amount of exercise a person does.
- People with Type 2 diabetes can regulate their blood glucose level by careful eating, regular exercise and losing weight. However, drugs are sometimes needed to help control blood glucose levels.

- Type 1 diabetes is the result of either:
  - an **auto-immune disease** (when a person's immune system destroys the pancreatic cells that produce insulin)
  - a genetic disorder (a **mutation** of the gene encoding the production of insulin).
- Recent research has indicated a strong correlation between obesity and the development of Type 2 diabetes.
- One way of determining if someone is overweight is to measure their **body mass index (BMI)**: $\text{BMI} \left(\frac{\text{kg}}{\text{m}^2} \right) = \frac{\text{mass (kg)}}{\text{height (m)}^2}$

Remember!

BMI is a measure of body fat that applies to normal-sized adult men and women. A body-builder's BMI will be high, but this does not mean he is overweight. His body will have a lot of muscle, which has a higher density than fat.

Improve your grade

Calculating BMI

Higher: Susan is a normal-sized adult woman. She is 1.6 m tall and has a mass of 82 kg.

Work out her BMI by using this equation: $\text{BMI} \left(\frac{\text{kg}}{\text{m}^2} \right) = \frac{\text{mass (kg)}}{\text{height (m)}^2}$

Use the graph opposite to explain how much of a risk Susan has of developing Type 2 diabetes.

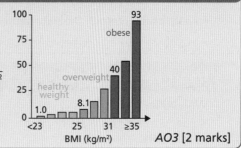

AO3 [2 marks]

Plant hormones

Plant movements

- Plants can move very slowly as a result of growth.
- When the movements are the result of stimuli coming mainly from one direction, then the response is called a **tropism**.
- The tropism is **positive** if plants grow towards the stimulus and **negative** if they grow away from it.

Auxin

- Plant **hormones** such as **auxin** are responsible for tropisms.
- **Phototropism** refers to the response of plants to the stimulus of light.
- **Gravitropism** (or **geotropism**) refers to the response of plants to the stimulus of gravity.
- Phototropism can be investigated using cress seeds. For example, by putting cress seeds on a sunny windowsill and watching as the shoots bend towards the light (positive phototropism).
- The discovery of auxin as the substance responsible for regulating shoot growth was made in the 1920s by Dutch biologist Frits Went.
- Went investigated the development of cereal **seedlings** and carried out many experiments to investigate the effects of auxin on shoot growth in response to light.

- In shoots, auxin is more concentrated in tissues on the side where light is least intense. The cells here grow more quickly than those on the brightly lit side. In this way, the shoot grows towards the brightest light.
- In roots where the concentration of auxin is high, the cells of the tissues grow more slowly. Auxin is more concentrated on the underside of roots, so the cells of the tissues of the underside grow more slowly than those on the upperside, causing the roots to grow down.

> ### EXAM TIP
> You may be asked why a control is important in experiments such as this. The control for this experiment would be some cress seeds placed in a dark area. If the shoots in the dark also bend, you know that it is not due to the light.

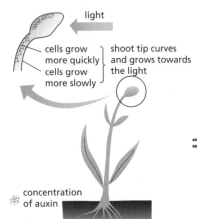

light

cells grow more quickly | shoot tip curves and grows towards the light
cells grow more slowly

concentration of auxin

The shoot grows more quickly where auxin is concentrated.

Plant hormones in food production

- Copies of plants can be made by taking **cuttings** and dipping the end in rooting powder. This contains plant hormones that encourages cut stems to develop roots.
- Fruit can be picked unripe and transported or stored in warehouses. A plant hormone called **ethene** gas is released into the air around the fruit to ripen it just before it is delivered to shops.
- Some types of **herbicide** contain plant hormones that stimulate the growth of plant stems. Because the rate of root growth does not keep pace with the stem, the roots are not able to absorb enough water to support the growing plant and it dies.
- Herbicides only affect the weeds because they are broad-leaved and absorb more herbicide than narrow-leaved crop plants.
- Growers can produce seedless fruits by smearing the plants' female sex organs with auxin paste, to stimulate the development of the fruit. However, the egg cells within the female sex organs have not been fertilised so seeds are not produced.

How science works

You should be able to:
- plan and execute an experiment to show how light affects the growth of seedlings
- analyse and interpret the data gathered from the experiment
- explain the difference between data and data interpretation.

Improve your grade

Weedkiller

Higher: Explain how plant hormones can be used as weedkillers that kill weeds only, without affecting the crops.

AO1 [3 marks]

Drugs, smoking and alcohol abuse

What are drugs?

- A **drug** is a substance from outside the body that affects the central nervous system and brings about changes in the body that can lead to **addiction**.
- There are different types of drugs:
  - **Painkillers**, such as morphine, deaden pain or affect the way we think about it.
  - **Hallucinogens**, like cannabis, LSD and solvents, produce sensations of false reality called hallucinations.
  - **Stimulants**, including caffeine, increase the speed of our reactions.
  - **Depressants**, such as alcohol, slow the activity of the brain and reaction times.

G–E

- A person can become addicted to a drug because:
  - It can give someone a false sense of well-being, which the person then craves when it goes away.
  - The body gets used to the changes taking place within its tissues.
- Addiction is expensive, because many drugs cannot be obtained without a prescription, so can only be bought from drug dealers.
- **Abuse** is a word often used to refer to the non-medical use of drugs.

D–C

Painkillers and their actions

- Painkillers block the release of neurotransmitter into the synapses which separate the neurones.
- Stimulants enhance the release of neurotransmitter.
- **Reaction time** is how long it takes for a person to respond to a stimulus. This depends on how quickly and how much neurotransmitter is released.

Remember!

Scientists can see how drugs affect reaction times by doing reaction-time tests on people before and after they take a drug, for example, by measuring how long it takes to press a button in response to a flashing light.

B–A*

Legal drugs

- Cigarette smoke contains many chemicals that are harmful:
  - Carbon monoxide reduces the amount of oxygen that red blood cells can carry.
  - Nicotine is an addictive stimulant that raises blood pressure and increases the risk of heart disease.
  - Tar contains substances that can cause cancer (carcinogens). It collects in the lungs and can cause emphysema.
- Alcoholic drinks contain ethanol, which can cause lowered inhibitions, slowed reaction times, blurred vision, and difficulty controlling the arms and legs.

Alcohol abuse

- Alcohol abuse usually refers to heavy drinking over a long period, or drinking large volumes of alcohol in a short time (**binge drinking**).
- It can cause liver disease, brain damage, heart disease, cancer and raised blood pressure.
- Sex, age, body mass and how quickly the body's cells break down alcohol affect how much an individual can drink safely.
- Four units of alcohol a day for men and three units for women is reckoned to be safe.
- A pregnant woman who drinks alcohol regularly increases the risk of her baby developing abnormally.

D–C

Smoking and disease

- Data collected between 1940 and 1980 established a link between smoking and disease.
- Deaths from lung cancer increased sharply, whereas deaths from other types of lung disease fell.
- A positive correlation was later found between the number of cigarettes someone smoked and their risk of dying from bronchitis and lung cancer.

⊙ Improve your grade

Drink driving

Foundation: Explain why it is dangerous to drink alcohol and drive.

AO1 [3 marks]

Ethics of transplants

Transplanting organs

- Transplant surgery replaces a diseased organ with a healthy one.
- The person supplying the healthy organ is known as the **donor**.
- The person receiving the organ is the **recipient**.
- Organ donors can be:
  - Living: live donors can donate tissues such as bone marrow or an organ such as a kidney, where there are two doing the same job.
  - Dead: people can give permission for their organs to be used if they are killed in an accident. Most organ donors are victims of accidents.
- **Rejection** of the organ is less likely to happen if the donor is related to the recipient.

Supply and demand

- There are far more people in need of organs for transplantation than there are donors.
- This has resulted in a search for alternative sources of organs. These include:
  - Animal donors (**xenotransplantation**). This was first tried in 1963 using a kidney from a chimpanzee, but the organ was rejected by the recipient.
  - **Genetically engineering** the organs of animals to stop them being rejected by the recipient. This practice is not yet widely used, but further research may enable it to become a powerful treatment for disease in the future.
  - **Transplantation tourism**, in which wealthy people needing a transplant pay for organs. Poor people in developing countries are often prepared to donate their organs for money, even if it is illegal to do so.
- There are many **moral** and **ethical** issues concerned with all of these options, including:
  - whether it is right to use animals as a source of organs
  - whether money should be an incentive in a decision to donate organs
  - wider human rights concerns relating to transplant tourism, such as the exploitation of the poor people in developing countries
  - the increased risk of transplanting diseased organs into recipients because poor donors do not receive regular health care.

Choosing who

- Modern medicine can have amazing effects, but it is expensive and resources are limited, including organs for transplant. This raises ethical concerns about how we **prioritise** transplants.

- A transplant might be needed for a problem that the sufferer has brought on themselves. Should a heart transplant for someone who is obese have the same priority as a life-saving transplant for someone suddenly taken ill?

- Who most 'deserves' the chance to live? Should 'deserve' even come into the equation? There are no easy answers to these difficult questions.

> ### EXAM TIP
> You may be asked to comment on 'moral' and 'ethical' issues. Morals are what people think is right or wrong. Ethics are the actions people take as a result of their moral judgement.

How science works

You should be able to:

- explain how and why scientists continue to research transplantation in areas that are considered controversial
- understand the social effects of such research.

Improve your grade

Ethical concerns

Higher: Jon and Margaret are both on the liver transplant waiting list. Jon is a 36-year-old father of three. He has cirrhosis caused by alcohol abuse. The cause of Margaret's liver failure is unknown. She is 83 years old. Doctors have to decide who receives the next available liver.

Choose who the liver recipient should be and argue your case.   *AO2* [5 marks]

Infectious diseases

Causes and spread of disease

- Organisms that cause infectious disease are called **pathogens**. We often call pathogens microbes (microorganisms), because most of them are only visible under a microscope.
- The human body is warm and moist, providing a perfect environment for pathogens to multiply.
- **Infectious** diseases are those caused by pathogens that spread from person to person.

G–E

- Cholera **bacteria** are found in water contaminated with sewage.
- **Viruses** that cause colds and flu are airborne – passed from person to person via moisture droplets from coughs and sneezes.
- *Salmonella* is a type of food poisoning that comes from chickens. Cooking food thoroughly and good hygiene decreases the risk of getting *Salmonella*.
- **HIV** is a virus that causes **AIDS**. It destroys some of the white blood cells that help defend the body against pathogens. HIV is spread by the exchange of body fluids.
- Athlete's foot is a fungal infection that thrives in the warm, moist environment of sweaty feet. Athlete's foot can be spread through skin contact and contact with contaminated surfaces.

D–C

- The bacteria that cause diarrhoea produce **endotoxins** (poisons). These stimulate the small intestine wall to contract violently and more frequently than normal.
- Diarrhoea prevents digested food and water being absorbed, which can cause severe dehydration that can lead to death if not treated.

B–A*

Insect-borne disease

- The term animal **vector** refers to animals that spread pathogens.
- Flies can transfer the bacteria which cause dysentery on to food via their feet.
- *Anopheles* mosquitoes are vectors for malaria. They feed on the blood of a victim and suck in the pathogen (a protozoan called *Plasmodium*) before biting another person and passing it on.

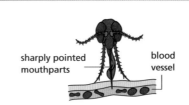

sharply pointed mouthparts   blood vessel

The head of a female *Anopheles* mosquito.

G–E

Stopping the spread of infection

- **Antiseptics** are chemicals that stop microbes from multiplying. We use them to swab a wound or clean skin to prevent infection.
- **Antibacterials** are substances that interfere with the growth of bacteria, e.g. antiseptics and antibiotic drugs. However, the term is more often used to describe cleaning products.

G–E

- We use **antibiotic** drugs to control infection caused by bacteria. Some kill the bacteria while others prevent them from multiplying.
- **Antifungal** drugs are used to treat fungal infections by killing the fungal cells but not the human cells.

Remember!
You can test how effective antibiotics are by inoculating agar plates with bacteria and adding small paper discs that have been soaked in antibiotics. An effective antibiotic will stop the growth of the bacteria.

D–C

Resistance in bacteria and antibiotic misuse

- Widespread use of antibiotics has led to strains of bacteria that cannot be treated with most antibiotics, e.g. **MRSA**.
- **Resistance** arises because of the high mutation rates of bacterial genes and the ongoing exposure of bacteria to antibiotics.
- Populations of bacteria always contain individuals with resistance genes. These individuals survive antibiotic treatment, reproduce and spread quickly.

B–A*

Improve your grade

Malaria prevention

Higher: The spread of malaria can be prevented cheaply and easily by covering beds with mosquito nets. Explain how this technique works.

AO2 [3 marks]

Defences and interdependency

Physical barriers

- Human skin forms a physical barrier to protect the body's interior from pathogens outside.
- The lungs contain mucus, which traps bacteria and other particles, and is swept away by hair-like cilia until it reaches the throat, when it is swallowed.
- Plant surfaces are also a physical barrier to pathogens.
- Plants may also have thorns as a defence against plant-chewing animals or hair-like structures that secrete sticky substances to trap insects.

Chemical defences

- Glands in the skin produce an oily substance called sebum, which kills bacteria and fungi. Glands in the stomach wall produce hydrochloric acid, which kills bacteria on food.
- Tears contain the enzyme lysozyme, which destroys bacteria.
- Some types of white blood cells bind to substances on the surface of pathogens and destroy them. Other types produce proteins called **antibodies**, which also bind to the pathogens.
- Platelets in the blood help form scabs over cuts in the skin, which stops blood loss and prevents pathogens entering.

New medicines

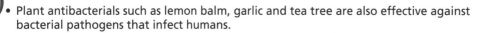

- Plants also use chemicals as a defence. Animals avoid bitter-tasting plants and prey, as the chemicals they contain can trigger vomiting.
- Bacterial attack is often a signal to the plants to produce antibacterial chemicals.
- Plant antibacterials such as lemon balm, garlic and tea tree are also effective against bacterial pathogens that infect humans.
- Scientists are searching for plants that could be new medicines. This is important, as bacterial pathogens are developing resistance to current antibiotic drugs.

Mutualism and parasitism

- All living things are interdependent – they have a dynamic relationship that ensures survival.
- **Mutualism** refers to a relationship where both species benefit. For example, cleaner fish feed on the dead skin and external parasites of other fish species. This keeps the **host** free of health-threatening parasites.
- **Parasitism** is a one-sided relationship between two species. A parasite obtains food at the other species' expense.
- Parasites can live on the outside (an **ectoparasite** such as a flea) or on the inside (an **endoparasite** such as a tapeworm) of its host.
- Mistletoe is a plant parasite, taking water and mineral salts from the tree on which it grows.

> ### EXAM TIP
> Make sure you can describe the difference between mutualism and parasitism and give an example of each.

Useful bacteria

- **Leguminous** plants such as peas, beans and clover have swellings on their roots called nodules. These contain **nitrogen-fixing bacteria**. The bacteria convert nitrogen from the air into compounds which the plants use to make proteins. The bacteria obtain sugars from the plant's roots.
- In hydrothermal deep-sea vents, the substances released by the underwater volcanic activity are the raw materials for another process carried out by bacteria, called **chemosynthesis**:

carbon dioxide + hydrogen sulfide ⟶ sugars + sulfur

- Chemosynthetic bacteria live in the bodies of giant tube worms. The worms supply the bacteria with oxygen, enabling the bacteria to make food that the worm needs.

Improve your grade

Interdependence

Foundation: Plants and humans are interdependent.

Explain what this statement means, giving an example.   *AO1* [2 marks]

Energy, biomass and population pressures

Food chains and energy flow

- A food chain begins with a **producer** (a plant, algae or some bacteria which produce food by photosynthesis).

- The next in a food chain is always an animal. Animals are **consumers**: they eat food – herbivores eat plants, carnivores eat other animals, omnivores eat both.

- Most carnivores are **predators**. They catch and eat other animals (**prey**) – often herbivores.

- **Scavengers** are carnivores that feed on the dead bodies of animals.

G–E

- A food chain represents one pathway of food energy through a community of organisms. A **food web** represents many pathways and is usually a more accurate description of feeding relationships.

- At each link in a food chain, energy is lost in waste products and as a result of **metabolism** in the form of heat. This means that there can be only a limited number of links in the chain.

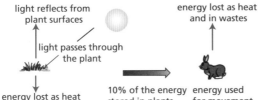

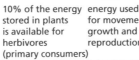

Energy flowing along a food chain.

light reflects from plant surfaces

light passes through the plant

energy lost as heat
1% of the light energy falling on the plant is used for photosynthesis

10% of the energy stored in plants is available for herbivores (primary consumers)

energy used for movement, growth and reproduction

energy lost as heat and in wastes

15% of the energy stored in herbivores is available for carnivores (secondary consumers)

energy used for movement, growth and reproduction

energy lost as heat and in wastes

food energy available dwindles to zero

D–C

Biomass

- We refer to the amount of tissue in an organism as **biomass**.

- **Pyramids of biomass** tell us about the biomass of producers and consumers.

- Different **trophic** (feeding) levels make up the pyramid. The amount of biomass decreases along the food chain (up the pyramid). This is because energy is lost at each link. Each trophic level has less biomass than the one below it.

B–A*

Population and resources

- The human population of the world is increasing as populations of developing nations like India are growing, even though populations of developed nations like France are levelling off.

- Population growth of a country depends on the birth rate, life expectancy and health care.

- Population pyramids reveal why growth may be high or low, as they show how many people of each age live in a country.

> **EXAM TIP**
>
> You may be asked to analyse, interpret and evaluate data on population growth, so make sure you are able to comment on what population pyramids show, e.g. one that shows a high percentage of children indicates an increasing population.

G–E

- Human population growth means that **resources** are in constant demand.

- Resources are the raw materials we take from the environment to run industry and our homes.

- These include the ores we use to extract metals and the oil we use to produce plastics. Both ores and oil are **non-renewable resources**. They cannot be replaced.

- Even renewable resources, like the wood for making paper, can be used at an unsustainable rate.

D–C

Waste: recycle or dump?

- Waste that isn't recycled needs to be incinerated or put into landfill.

- We are running out of landfill sites and they need careful management to stop them polluting water supplies or releasing methane.

- When paper and plastics are incinerated, some of the energy produced can be used as heat for industrial processes and to warm homes. However, the process can release pollutant gases.

- Recycling paper, plastic and metals saves the energy used to make them, avoids the need for raw materials and solves the problem of disposal.

B–A*

Improve your grade

Metal recycling
Higher: Evaluate the use of metal recycling as an alternative to landfill.

AO3 [4 marks]

Water and air pollution

Water pollutants

- Chemicals that are harmful to our health and to wildlife are called **pollutants**. These can be released into our environment, causing **pollution**.
- Nitrates and phosphates are pollutants in fertiliser, which is used to increase crop yield.
- These chemicals can pollute groundwater, ponds and rivers when they are not absorbed by crops.
- Groundwater provides one-third of Britain's drinking water. High nitrate and phosphate concentrations in drinking water are a health hazard.

Eutrophication and indicator species

- Nitrate- and phosphate-rich water in ponds and rivers (from fertilisers or sewage) stimulates the growth of algae and water plants, which clog the water.
- When the vegetation dies, bacteria decompose the organic material. This uses up the oxygen in the water. Ammonia and other poisonous substances are also released.
- Wildlife living in the water dies through lack of oxygen or poisoning.
- The process is called **eutrophication**.

- The more polluted a river is with sewage, the less oxygen there is in solution because of eutrophication. Fewer species survive in the polluted parts.
- The presence or absence of different species indicates how polluted (and therefore how eutrophic) the water is.
- Scientists use these **indicator species** to assess pollution levels.
- Stonefly and shrimps are clean-water indicators because they cannot survive in water with low oxygen concentrations.
- Bloodworms and sludgeworms are polluted-water indicators. They can survive at low levels of oxygen because they are tolerant to pollution.

Sulfur dioxide

- Burning fossil fuels releases gases such as sulfur dioxide.

| sulfur | + | oxygen | $\rightarrow$ | sulfur dioxide |
| (from fossil fuel) | | (from air) | | (gas) |

- Pollution with sulfur dioxide reduces air quality and dissolves in water vapour to form **acid rain** or acid snow, which passes into lakes and rivers.

- Acidic water causes fish to produce too much mucus. This clogs the gills and kills the fish through oxygen deprivation.
- Acid rain also washes important substances out of the soil. Poisons are released from the soil and trees die.
- **Lichens** are an indicator species for air pollution. There are different types: shrubby, leafy and slightly leafy.
- The number of lichen species varies according to the level of sulfur dioxide in the air. A greater variety is seen where sulfur dioxide pollution is low.
- Black spot is a fungal disease that covers rose leaves. Its presence is an indicator of good air quality.

> **Remember!**
> You can investigate the effects of sulfur dioxide on plant growth by growing germinated cress seeds in a box containing a chemical that gives off the gas. You will also need a control in which the seeds grow with no pollutants, so you can compare them.

- For much of the year the prevailing wind blows from the west/south-west to the east/north-east across Europe.
- These prevailing winds carry acid water vapour from the UK, France and other countries, causing acid rain or acid snow to fall on Norway and Sweden, hundreds of kilometres from the source of the pollution.

🔘 Improve your grade

Pond pollution

Foundation: A farmer grows wheat on his field. He notices that the water in a small pond next to the field has turned green and the fish have all died.
Explain what has happened.

AO2 [5 marks]

Recycling carbon and nitrogen

Decomposition

- Decay and **decomposition** are caused by fungi and bacteria called **decomposers**.
- **Nutrients** such as carbon, nitrogen and the compounds they form are released because of their activities.
- The nutrients are absorbed in solution by plants and pass to animals as the result of feeding.

The carbon cycle

- Carbon is recycled as carbon dioxide (CO_2) through **respiration** and **photosynthesis** in the carbon cycle.
- Plants absorb CO_2 from the environment, which enables their cells to produce sugars by photosynthesis. The sugars can be used to form the other carbohydrates, lipids (fats and oils) and proteins that build plant bodies.
- When plants are eaten by animals, the carbon in the plant tissues becomes part of the animal bodies. This transfer of carbon continues as animals are eaten by other animals.
- During respiration, organisms release carbon dioxide into the atmosphere. It is also released by the burning of fossil fuels.
- Chalk is formed from the fossilised remains of sea creatures. Exposed to rain (which is slightly acid), the chalk dissolves and more carbon dioxide is released.

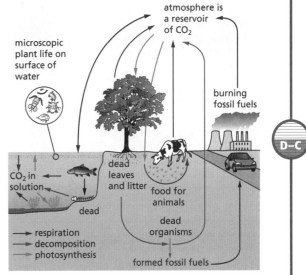

The carbon cycle.

The nitrogen cycle

- Nitrogen is an essential part of the proteins which build bodies, but most living things cannot use nitrogen in the air.
- **Nitrogen-fixing bacteria** in the root nodules of leguminous plants or in the soil can use this gaseous nitrogen, though. They 'fix' (to make part of) gaseous nitrogen as ammonia (NH_3), which forms ammonium compounds.
- Plants absorb the compounds in solution from the soil through their roots.
- Animals obtain nitrogen from food they eat.
- Proteins are a major part of the remains of dead animals and plants and animal wastes. Decomposers convert these proteins and urea into ammonia.
- **Nitrifying bacteria** convert the ammonia from decaying and waste matter to nitrates, which are also absorbed by plants.
- Lightning breaks apart nitrogen molecules in the atmosphere, and the nitrogen reacts with atmospheric oxygen to form nitrogen oxides. These dissolve in raindrops.
- Nitric acid (HNO_3) and nitrous acid (HNO_2) are produced. These acids react with compounds in the soil and form nitrates.
- Nitrates not absorbed by plants are converted by **denitrifying bacteria** in the soil to nitrogen gas, which is released to the atmosphere.

EXAM TIP

Different processes recycle nitrogen between the environment, the dead and the living: nitrogen fixation ⟶ decomposition ⟶ nitrification ⟶ denitrification. Remembering these terms and the role of the bacteria at each stage will help you to recall the nitrogen cycle.

◉ Improve your grade

Carbon dioxide levels

Foundation: Scientists around the world are monitoring the amount of carbon dioxide in the atmosphere and collecting data such as that shown in the graph opposite.

Describe the trend in the graph and suggest a reason for it.

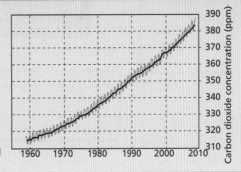

Atmospheric carbon dioxide measured at Mauna Loa, Hawaii.

AO3 [3 marks]

B1 Summary

Living things are put into groups according to how closely they are related to one another. The kingdom is the largest group and species the smallest. Each species is given a two-part (binomial) name.

Living things have characteristics that enable them to live in their environment. This is called adaptation.

Members of a species show differences called variation, which can be due to genetics or the environment, and which can be continuous or discontinuous.

Classification, variation and inheritance

Darwin's theory of natural selection explains how living things evolved due to variation and survival of the best-adapted.

Alternative forms of genes called alleles are passed from parents to offspring. A dominant allele masks the presence of a recessive allele.

Disorders such as sickle cell disease and cystic fibrosis are inherited. Genetic diagrams help us to analyse who in a family is at risk of having the disorder or being a carrier of the affected allele.

The amount of water and glucose in the body and body temperature are kept constant by a process called homeostasis.

Sensory neurones carry electrical impulses to the central nervous system from receptors in sense organs. Motor neurones carry messages from the CNS to effectors (muscles and glands).

Hormones are produced in endocrine glands and are transported in the blood to target organs, where they have an effect.

Responses to a changing environment

Insulin is a hormone that regulates the amount of glucose in the blood. People with Type 1 diabetes do not make insulin so have to inject it. Type 2 diabetes is caused by resistance to insulin, and can be controlled via diet.

Plant hormones cause their shoots to grow towards the light (positive phototropism) and roots to grow towards gravity (positive geotropism).

Plant hormones can be used commercially as selective weedkillers, to grow seedless fruit, to ripen fruit and as rooting powder.

Cigarette smoke contains chemicals that are damaging to health including tar (causes cancer), nicotine (an addictive stimulant) and carbon monoxide (reduces the amount of oxygen in the blood).

Infectious diseases are caused by pathogens. The human body uses physical barriers and chemical defences in the fight against pathogens.

Problems of, and solutions to a changing environment

Energy is wasted at each stage in a food chain, which results in less biomass at each trophic level. This is represented as a pyramid of biomass.

An increasing human population contributes to air and water pollution and a growing demand for resources.

Both nitrogen and carbon can exist in different compounds in the air and bodies of living things. These elements are continually recycled.

Living things rely on each other – they are interdependent. Some relationships are parasitic, others are mutualistic.

Seeing cells and cell components

Microscopes

- Most cells are too small to be seen with the naked eye but can be seen using a light microscope. In a light microscope, a beam of light is passed through the cells.

- Electron microscopes pass a beam of **electrons** through the cells. They enable us to see much more detail.

- You can work out the magnification of a light microscope by carrying out this calculation:

total magnification = magnifying power of eyepiece lens × magnifying power of objective lens

- The greater the **resolving power** of a microscope, the clearer the image it forms. Electron microscopes have better resolving powers than light microscopes.

- Resolving power depends on the wavelength of the electromagnetic radiation (e.g. light or electrons) that is used:

$$\text{Resolving power} = \frac{\text{wavelength}}{2}$$

Cells – components and their functions

- **Multicellular** organisms are made up of many different types of cell.

- Each cell contains components. Some of these are found in all cells, others are only found in a few types.

EXAM TIP

Make sure you remember which components are found in both plant and animal cells and which are found only in plant cells.

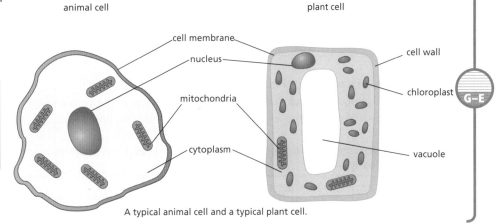

A typical animal cell and a typical plant cell.

- The table below shows the components of animal cells and their functions.

Cytoplasm	Where most of the cell's chemical reactions take place
Cell membrane	Controls the movement of chemicals in and out of the cell
Nucleus	Contains chromosomes
Mitochondria	Where sugars are broken down, releasing energy

- Plant cells have the same components as animal cells, plus those in the table below.

Cell wall	Made of cellulose to strengthen the cell
Vacuole	Keeps the cell turgid
Chloroplasts	Contain chlorophyll and used in photosynthesis

- Bacterial cells are different to plant and animal cells:

  - They do not have mitochondria, chloroplasts or a nucleus (chromosomal DNA and loops of DNA called **plasmids** lie loose in the cytoplasm).

  - The cell wall is not made of cellulose.

  - Some bacteria have a **flagellum**, which propels the cell through liquid.

Improve your grade

Looking at cells

Foundation: The image opposite shows some cells as seen down a microscope.

Are these animal or plant cells? Explain how you decided.

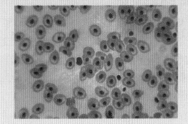

AO2 [2 marks]

DNA

DNA and its structure

- A cell's nucleus contains **chromosomes**, which are made up of **deoxyribonucleic acid** (DNA) wrapped around a core of protein molecules.

- DNA is a double-stranded molecule twisted into a spiral called a double helix.

- The strands of DNA may consist of thousands of building units called **nucleotides**.

- Each nucleotide includes one of four **bases**: guanine (G), thymine (T), adenine (A) and cytosine (C).

- The bases can be in any order, but A always bonds with T and G always bonds with C.

- A **gene** is a section of a strand of DNA which carries the information in the sequence of its bases, enabling a cell to make a protein or part of a protein.

first twist   second twist

> ### EXAM TIP
> You can remember which bases pairs up with which by using this sentence:
>
> **T**igers   **A**re   **G**reat **C**ats
> T pairs up with A   G pairs up with C

Part of a DNA molecule showing the two strands of DNA joined through their bases.

- DNA can easily be extracted from cells in the following way:
  - Use a detergent/salt mixture to break up the membrane of the cells and release the chromosomes.
  - Use a protein-digesting enzyme to break down the protein part of the chromosomes, releasing their DNA.
  - Add cold methanol, which precipitates the DNA (makes it come out of solution). The strands can now clearly be seen.

Complementary base pairing

- The arrangement where the two strands of a DNA molecule are joined together through their bases (A to T and G to C) is called **complementary base pairing**.

- Weak hydrogen bonds join a base with its complementary partner. Because the bonds are weak, they are easily broken, enabling a DNA molecule to separate into two strands.

- This is important when cells make protein and when they divide to form new cells.

Discovering DNA

- The structure of DNA was discovered by scientists building upon each other's work.

- In 1952, Rosalind Franklin and Maurice Wilkins used X-ray crystallography to discover the arrangement of the atoms of DNA molecules.

- In 1953, James Watson and Francis Crick used this information to propose that the structure of a molecule of DNA is a double helix.

The genetic code

- The **sequences** of three bases is called a **codon**. Each codon specifies a particular amino acid.

- This **genetic code** is universal. It works in the same way in the cells of all living things.

How science works

You should be able to:

- describe how we came to our current understanding about the structure of DNA through scientists collaborating and developing each other's ideas.

Improve your grade

Cell division

Higher: Why must the two strands in the DNA molecule separate during cell division?   *AO2* [2 marks]

Genetic engineering and GM organisms

Genetic engineering using bacteria

- **Genetic engineering** involves transferring genes from one type of organism to another.

- A gene controlling the production of a useful protein such as human insulin can be inserted into bacterial cells.

- The cells grow in a solution called a **culture** in huge containers called **fermenters**. They produce large amounts of the protein very quickly.

- The genes are transferred from cell to cell using bacterial enzymes. The diagram opposite shows the process.

Remember!
An organism that has had genes from another type inserted into its cells is called a **genetically modified** (GM) organism.

- Genetically engineered insulin has several advantages:
  - It is cheap to produce and is available in large quantities.
  - It is human insulin, so users experience no allergic reactions or intolerances.
  - It does not use animal products and so is not a problem for certain religious groups or vegetarians.

- However, some people are concerned that GM organisms could have unknown and unforeseen effects on other organisms, including humans.

strand of DNA carrying a gene which enables cells to produce useful proteins

bacterial cell
bacteria have pieces of circular DNA called plasmid DNA

the DNA strand is cut out using a **restriction enzyme** to isolate the 'useful' gene

plasmid is cut open with the same enzyme used to cut out the 'useful' gene

the 'useful' gene is inserted into the plasmid using **ligase** enzyme

plasmid is put back into the bacterial cell

bacteria multiply and produce millions of identical clones, all with the DNA coding for the required protein

bacteria grow in special tanks called fermenters. The end product is removed from the fermenter

A summary of producing genetically engineered bacteria.

(Grade indicators: G–E, D–C, B–A*)

Feeding the world

- Developments in GM crops include those that can:
  - grow in places with low rainfall
  - produce their own chemicals to kill insects that damage them
  - resist diseases
  - resist the effects of **herbicides** (weedkillers); farmers can then destroy competing weeds without destroying the crop
  - produce their own fertiliser.

- Some people are concerned about GM crops. Their worries are that:
  - it's not natural
  - eating GM food may affect our health
  - GM crops may harm wildlife
  - pollen from crops modified to resist herbicides may transfer to weeds.

(Grade indicator: G–E)

- **Vitamin A** deficiency is common among millions of poorer people and can cause blindness.

- Golden rice is a variety that has been genetically modified to produce more **beta-carotene** in the rice grain. This is converted to vitamin A in our cells.

- There are arguments for and against using golden rice.

For	Against
Human cells convert beta-carotene into vitamin A very efficiently.	Aiming for a balanced diet is a better solution to vitamin A deficiency.
Golden rice is not meant to be the only solution to the vitamin A problem.	Trying to deal with the vitamin A problem with a single GM solution is too limiting.
We are only trying to deal with a part of the bigger problem of making a healthy balanced diet available to poor people.	Golden rice has never undergone trials to check that it is safe for people to eat.

(Grade indicator: D–C)

How science works

You should be able to:
- discuss the benefits and drawbacks of genetic modification in the contexts of using bacteria to make human insulin, the use of golden rice and herbicide-resistant crops.

Improve your grade

GM protest
Foundation: Fifty people turned up to protest on a piece of land that was growing GM wheat. Outline the concerns they have.
AO1 [3 marks]

Mitosis and meiosis

Dividing cells

- When parent cells divide, new cells called **daughter cells** are formed.
- The nucleus of the parent cells can divide in one of two ways: **mitosis** or **meiosis**.
- Mitosis results in two daughter cells with identical chromosomes to the parent cells. If the parent cells have two sets of chromosomes (**diploid**) then the daughter cells will also be diploid.

G–E
- Mitosis is used in order for organisms to:
  - *repair damage*: damaged or old skin cells are replaced by mitosis with identical new skin cells.
  - *grow*: the mass of a plant root increases because the existing root cells produce more by mitosis.

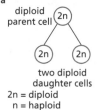

a

diploid parent cell (2n)

two diploid daughter cells
2n = diploid
n = haploid

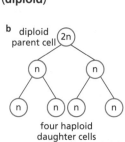

b diploid parent cell (2n)

four haploid daughter cells

Reproduction

- Asexual reproduction also happens via mitosis. It involves only one parent, which produces new cells to form offspring. The offspring are therefore genetically identical to each other and the parent. They are **clones**.
- Meiosis is the process that is used to form **gametes**.

D–C
- In meiosis, the four daughter cells each have half the number of chromosomes of the parent cell, resulting in genetically different **haploid** gametes.

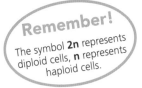

Remember!
The symbol **2n** represents diploid cells, **n** represents haploid cells.

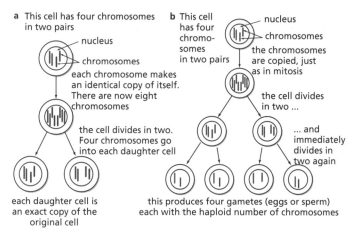

a This cell has four chromosomes in two pairs

nucleus

chromosomes

each chromosome makes an identical copy of itself. There are now eight chromosomes

the cell divides in two. Four chromosomes go into each daughter cell

each daughter cell is an exact copy of the original cell

b This cell has four chromosomes in two pairs

nucleus

chromosomes

the chromosomes are copied, just as in mitosis

the cell divides in two ...

... and immediately divides in two again

this produces four gametes (eggs or sperm) each with the haploid number of chromosomes

a Mitosis and b meiosis: the pattern of chromosomes compared.

- When a parent cell is about to divide, its chromosomes **replicate** (copy) themselves.
- This results in chromosomes with two identical strands called **chromatids**.
- During meiosis, each chromosome pairs up with its corresponding partner along the centre of the cell.
- The pairs of chromosome copies exchange pieces of DNA with one another before the cell divides into two.

B–A*
- Another division then takes place, where the chromatids are split in half. Each daughter cell receives a different chromosome. This results in gametes that are haploid and genetically different from one another.
- During fertilisation, a haploid male gamete (sperm) fuses with a haploid female gamete (egg). The chromosomes of each cell combine.
- The result is a diploid **zygote** (fertilised egg). This has inherited a new combination of chromosomes – and therefore genes – contributed 50:50 from the parents.

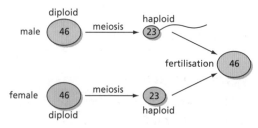

diploid
male 46 → meiosis → haploid 23

fertilisation → 46

female 46 → meiosis → 23
diploid   haploid

Fertilisation restores the diploid number.

Improve your grade

Zygote to foetus

Foundation: Explain why mitosis is an essential process in the formation of a baby from a fertilised egg.

AO1 [3 marks]

Cloning plants and animals

Vegetative reproduction

- In flowering plants, parts of the root, leaf or stem can grow into new plants. This type of asexual reproduction is sometimes called **vegetative reproduction**.

- It produces new plants which are genetically identical (clones) to the parent plant. This is useful to gardeners and farmers who want stocks of plants with preferred characteristics such as disease resistance, fruit colour, flower shape, and so on.

- A simple type of vegetative reproduction is to take **cuttings**.

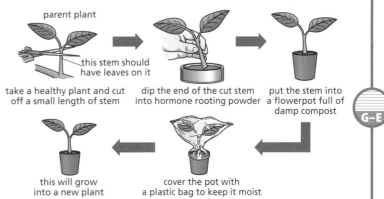

parent plant

this stem should have leaves on it

take a healthy plant and cut off a small length of stem

dip the end of the cut stem into hormone rooting powder

put the stem into a flowerpot full of damp compost

this will grow into a new plant

cover the pot with a plastic bag to keep it moist

Making a cutting.

G–E

Tissue culture

- **Tissue culture** is a process that involves cutting small pieces of tissue from the parent that is to be cloned.

- The pieces are grown in a sterile liquid or gel, which provides all the substances needed for their development.

D–C

Embryo transplants

- **Embryo** transplants begin in the laboratory and end in normal births:
  - **Donor eggs** are taken from female animals and fertilised in the laboratory.
  - Each embryo that forms is split up into its separate cells.
  - Some of the separated cells are transplanted into the womb of a **host mother**, where they develop into identical embryos.
  - The host mother later gives birth to several genetically identical youngsters. They are clones.

EXAM TIP

You may be asked to discuss the advantages, disadvantages and risks of cloning mammals, so make sure you can apply some of the points here to different situations.

G–E

Cloning

- The benefits and dangers of cloning animals have been hotly debated.
  - Cloning allows scientists to produce animals with desirable characteristics quickly and reliably.
  - It helps to build up populations of rare animals which might otherwise be threatened with extinction. Host mothers can carry transplanted embryos of different species even after the original parents have died, as fertilised eggs can be kept frozen for many years.
  - There is evidence that cloned animals have medical issues. Should we produce clones that may have short and painful lives?

- Although it is currently illegal, it is possible to clone human cells. Healthy cells from a sick person can be cloned and used to repair that person's damaged tissues.

- A person needing a transplant could use a brain-dead clone of themselves as a source of tissues and organs for transplant. The transplanted material would not be rejected because it is genetically identical.

- Dolly the sheep was the first cloned mammal. She suffered medical issues that eventually caused her to be put down.

- Such points raise issues about the safety and ethics of cloning.

D–C

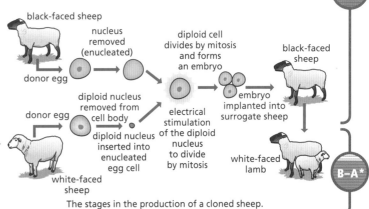

black-faced sheep

nucleus removed (enucleated)

donor egg

diploid cell divides by mitosis and forms an embryo

black-faced sheep

donor egg

diploid nucleus removed from cell body

diploid nucleus inserted into enucleated egg cell

white-faced sheep

electrical stimulation of the diploid nucleus to divide by mitosis

embryo implanted into surrogate sheep

white-faced lamb

B–A*

The stages in the production of a cloned sheep.

Improve your grade

Cloning Daisy

Foundation: Daisy the cow produces the most milk in her herd. Her farmer is considering using her eggs for embryo transplants.

Explain to him why cloning her might be an even better idea.

AO2 [3 marks]

Stem cells and the human genome

Stem cells

- After fertilisation, cell division takes place and a hollow ball of cells called an embryo is formed.
- The cells on the inside of an embyro are called **embryonic stem cells**.
- They are unspecialised (not designed for a particular job). As the embryo develops the cells begin to **differentiate** and change into different types of cell.
- As the cells mature, they can no longer differentiate, but some of our stem cells remain into adulthood. For example, there are adult stem cells in our bone marrow which give rise to new blood cells. Small numbers of stem cells remain in other body tissues as well.
- If stem cells can be made to multiply and differentiate, we would have an unlimited supply of different types of cells, which could be transplanted into people whose tissues are damaged. This is called stem cell therapy.

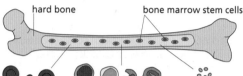

Remember!
Once stem cells mature, they lose their ability to differentiate and their role stays with them for life.

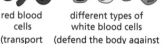

red blood cells (transport oxygen)   different types of white blood cells (defend the body against disease-causing microbes)   platelets (help to clot blood, stopping bleeding)

Section of a long bone cut lengthways. The bone marrow is a source of stem cells, which differentiate into red blood cells, white blood cells and platelets.

Stem cell therapy

- Because embryonic stem cells can differentiate into many more types of cell than adult stem cells, they are ideal for therapies that repair damaged tissues. Treating Parkinson's disease and diabetes are examples.
- Sourcing embryonic stem cells destroys the embryo they come from. Some people think that it is unethical to destroy embryos. Using adult stem cells is less controversial.

- Risks of stem cell therapy include:
  - rejection of the embryonic stem cells
  - the possibility that adult stem cells may carry genetic mutations for disease or may become defective
  - the appearance of side-effects and complications in the recipient; stem cell therapy may trigger adverse immune responses or the development of cancers
  - claims of the effectiveness of the therapies and treatments offered are sometimes from unregulated sources, whose treatment may be dangerous.
- Scientists are researching new ways of producing stem cells that offer the benefits of embryonic stem cells but do not destroy embryos.

The human genome

- **Genome** refers to all of the DNA in each cell of an organism.
- The **Human Genome Project** (HGP) began in 1989. A group of scientists from all over the world collaborated to work out the human genome. The result was announced in April 2003.
- The scientists broke up chromosomes of cells to get at their DNA. Thousands of copies of the pieces of DNA were placed inside machines called **sequencers**, which display the most likely order of the bases.
- Powerful computers were used to help match the base sequences of genes with the proteins for which they are the code.
- Understanding the human genome enables scientists to look at how genes control our vulnerability to particular diseases and to personalise drug treatments to work with an individual's genome (**pharmacogenomics**).
- The human genome revealed that some races are more or less vulnerable to certain diseases than others. Some people are concerned that if genetic data identifying ethnicity were available it might encourage discrimination against certain groups of people.

How science works

You should be able to:
- discuss the potential applications of stem cell therapy and the results of the Human Genome Project, as well as their potential benefits and drawbacks.

Improve your grade

Future applications of the HGP

Higher: In the future we may be able to use an individual's genome to calculate the likelihood of them developing diseases such as cancer.

Evaluate this potential application of the Human Genome Project.   *AO2* [4 marks]

Protein synthesis

Making proteins

- Cells make, or synthesise, **proteins** by joining together amino acid units in the correct order.

- Proteins have a complicated shape that helps them to carry out their jobs. Protein molecules that are the wrong shape cannot perform their functions correctly.

- DNA makes sure that the correct number of amino acid units joins together in the right order.

- The more amino acid units joined together, the larger the molecule: **peptides** are chains of 2–20 amino acids; **polypeptides** contain 21–50; proteins contain more than 50 amino acid units.

Ribonucleic acid

- **Ribonucleic acid (RNA)** is a chemical like DNA. However, RNA is a single strand and has U base instead of T.

- RNA has two roles in protein synthesis:
  - **Messenger RNA (mRNA)** carries the protein-making information from the DNA inside the nucleus of the cell to the **ribosomes** in the cytoplasm, where the protein is made.
  - **Transfer RNA (tRNA)** carries the amino acids needed to form the protein to the ribosomes.

Protein synthesis

- There are two stages in protein synthesis: transcription and translation. Each step numbered below is shown in the diagram.

- **Transcription**
  1 The strands of DNA separate.
  2 Strands of mRNA form as the bases of RNA nucleotides combine with their complementary bases of the single-stranded DNA.
  3 The strands of mRNA separate from their respective complementary strands of DNA. They pass from the nucleus through gaps.

- **Translation**
  4 Each strand of mRNA binds to a ribosome, forming an mRNA–ribosome complex.
  5 Each type of tRNA molecule binds to its particular type of amino acid dissolved in the cytoplasm, depending on the triplet of bases (codon) it carries.
  6 tRNA/amino acid combinations pass to the mRNA–ribosome complex. The exposed bases of each tRNA bind to their complementary bases on the mRNA. Chemical bonds form between the amino acids next to each other
  7 Once the bonds form, each tRNA separates from its amino acid and the mRNA strand.
  8 The linked amino acids form a polypeptide.

> **Remember!**
> RNA has the base uracil (U) instead of thymine (T). Therefore during transcription, any A bases on the DNA strand will be paired up with a U to form the mRNA.

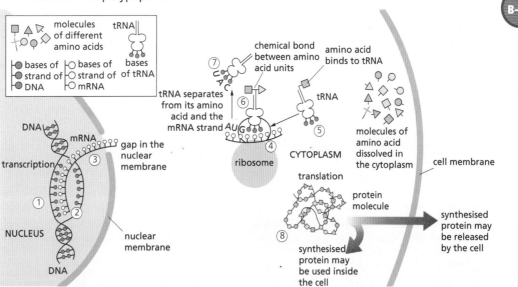

Protein synthesis simplified.

Improve your grade

Sickle cell mutation

Higher: Haemoglobin is a protein that is found in red blood cells. Sickle cell disease is a genetic illness where the red blood cells have a distorted shape. It is caused by a mutation in the gene for haemoglobin that converts a GAG codon into a GTG.

Explain how this causes a change in the shape of the haemoglobin molecule. *AO2* [4 marks]

Mutations

Variation and mutation

- If a sperm or an egg carries a mutated gene, the **mutation** will be inherited by offspring after fertilisation has taken place.

- Mutations can be harmful, as altering the proteins produced can disturb the activity of cells. Affected organisms are therefore less likely to survive.

- Some genes that are now 'normal' were once mutants. The mutations added genetic variation that happened to be beneficial.

- This meant that the organisms carrying the mutated genes survived. Their descendants inherited the genes and now they are the normal versions.

- Some mutations are neutral – they do not affect an organism's chances of survival one way or another.

How mutations change DNA

- Mutations occur because of copying errors in the sequence of bases during DNA **replication**.

- A base may be deleted or inserted. This changes the sequence of bases along the gene from where the mutation occurs.

- The diagram opposite shows a normal DNA base sequence mutated by a deletion (removal of a base) and an insertion (addition of a base).

- The order of amino acid units from where the mutation occurs changes in each mutated gene. This affects the structure of the protein.

- The structure (and therefore shape) of a protein affects its function. Changes in structure can therefore affect how well the protein works or may even prevent it from working at all.

The deletion or insertion of a base causes a mutation. The amino acid units and their sequence controlled by the particular short sequence of DNA bases shown here are named as their internationally recognised abbreviations.

Silent mutations

- A codon is a section of DNA or RNA that codes for an amino acid. Almost all amino acids are specified by more than one codon (there are two exceptions to this).

- If a mutation changes a codon to an alternative (substitution) that still specifies the same amino acid, and the sequence of codons (including the mutated codon) is unchanged, then the amino acid sequence and the structure of the protein remains unchanged.

- This is known as a **silent mutation**.

EXAM TIP

There are 20 different amino acids whose names can be abbreviated, e.g. valine becomes val. You don't need to learn any of the names for your exam.

A silent mutation alters the base sequence of a gene but not the sequence of the amino acid units of the protein encoded by the gene.

Improve your grade

Sex cell mutation

Foundation: A mutation occurs in the DNA of an organism's sperm cells.

Explain how this mutation will be passed to its offspring. *AO1* [2 marks]

Enzymes

Rates of reaction

- **Enzymes** are biological **catalysts**. They increase the rate of chemical reactions inside and outside cells.
- Enzymes are specific in their action – each enzyme only catalyses a particular chemical reaction or type of chemical reaction.
- During digestion, enzymes break down large insoluble food molecules into smaller, soluble ones that can dissolve into the blood.

How enzymes work

- The diagram opposite shows an enzyme working. The **substrate** binds to a part of the enzyme called the **active site**.
- Notice how they fit together like a lock and key. An enzyme will only catalyse a particular reaction when the shape of its active site matches the shape of the substrate molecule.
- The enzyme catalyses the breakdown of the substrate into the **products**, which then leave the enzyme. The enzyme is then free to join to another substrate molecule.

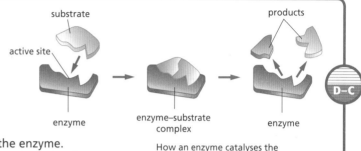

How an enzyme catalyses the breakdown of a molecule.

- Two examples of enzymes at work in the body include:
  - **DNA polymerase**, which breaks up the double helix before DNA replication. It is also involved in checking the copying of the DNA strand.
  - Speeding up the rate of joining together the individual amino acids during protein synthesis.

Factors affecting enzymes

- Because most enzymes are proteins, they are sensitive to changes in temperature and pH.
- The activity of enzymes increases as the temperature goes up. When the activity of the enzyme is at a maximum, we say this is the optimum temperature. This is around 37 °C for enzymes that exist in the human body. After this point, as the temperature increases the activity will decrease.
- Different enzymes have different optimum pHs (the pH at which their activity is highest). For example, the enzyme **amylase** has an optimum pH of around 8.

EXAM TIP

The activity of an enzyme increases with temperature because a rise in heat energy increases the movement of the enzyme and substrate molecules, so there is more chance of them colliding and forming an enzyme-substrate complex.

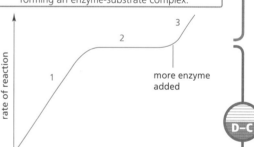

Enzyme activity varies with the concentration of substrate.

- Enzyme activity is also affected by substrate concentration, as shown in the graph.
  1. When there is more than enough enzyme, the **rate of reaction** is proportional to the concentration of substrate.
  2. When all of the enzyme's active sites are filled with substrate molecules, the rate of reaction levels off.
  3. Adding more enzyme increases the rate of reaction because more active sites are available to substrate molecules, which fill them.

Protein synthesis

- At extremes of temperature or pH an enzyme will become **denatured**.
- Denaturing is a permanent change in shape of the protein molecule. It is caused by the breaking up of the hydrogen bonds that hold the structure together.
- A change in a protein's shape will affect its activity because the active site will change, so the substrate will no longer fit.

Improve your grade

Understanding enzymes

Higher: Biological washing tablets contain enzymes that help break down stains found on clothes. Mark's clothes were very dirty so he decided to wash them at a much higher temperature than recommended on the instructions. The stains did not come off his clothes.

Use your understanding of enzymes to explain why.

AO2 [3 marks]

Topic 1: 1.26, 1.27, 1.28, 1.29, 1.30, 1.31, 1.32

Unit B2   31

Respiring cells and diffusion

Respiration

- We exhale less oxygen and more carbon dioxide than we inhale.

- This is the result of cells carrying out the chemical reaction **aerobic respiration**. This uses oxygen to break down glucose molecules to release energy, carbon dioxide and water:

  glucose + oxygen → carbon dioxide + water + energy

- All of the available energy is released from a glucose molecule during aerobic respiration.

- **Anaerobic respiration** does not use oxygen. For example, in muscle tissue:

  glucose → lactic acid + energy

- The energy released in anaerobic respiration is much less than in aerobic respiration, as the glucose is not fully broken down.

- The energy released during aerobic respiration is used to keep us warm and drive life processes, such as movement and reproduction.

Remember!

All living cells carry out respiration. A common misconception is that plants carry out photosynthesis instead, but in fact they carry out both processes when it is light, and only respiration when it is dark.

- Exercising hard results in the muscles carrying out anaerobic respiration, as the heart and lungs cannot work fast enough to get the required amount of oxygen for aerobic respiration.

- The lactic acid produced in anaerobic respiration accumulates in the muscles and makes them tired and sore.

- After exercise, rapid breathing draws more air into the lungs and the fast-beating heart sends the oxygen to the muscle cells, where it helps break down lactic acid into carbon dioxide and water.

- This is called **excess post-exercise oxygen consumption (EPOC)**.

- The time taken for the lactic acid to be removed and breathing and heart rates to return to normal is the **recovery period**.

What is diffusion?

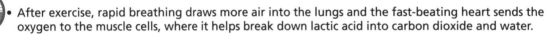

- Molecules in liquids and gases are in constant random motion. Some molecules will spread from areas where they are highly concentrated to areas of lower concentration. As a result there is a net movement of molecules in this direction. This is called **diffusion**.

- The greater the difference between the regions of high and low concentration, the faster the substance's rate of diffusion.

- Substances move into and out of cells of living things by diffusion.

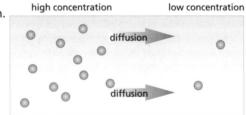

high concentration   low concentration

diffusion

diffusion

Diffusion: molecules of a substance move from where the substance is in high concentration to where it is in low concentration.

- **Capillary vessels** supply body tissue with blood via the circulatory system.

- Substances such as glucose, oxygen and hormones pass between the blood and tissues via diffusion.

- Gaseous exchange is the process by which oxygen enters the blood and carbon dioxide leaves. It takes place across the walls of the alveoli (air sacs) in the lungs.

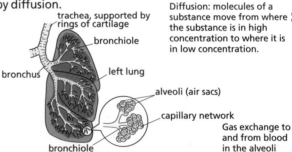

trachea, supported by rings of cartilage

bronchiole

bronchus

left lung

alveoli (air sacs)

capillary network

Gas exchange to and from blood in the alveoli

bronchiole

Concentration gradients

- The **concentration gradient** is the difference in concentration of a substance between high and low concentration regions.

- The greater the difference between the regions, the greater the concentration gradient. As a result the rate of diffusion is maximised.

- The diffusion of glucose and oxygen to respiring cells relies on a high concentration gradient between the cells and the blood capillaries.

- This is maintained because the cells are constantly respiring, breaking down the glucose and oxygen and lowering their concentration inside the cells.

Improve your grade

The race

Foundation: You take part in a race. At first you sprint off feeling full of energy. However, half way through your legs start to ache and you have to stop. Explain why this happened.   *AO1* [3 marks]

Effects of exercise

Exercise and rates

- Exercise increases the **heart rate** and breathing rate.

- During exercise aerobic respiration in the muscle cells releases energy, enabling muscles to contract quickly and strongly.

- Respiration produces carbon dioxide, which passes from the muscle cells to the blood, raising its acidity and lowering its pH below 7.0.

- The lowered pH stimulates an increase in the heart rate and breathing rate.

- Heart and breathing rates remain high for some minutes after exercising. As a result, more blood – with its load of carbon dioxide – passes to the lungs, where it is exhaled.

- The concentration of carbon dioxide in the blood decreases, restoring the pH of the blood to its normal value of 7.4. Heart rate and breathing rate return to normal.

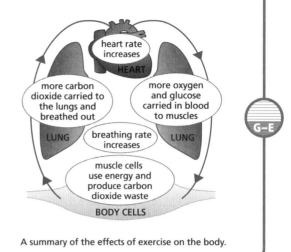

G–E

A summary of the effects of exercise on the body.

Investigating the effects of exercise

- Breathing rate can be investigated by using limewater to test for carbon dioxide.

- An easy way to measure your carbon dioxide output is to place a straw in limewater and note the time taken for the limewater to turn cloudy as you breathe out through the straw.

- Counting the number of times your back rises and falls in a minute gives the breathing rate.

- Taking your **pulse** is an easy way of measuring heart rate (the number of pulses per minute).

D–C

Breathing and heart rate

- The more air we breathe in, the more oxygen reaches the muscles and the more energy is released through aerobic respiration.

- The muscles contract more vigorously, enabling us to exercise more.

- The increased rate of aerobic respiration in the muscle cells produces more carbon dioxide. The increased breathing rate rapidly removes the carbon dioxide from the lungs.

- The larger the volume of air moving in and out of our lungs with each breath, the higher the volume of oxygen that can reach the muscles.

- The following equation can be used to calculate this:

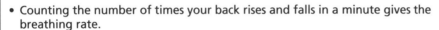
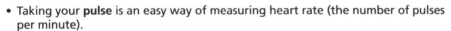

number of breaths in a minute (breathing rate) × volume of air per breath = volume of air exchanged per minute

- One complete contraction and relaxation of the heart produces one **heartbeat**.

- The volume of blood pumped from the heart each minute (called the cardiac output) depends on the heart rate and volume of blood pumped out with each beat (the stroke volume).

- Heart rate, stroke volume and cardiac output measure the heart's effectiveness and fitness. Each can be calculated using the equation:

cardiac output = stroke volume × heart rate

B–A*

Remember!
Both the volume of air per breath, the number of breaths in a minute and heart rate will increase with exercise.

Improve your grade

Stroke volume

Higher: Ben is a professional runner. Through training he has been able to increase the stroke volume of his heart.

Explain how this enables Ben to run faster.

AO2 [5 marks]

Photosynthesis

Light and photosynthesis

- Plants use sunlight, carbon dioxide and water to produce glucose, through the process of **photosynthesis**.

$$\text{carbon dioxide} + \text{water} \xrightarrow{\text{light energy}} \text{glucose} + \text{oxygen}$$

- Plants are green because of the green pigment **chlorophyll** inside the **chloroplasts** in their cells.

- Chlorophyll absorbs the light energy required to drive photosynthesis.

EXAM TIP

Notice that the chemical equation for photosynthesis is the same as the one for respiration, but in reverse. This means that if you only learn one for the exam, you will also know the other.

Leaves and photosynthesis

- Leaves are thin and flat, exposing a large surface area. This maximises the absorption of light.

- The palisade cells, just under the upper surface of the leaf where the light is brightest, are packed with chloroplasts containing chlorophyll for a maximum rate of photosynthesis.

- Air spaces enable gases including water vapour to circulate within the leaf, so the reactants for photosynthesis can reach the cells that need them.

- Oxygen, carbon dioxide and water vapour diffuse between the leaf's air spaces and the atmosphere through the gaps called **stomata** that perforate the underside of the leaf.

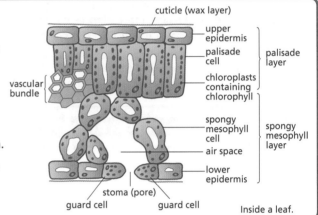

Inside a leaf.

The rate of photosynthesis

- The rate at which plants make glucose is affected by conditions of:
  - temperature
  - light intensity
  - carbon dioxide
  - water.

- If levels of any of these factors drop too low, photosynthesis slows even if the others are in abundant supply. This is called a **limiting factor**.

Limiting factors

- You can measure the rate of photosynthesis using the technique shown in the diagram opposite.

- The rate is measured by counting the number of bubbles of oxygen produced by the water-weed in a given time.

- This set-up works for investigating the effects of changing light intensity, carbon dioxide concentration and temperature on the rate of photosynthesis.

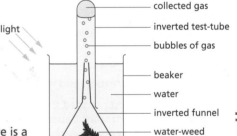

An experimental set-up to investigate the rate of photosynthesis. What is the gas collected?

- Most plants grow best in warm, light conditions and when there is a high concentration of carbon dioxide and plenty of water. Growing plants in greenhouses can help maximise these conditions.

- The higher the temperature, the faster the rate of photosynthesis and the faster the production of materials that enable plants to grow.

- If the temperature continues to increase beyond an optimum, photosynthesis slows because the enzymes controlling the different reactions of photosynthesis are **denatured**.

- Plants grow more vigorously in bright sunlight because high light intensity maximises the rate of photosynthesis. The rate of increase is up to a maximum value (called the optimum light intensity). Even though light intensity increases further, the rate of photosynthesis does not.

Improve your grade

Weed removal

Foundation: Suzanne has weeds growing in her flowerbeds and notices that her plants are not growing. Explain why this is.

AO2 [3 marks]

Transport in plants, osmosis and fieldwork

Transport systems

- **Xylem** (zy-lem) tissue consists of columns of hollow, dead cells. It carries water and dissolved mineral salts from the roots, through the stem and out into every leaf and flower.

- **Phloem** (flow-em) tissue runs by the side of the xylem. Its tube-like cells carry dissolved glucose and other substances to all parts of the plant.

- Water evaporates from stomata in a process called **transpiration**.

- As water is lost from the leaves, more is drawn up through the xylem tissue from the roots, which absorb more water from the soil. This continuous movement of water is called the transpiration stream.

Osmosis

- **Osmosis** is the movement of water from a high water concentration to a lower one across a partially permeable membrane (one that will only let water molecules across).

- You can investigate osmosis by studying cells under a microscope. Cells left in a concentrated salt or sugar solution will lose water by osmosis. They will become **flaccid** (limp).

- Visking tubing is a partially permeable membrane that can be used to investigate the movement of substances into and out of cells.

- In experiment **a** opposite there is a higher water concentration outside the tubing than inside. Over time the water will enter the tubing by osmosis, causing the pressure inside to increase and the tubing to become **turgid**.

- Experiment **b** shows the opposite happening, as water flows out of the tubing, leaving it flaccid.

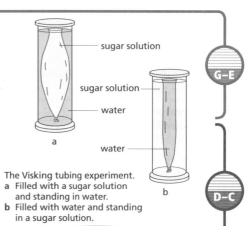

The Visking tubing experiment.
a Filled with a sugar solution and standing in water.
b Filled with water and standing in a sugar solution.

Remember!
A solution that is highly concentrated, e.g. has a high sugar concentration, will have a low water concentration.

Root hairs

- Root hair cells are fine, hair-like extensions of a root.

- Water flows into root hair cells by osmosis. Their large surface area is an adaptation that enables plants to maximise their absorption of water from the soil.

Water absorption through a plant's root system.

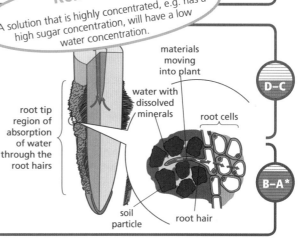

- Root hairs also take up mineral salts in solution. The solutions are much more concentrated in the cells of root tissue than in the soil. Therefore, mineral salts cannot pass into the roots by diffusion. **Active transport** is used, which requires energy from aerobic respiration.

Organisms and their environment

- Fieldwork investigations are designed to find out more about where organisms live (their distribution) and why they live where they do.

- Techniques used include:
  - pooters, nets and traps to collect animals in order to estimate their distribution
  - quadrats to count the number of animals or plants in a known area
  - probes to measure temperature, pH and light intensity.

- **Ecosystems** and their **populations** are usually too large for us to study everything about them. Instead we study small parts called samples.

- Errors in sampling techniques can be reduced by taking a number of random samples and standardising the samples taken (e.g. at the same time of day or in the same season/weather conditions).

Improve your grade

Preserving fish

Foundation: Covering fish with salt and leaving it causes the fish to dry out and become hard. Use osmosis to explain why this happens. *AO2* [3 marks]

Topic 2: 2.17, 2.18, 2.19, 2.20, 2.21, 2.22, 2.23   Unit B2   **35**

Fossil record and growth

The fossil record

- **Fossils** are the remains or impressions made by dead organisms. They are usually found in **sedimentary rocks**. They are preserved over millions of years as rock particles from ancient seas fell on dead organisms on the seabed.

- Each layer of fossils records life on Earth at the time the layer formed. This helps us trace the history and evolution of life. Fossils provide evidence for Darwin's theory of **natural selection**.

- Fossil records do not show a continuous series of changes between ancestors and their descendants. There are gaps. This is because:
  - most organisms **decompose** quickly when they die; not all of them find their way into an environment where they will be preserved and so only a small number of fossils form
  - many fossils are yet to be found
  - even if a fossil forms, it may not survive geological cycles.

- Most vertebrates today have a **pentadactyl limb** – a forelimb with five 'fingers' or 'toes'.
- The discovery of pentadactyl limbs in fossils has led scientists to believe that all vertebrates directly descend from a **common ancestor**. They use this as evidence of **evolution**.

Growth

- Growth is measured as an increase in an organism's size, length and mass. The increase is the result of:
  - cell division: the number of cells increases
  - cell elongation: the length of cells increases
  - synthesis of organic materials (**carbohydrates**, proteins, fats and oils): the mass of cells increases.

- Plants grow throughout their life from cell division in tissues called **meristems**.

- Behind the meristems are regions where cells elongate and increase in size by water and other organic materials flowing into them.

- These cells are undifferentiated. As growth continues, differentiation of cells begins producing the types of cell that make up the tissues and organs of the plant.

- Cell division in animals occurs in all the tissues of the body.

- In young animals, tissues grow because cell division produces more cells than die through age or damage.

- Animals continue to grow until the gain of cells balances the loss of cells.

- Growth then stops, marking the start of becoming an adult. However, the mass of an individual may continue to increase as protein synthesis adds more mass to cells and the tissues that the cells form.

> **Remember!**
> Plant growth involves cell division, cell elongation and differentiation. Cell division and differentiation contribute to growth in animals.

- Growth charts help parents and doctors to monitor children's development.

- The figures on the chart are different **percentiles**, each representing the spread of values for the characteristic (such as height or mass) selected. The 50th percentile represents the average value.

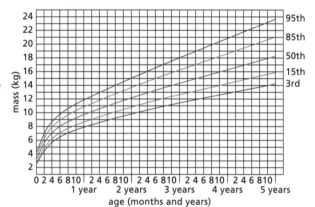

A growth chart for mass of boys aged up to 5 years
(Source: WHO Child Growth Standards.)

Improve your grade

Growth chart

Higher: Adam is four years old and has a mass of 13 kg.

Use the growth chart above to comment on his mass.   *AO3* [3 marks]

Cells, tissues, organs and blood

Cells join together

- Cells are the building blocks from which humans and all other living things are made

- **Tissues** are a group of similar cells with a particular function.

- An **organ** is a group of different tissues that work together. An organ has a particular function.

- An organ system is a group of different organs that work together. Organ systems also have specific functions.

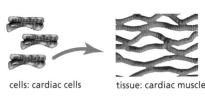

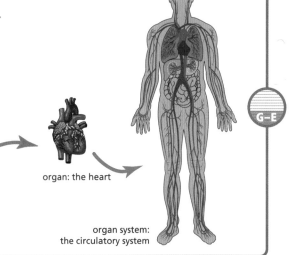

cells: cardiac cells → tissue: cardiac muscle → organ: the heart

organ system: the circulatory system

Cells form tissues which form organs which form organ systems.

 G–E

Differentiation

- All the different types of human cell are the result of cell division (mitosis) and **differentiation** during the development of the egg to the **embryo** to the **foetus**.

- Each type of human cell is specialised to enable it to carry out a particular function. For example, neurones (nerve cells) transmit nerve impulses and muscle cells contract (shorten).

D–C

- The process of mitosis produces daughter cells. These are genetically identical to one another and to their parent cell. However, most adult cells are differentiated.

- Genetically the cells may be the same, but the pattern of genes switching on and off (gene activity) is different.

- This process occurs in the development of all living things.

B–A*

Blood

- Blood contains the following components:
  - *Red blood cells* contain a red pigment called **haemoglobin**. They do not have a nucleus.
  - *White blood cells* have a nucleus. They contain cytoplasm, which allows them to access tissues so they can protect the body by attacking and destroying bacteria and viruses.
  - *Platelets* are fragments of cells with no nucleus. Platelets contain proteins.
  - *Plasma* is a straw-coloured liquid that transports carbon dioxide, soluble food products and urea (and waste products from the liver) in solution. Plasma also circulates the heat released by the chemical reactions in body cells, and this helps to maintain body temperature.

 G–E

- The function of red blood cells is to transport oxygen from the lungs to respiring tissues.

- In the lungs, where oxygen concentration is high, haemoglobin combines with oxygen to form **oxyhaemoglobin**.

- Oxyhaemoglobin breaks down to release oxygen to respiring tissues where the concentration of oxygen is low.

 D–C

> **Remember!**
> Blood containing a lot of oxyhaemoglobin is called **oxygenated blood** and is bright red. Blood with little oxyhaemoglobin is called **deoxygenated blood** and is a deep red-purple colour (not blue!).

- When platelets are damaged by a cut or torn tissue, they release a substance that starts a chain of chemical reactions in the blood. These reactions end with the soluble plasma protein called fibrinogen changing into insoluble **fibrin**.

- Fibrin forms a mesh of fibres across the wound and traps red blood cells, forming a clot.

- The clot plugs the wound and stops bleeding. It also prevents bacteria and viruses from entering the body.

 B–A*

Improve your grade

The heart
Foundation: Why is the heart classed as an organ?

AO1 [2 marks]

The heart and circulatory system

The heart pumps blood

- The heart lies inside the chest cavity, protected by the rib cage. Much of the wall of the heart is made of **cardiac muscle**. This muscle contracts and relaxes to pump blood through the circulatory system.

- The heart has four chambers: two **atria** (singular atrium) and two **ventricles**.

G–E

- The wall of the left ventricle is thicker than that of the right ventricle because it has to pump blood to all parts of the body. The right ventricle only pumps blood to the lungs, so less effort is required.

- The heart also has four major blood vessels: pulmonary artery, pulmonary vein, vena cava and aorta.

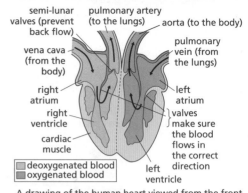

A drawing of the human heart viewed from the front. The black arrows show the direction of blood flow.

Blood circulates

- The heart is a double pump: each side pumps blood along a different route.

D–C

- The diagram opposite shows a simplified arrangement of the circulation of blood:
  - The left atrium and ventricle pump **oxygenated blood** from the lungs around the rest of the body.
  - The right atrium and ventricle pump **deoxygenated blood** to the lungs, where it can be oxygenated.

Remember!

Arteries carry blood away from the heart, veins carry blood towards it. Arteries (apart from the pulmonary artery) carry oxygenated blood; veins (apart from the pulmonary vein) carry deoxygenated blood.

B–A*

- When the muscular walls of the heart relax, blood fills the chambers. When the muscles contract, blood is forced from the chambers.

- The valves control the flow of blood through the heart and into the arteries leading from the heart, preventing backflow (flow in the opposite direction).

The heart and circulatory system, showing the lung circuit and the head and body circuit.

The circulatory system

- The circulatory system is a network of tube-like vessels called **arteries** and **veins**.

- The heart pumps blood through arteries to body tissues.

G–E

- Blood drains from the tissue through the veins, back to the heart.

- Smaller vessels branch from arteries and veins. The smallest are called **capillaries**. They link arteries and veins.

- Blood in veins flows more slowly than blood in arteries because it is at lower pressure. The large diameter of a vein enables the blood to flow easily.

- Blood flow through veins is helped by the contractions of the muscles in the arms and legs through which the veins pass.

D–C

- The heart pumps blood into arteries at high pressure, as the blood needs to reach the extremities of the body.

- Elastic fibres in the artery wall help maintain the flow of blood away from the heart and prevent backflow, so no valves are needed.

- Capillaries form dense networks, called **capillary beds**, in the tissues of the body.

- They provide a large surface area for the efficient exchange of materials between the blood and tissues.

B–A*

- The blood is at a higher pressure at the artery end of the capillary bed. The higher pressure forces plasma through the thin capillary walls. The liquid, called **tissue fluid**, carries nutrients and oxygen to the surrounding cells.

Improve your grade

Capillaries

Higher: Capillaries are blood vessels that are very thin (0.005 mm in diameter) and whose walls are only one cell thick. Explain how these features enable them to carry out their function. *AO2* [4 marks]

The digestive system

Make-up of the digestive system

- The digestive system is made up of the alimentary canal (a muscular tube through which food passes from mouth to anus), liver and **pancreas**.

- The different parts of the digestive system are:
  - *Mouth*: food is taken in (ingestion), chewed into smaller pieces and mixed with saliva. This begins the breakdown of food.
  - *Oesophagus*: this muscular tube pushes food into the stomach.
  - *Stomach*: muscles in the stomach wall contract and relax to mix food with digestive juices.
  - *Pancreas*: produces pancreatic juice containing digestive enzymes that pass to the small intestine.
  - *Small intestine*: where digestion (breaking food down into soluble products) and absorption (diffusion of soluble products into the blood) takes place.
  - *Liver*: processes the nutrients from the small intestine and produces **bile**, which helps digest fat.
  - *Large intestine*: absorbs water from the remaining indigestible food matter.
  - *Anus*: undigested food is removed as faeces (egestion).

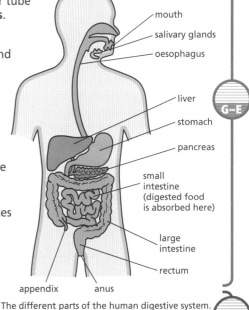

mouth
salivary glands
oesophagus
liver
stomach
pancreas
small intestine (digested food is absorbed here)
large intestine
rectum
appendix   anus

The different parts of the human digestive system.

G–E

- Contraction and relaxation of the muscle layers in the wall of the alimentary canal moves food through the digestive system. This muscular action is called **peristalsis**.

D–C

- The **gall bladder** is a small sac-like structure connected to the small intestine by the bile duct. It stores the greenish alkaline liquid called bile produced by the liver.

circular muscles contract, squeezing food into the next section where the circular muscles are relaxed

when longitudinal muscles contract the canal shortens, pushing the food along

food passing through the alimentary canal

Peristalsis – the alimentary canal narrows when the circular muscles contract and shortens when the longitudinal muscles contract.

B–A*

Digestion and absorption

- **Enzymes** break down large, insoluble molecules of carbohydrates, fats and protein into smaller molecules which the body can absorb, as summarised in the table below.

> **Remember!**
> Digestion is both chemical (the action of enzymes) and mechanical (teeth grinding food, muscle contraction).

Enzyme group	Examples	Location	Food component acted on	Substance produced
Carbohydrases digest carbohydrates	**Amylase**	Mouth and small intestine	Starch	Glucose (simple sugars)
Proteases digest proteins	**Pepsin**	Stomach	Proteins	Amino acids
Lipases digest fats and oils	Lipase	Small intestine	Fats and oils	Fatty acids and glycerol

G–E

- Visking tubing (see page 35) can be used as a model of the small intestine.

- Add a mix of enzyme(s) and large food molecule(s) into the tubing and suspend it in warm water (which acts like the blood supply). You can then detect the presence of the soluble products of digestion in the water.

D–C

Bile and villi

- Bile breaks down fats into small droplets (**emulsification**), which increases the surface area, speeding up the action of lipase.

- Bile also neutralises the stomach acid present in the food, which enters the small intestine to allow enzymes to work at their optimum pH of around 8.

- Tiny projections called **villi** (singular villus) line the small intestine. They increase its surface area, allowing more efficient absorption of the soluble products of digestion.

B–A*

Improve your grade

Enzyme experiment

Foundation: Dipesh mixed some starch with amylase in a beaker and left the mixture in a water bath at 37 °C. After 30 minutes he tested the mixture to see if there was any starch present. Predict what Dipesh will find and give a reason for your answer.   *AO3* [3 marks]

Functional foods

What are functional foods?

G–E

- **Functional foods** are foods that have health-promoting benefits over and above their basic nutritional value.
  - **Probiotic** foods contain bacteria such as *Bifidobacteria* and lactic acid bacteria *Lactobacillus* that are believed to maintain a healthy digestive system.
  - **Prebiotic** foods contain added sugars called oligosaccharides. These cannot be digested, but act as a food supply to the 'good' bacteria in the alimentary canal.
  - **Plant stanol esters** have been clinically proven to reduce the absorption of harmful **cholesterol**.

D–C

- The bacteria we carry in our digestive system can be divided into:
  - 'bad' bacteria, which can lead to diseases of the alimentary canal
  - 'good' bacteria, which suppress the activities of the 'bad' bacteria.
- Poor diet, stress, food poisoning and the use of antibiotics can disturb the balance so there are more 'bad' than 'good' bacteria.
- Prebiotics and probiotics are foods which aim to boost the numbers of 'good' bacteria that suppress the activity of the 'bad' bacteria.
- The margarine Benecol has had plant stanol ester added.
- Studies have shown that people who include plant stanols in their diet over a year might expect the cholesterol levels in their blood to fall by up to 10%.
- Lowering blood cholesterol reduces a person's risk of heart disease.
- Manufacturers of functional foods say that they prevent, treat or cure disease, but many scientists think that the foods should be tested in the same way that new drugs are, to ensure that these claims are valid.

Evaluating functional foods

B–A*

- In the past, the public's interest has led to food producers making health claims for their products that were unsupported by clear scientific evidence.
- However, there are concerns about the effectiveness of functional foods. The use of *Lactobacillus* and *Bifidobacterium* bacteria in some dairy products is an example. There are concerns involving:
  - how well the bacteria survive the manufacture and storage of probiotics before sale
  - their passage through the digestive system
  - competition with the trillions of other microorganisms already in the gut.
- The health claims made for most functional foods remains in doubt. Much more research is still needed.

> **Remember!**
> It is the balance of 'good' bacteria and 'bad' bacteria that influences the health of the digestive system. Both probiotics and prebiotics aim to increase the number of 'good' bacteria which suppress the activity of the 'bad'.

How science works

You should be able to:

- understand why there are doubts about the effectiveness of functional foods
- evaluate claims made by functional food producers that they promote good health.

Improve your grade

Probiotics vs prebiotics

Higher: Explain why some people believe that prebiotics are more likely to affect the health of the gut than probiotics.

AO1 [5 marks]

B2 Summary

Light and electron microscopes are used to magnify cells so we can study them and their components.

Cells can be animal, plant or bacterial. They all share the components of a cell membrane, cytoplasm and DNA, but have their own unique components that enable the cells to carry out processes, e.g. chloroplasts in plant cells carry out photosynthesis.

Advances in the understanding of DNA and cells have led to the Human Genome Project, cloning mammals, stem cell therapy and the production of GM organisms. Technology such as this has advantages and disadvantages.

The building blocks of cells

Mitosis results in two daughter cells identical to the parent cell. It is used for growth, repair and asexual reproduction. Gametes (sex cells) are produced during meiosis.

Enzymes are biological catalysts whose activity is affected by temperature and pH. They are specific in their action.

A DNA molecule consists of two strands linked by bases (a double helix). The bases always pair up in the same way (A with T and G with C), and their order determines the order of amino acids in the protein the DNA codes for.

Respiration takes place in all cells and is the release of energy from glucose.
The word equation for aerobic respiration is:
glucose + oxygen → carbon dioxide + water + energy
During exercise, heart and breathing rate increases to maximise the rate of respiration.

Oxygen diffuses from the alveoli into the blood. Carbon dioxide diffuses in the opposite direction.
A lack of oxygen in the muscles will result in anaerobic respiration:
glucose → lactic acid + energy

Sampling techniques such as quadrats are used to investigate the distribution of organisms in an ecosystem.

Organisms and energy

Plants produce glucose by photosynthesis (water + carbon dioxide → oxygen + glucose). The rate is controlled by limiting factors: temperature, light intensity and carbon dioxide concentration.

Osmosis is the diffusion of water and is how water moves into plant roots. The uptake of minerals by the roots requires energy and is known as active transport.

Plant tissues called xylem and phloem transport the reactants and products of photosynthesis. Leaves are adapted to maximise the rate.

Fossils provide evidence for Darwin's theory of evolution by natural selection.

All organisms grow. There are differences between how plants and animals grow, but both involve mitosis and differentiation.
Percentile charts help us to monitor growth in children.

Functional foods are those that have health benefits over their basic nutritional value. Examples include prebiotics, probiotics and foods that contain plant stanol esters such as Benecol margarine.

Common systems

Blood contains red blood cells (for the transport of oxygen), white blood cells (for defence against pathogens), plasma (which transports substances in solution) and platelets (for clotting).

The function of the digestive system is to break down food into simple soluble products. This is done by mechanical processes, such as the chewing of food, and the chemical breakdown of food molecules catalysed by enzymes.

The heart and blood vessels (arteries, veins and capillaries) make up the circulatory system. Its function is to transport blood to every cell in the body.

Removing wastes

Cell metabolism produces wastes

- Metabolic reactions inside cells break down compounds and form new ones.

- Some of the new compounds are waste substances and harmful if not removed from the body. Their removal is called **excretion**.

- Examples of waste substances include carbon dioxide and water (produced by aerobic respiration) and urea (a waste product produced when the liver breaks down excess amino acids).

- Carbon dioxide is excreted by gas exchange in the lungs.

- Water and **urea** are excreted in the kidneys, which also have a role in **homeostasis** as they regulate the amount of water and other useful substances in the blood.

Remember!
The term excretion only applies to the removal of waste substances made by cell metabolism. Faeces (food which is not digested) are not excreted, they are egested.

The urinary system

- Water and salts are needed for the cells of the body to work properly. The surplus is removed in the **urine**. We also lose some through sweating.

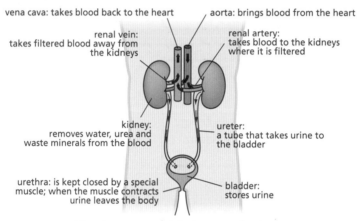

vena cava: takes blood back to the heart

aorta: brings blood from the heart

renal vein: takes filtered blood away from the kidneys

renal artery: takes blood to the kidneys where it is filtered

kidney: removes water, urea and waste minerals from the blood

ureter: a tube that takes urine to the bladder

urethra: is kept closed by a special muscle; when the muscle contracts urine leaves the body

bladder: stores urine

The urinary system and the functions of each part.

- Each kidney consists of tiny tubules called **nephrons** in which filtration and reabsorption take place.

- Filtration takes place in the **Bowman's capsule** which surrounds a knot of capillaries called the **glomerulus**.

- The blood is under high pressure so water and dissolved substances such as urea and glucose are forced into the Bowman's capsule. Large molecules and blood cells remain in the blood.

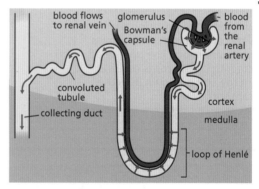

blood flows to renal vein

glomerulus
Bowman's capsule

blood from the renal artery

convoluted tubule

collecting duct

cortex

medulla

loop of Henlé

The nephron at work.

- The solution travels along the rest of the nephron. At the **loop of Henlé** and **collecting duct** water is reabsorbed back into the blood. Glucose is reabsorbed at the **convoluted tubules**.

- Reabsorption is selective as urea and other wastes are not reabsorbed.

- **Osmoregulation** is the control of the body's water balance. The amount of water reabsorbed depends on how much the body needs, and this is regulated by a hormone.

- The liquid in the collecting duct is urine, which trickles down to the ureter and eventually to the bladder, where it is temporarily stored before being released.

Improve your grade

Osmoregulation

Higher: Describe the role of the kidney in regulating the water content of the blood (osmoregulation)

AO2 [3 marks]

Helping the kidneys to function

Kidney failure

- Kidney failure can be short- or long-term.
- Controlling the amount of protein in the diet helps to reduce the amount of urea produced by the liver.
- If the urea content of the blood gets too high it can be life-threatening, so treatment is needed before this happens.

- One treatment for failing kidneys is **dialysis**.
- Blood containing urea passes from the person into the machine.
- Inside, the blood passes through tubes made of a partially permeable membrane which is surrounded by **dialysis fluid**.
- The dialysis fluid has the same concentration of salts and sugars as the blood but no urea.
- Urea diffuses from the blood into the dialysis fluid (from a high to low concentration). The dialysis fluid is in a continuous stream to remove urea and maintain a high concentration gradient for diffusion.
- 'Clean' blood returns to the person.
- Kidney transplantation is an option; however, the supply of suitable donor kidneys is limited. Rejection of transplants is a risk, and drugs must be taken to combat this.

> **Remember!**
> Diffusion is the movement of particles from a higher concentration to a lower concentration. In this case, because the concentration of sugars and salts in both the blood and dialysis fluid are the same there is no net movement of these substances.

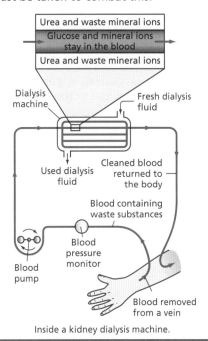

Inside a kidney dialysis machine.

Regulating water content

- The reabsorption of water from the kidney back into the blood is an example of **negative feedback**.
- Receptor cells in the hypothalamus of the brain detect how much water is in the blood. Nerve impulses from the receptor cells pass to the **pituitary gland**, which then releases more or less **ADH (antidiuretic hormone)** depending on the water content of the blood.
- If there is an excess of water in the blood:
  - less ADH is released
  - the walls of the collecting ducts of the nephrons become less permeable to water
  - less water is reabsorbed back into the blood
  - more water is removed in the urine from the body.
- If there is too little water in the blood more ADH is released and the opposite happens.

Improve your grade

Dialysis

Higher: Explain how dialysis is designed to maximise the rate of diffusion of urea from the blood.

AO2 (4 marks)

Controlling the menstrual cycle

What is the menstrual cycle?

- Between the ages of about 11 and 17 years, a girl's ovaries begin to release eggs, and her periods begin (**menstruation**).

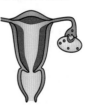

1. On the first day of the cycle, menstruation begins. The thick lining of the uterus breaks down and is lost through the vagina

2. One week into the cycle, the uterus lining is just starting to build up again. An egg is ripening in the ovary

   Follicles, each containing an egg, begin to develop in one of the ovaries

3. Two weeks into the cycle, an egg is released from the ovary (ovulation). The lining of the uterus is soft and thick, ready to receive the egg if it is fertilised

4. Three weeks into the cycle, the egg has almost reached the uterus. If it hasn't been fertilised, it will die

The menstrual cycle: the timing of events varies depending on the individual.

The role of hormones in the menstrual cycle

- Oestrogen and progesterone are hormones produced by the ovaries, which control the menstrual cycle.

- At the start of the cycle, levels of oestrogen rise. Oestrogen stimulates growth and repair of the uterus lining, and the development of egg-containing follicles in the ovaries.

- Just before ovulation the concentration of progesterone increases and the concentration of oestrogen falls. Progesterone maintains the thickness of the lining.

- If the egg is fertilised, then the pregnant woman does not menstruate. The embryo attaches to the uterus lining.

- High levels of blood progesterone continue during pregnancy. This prevents development of more follicles and the release of eggs.

> ### EXAM TIP
> You may find it helpful in your revision to write out the events in the menstrual cycle as a flow chart with different coloured text to represent the effects of the different hormones.

- **Follicle stimulating hormone (FSH)** and **luteinising hormone (LH)**, released by the pituitary gland, also control the menstrual cycle.

- Days 1–7: FSH is released and stimulates the maturation of follicles and the release of oestrogen. A high level of oestrogen stimulates secretion of LH and inhibits the release of FSH (an example of negative feedback).

- Days 8–14: A surge of LH triggers ovulation at around day 14.

- Days 15–21: The follicle, empty of its egg (the corpus luteum), secretes progesterone, which maintains the lining of the uterus and inhibits the secretion of FSH and LH, preventing the growth and development of more follicles (negative feedback).

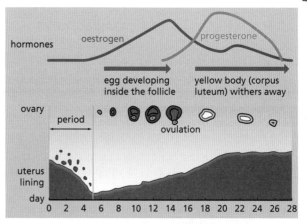

How hormones affect the menstrual cycle.

- Days 22–28: If the egg is not fertilised the levels of oestrogen and progesterone drop, triggering menstruation. Low progesterone levels allow an increase in secretion of FSH, which enables the development of follicles to begin again.

Improve your grade

Oestrogen
Foundation: State two functions of oestrogen in the menstrual cycle.   *AO2* (2 marks)

Sex cells and fertilisation

Sex cells

- The term **gametes** refers to sperm (male sex cells) and eggs (female sex cells).

- Millions of microscopic sperm are released with seminal fluid from the penis. They are adapted to swim to and fertilise an egg.

- An egg cell is bigger than a sperm. Its cytoplasm contains nutrients for the embryo that develops after fertilisation but before it attaches to the uterus wall.

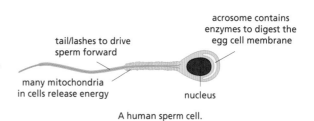

tail/lashes to drive sperm forward

many mitochondria in cells release energy

acrosome contains enzymes to digest the egg cell membrane

nucleus

A human sperm cell.

Remember!

In humans a diploid body cell contains 46 chromosomes (23 pairs, one from each pair coming from each parent). Gametes are haploid, which means they only contain 23 chromosomes.

cells surround the egg

cytoplasm containing nutrients

nucleus

granules behind the cell membrane

cell membrane

A human egg cell.

- Sperm and egg cells are haploid. This means they only have half the number of chromosomes of most of the other (diploid) cells of the body.

Fertilisation

- When a sperm reaches an egg, the **acrosome** releases enzymes which break down the cells surrounding the egg, helping the sperm to penetrate it.

- The head of the sperm enters the cytoplasm of the egg.

- A substance released by granules behind the egg cell membrane seals it so no more sperm can enter.

- The nucleus of the sperm head is released and fuses with the egg nucleus. This is fertilisation. A diploid **zygote** is formed. It has a full set of chromosomes.

Treating infertility

- Male infertility is caused by a low sperm count. This can be treated by taking testosterone or **insemination** of the woman with the semen from another man (donor).

- Insufficient FSH is one cause of female infertility. Taking a drug that makes the pituitary gland insensitive to oestrogen can raise FSH levels (this works because oestrogen inhibits the secretion of FSH).

- During *in vitro* **fertilisation (IVF)** the woman is treated with hormones that bring on ovulation (or **donor eggs** are used). Eggs are retrieved and mixed with sperm from her partner (or donor) outside the body. One or two of the embryos produced are placed in the woman's uterus.

- **Surrogate mothers** carry a baby and give it to the couple after birth. The surrogate's own egg can be fertilised with the father-to-be's sperm using IVF, or she carries the genetic child of the infertile couple conceived through IVF.

- These treatments allow couples to have a baby that carries their own genes. Disadvantages include the possible drug side-effects and the cost and availability of treatment. Using donor eggs/sperm or surrogate mothers can create emotional issues. The storage and potential use of embryos also raises ethical questions.

How science works

You should be able to:

- discuss the advantages and disadvantages of infertility treatments.

Improve your grade

Sperm cell adaptation

Foundation: Explain how a sperm cell is adapted to its function.

AO2 (4 marks)

Sex and sex-linked genetic disorders

Inheritance of sex

- The X chromosome and the Y chromosome are known as the sex chromosomes.

- Females have 2 X chromosomes (XX) and males have an X and a Y chromosome (XY).

- In a normal female, 1 X chromosome becomes inactive and the other controls female development.

- In the male, the Y chromosome causes the male genital system to develop.

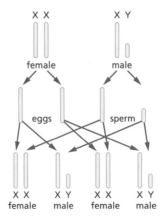

A genetic diagram showing how the sex of offspring is determined.

EXAM TIP

You can also use a Punnett square to show the same information if you find it clearer. You can see how the probability of having a boy or girl is 50%.

	Male gametes	
	X	Y
X	XX	XY
X	XX	XY

(Female gametes)

- Sex cells are produced during meiosis.

- The body cells of a woman carry 2 X chromosomes so the egg cells produced can only carry an X chromosome.

- Each body cell of a man carries an X chromosome and a Y chromosome, so during meiosis 50% of the sperm cells carry an X chromosome and 50% carry a Y chromosome.

- Whether the egg is fertilised by a sperm carrying an X chromosome or a Y chromosome determines a baby's sex.

Sex-linked disorders

- **Haemophilia** is a sex-linked genetic disorder that causes a person's blood not to clot properly. The person fails to produce a clotting agent because of a mutation in one of the alleles of the gene controlling its synthesis.

- The mutant allele is recessive and located on the X chromosome.

- A woman carrying the mutant allele on one of her X chromosomes is not a sufferer because the normal allele of the other X chromosome is dominant. She is a **carrier**.

- She is able to pass it on to her children. If a man inherits the recessive mutant allele for haemophilia on the X chromosome, there is no dominant allele on the Y chromosome to hide its effect so the man suffers from haemophilia.

	Mother	
	X^h	X^H
X^H	$X^H X^h$	$X^H X^H$
Y	$X^h Y$	$X^H Y$

(Father / Children)

The Punnett square shows the outcome possibilities for offspring of a haemophilia-carrier mother and a non-haemophiliac father. The son with the genotype $X^h Y$ has haemophilia.

- Another sex-linked disorder caused by a recessive mutant allele on the X chromosome is red–green **colour blindness**. Women with a single recessive allele on the X chromosome are carriers. They only have the disorder if they inherit two recessive alleles. This is rare.

How science works

You should be able to:

- use genetic diagrams to show how sex-linked genetic disorders are inherited
- interpret genetic diagrams to calculate probabilities, ratios and percentages.

Improve your grade

The inheritance of colour blindness

Higher: A red–green colour blind man and a woman who is a carrier of the allele have children. What is the probability of them having a girl with red–green colour blindness? Use a genetic diagram to help you to answer.

AO2 [4 marks]

Immunisation

Vaccinations

- Edward Jenner came up with a theory that people infected with **cowpox** were protected from the more deadly **smallpox**.

- He infected a boy who had just recovered from cowpox with smallpox pus. He survived because of this **immunisation (vaccination)**. Jenner's theory was supported.

- We now know that it worked because the virus causing cowpox is very similar to the smallpox virus.

- All vaccines have side-effects. However, they are very rare, so the risk from not being vaccinated and then dying from the disease is greater.

- If enough people in the population are immunised then the whole population is protected. This is called the **herd effect**.

G–E

The immune response

- Organisms that cause disease are called pathogens.

- The body recognises pathogens because their surfaces are covered in 'foreign' molecules called **antigens**.

- White blood cells are part of the body's immune system; their actions are the **immune response**.

- **B-lymphocytes** produce proteins called **antibodies**. These bind to antigens and destroy the pathogens.

- Phagocytes ingest pathogens.

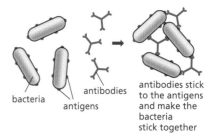

bacteria   antigens   antibodies   antibodies stick to the antigens and make the bacteria stick together

The immune response in action.

> **Remember!**
> Many words in biology are very similar. Antibody, antigen and antibiotic all sound similar but have very different meanings. Make sure you use them correctly.

 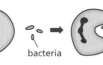 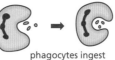

phagocyte

nucleus   bacteria   phagocytes ingest the bacteria   the bacteria are trapped   the bacteria have been digested

A phagocyte ingesting bacteria.

D–C

- Antigens also trigger the production of **memory lymphocytes**, which quickly produce antibodies again if they detect the same antigens at a later date.

- A **vaccine** contains a pathogen that has been made harmless by killing it, weakening it or using only a part of it.

- The harmless antigens trigger the production of antibodies and memory cells. If the harmful form of the pathogen infects the body, antibodies are made quickly.

- The vaccine has made the person immune to the particular pathogen and the disease it causes.

- The first time the body is infected by a particular infection, B-lymphocytes take some time to produce the correct antibody. This is the **primary immune response**. We might feel ill for a few days and then recover.

- If we are attacked by the same pathogen again, **the secondary immune response** is much quicker. This is because memory lymphocyte cells left over from the primary immune response quickly divide on re-exposure to the same antigen. The blood plasma concentration of antibodies increases very quickly and the pathogen may be destroyed before it can multiply.

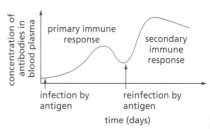

concentration of antibodies in blood plasma

primary immune response   secondary immune response

infection by antigen   reinfection by antigen

time (days)

The graph shows how the concentration of antibodies in blood plasma varies in response to the first and subsequent infections by the same antigen.

B–A*

How science works

You should be able to:

- evaluate the use of vaccination by discussing its risks and benefits.

Improve your grade

How immunisation works

Foundation: Explain how having the whooping cough vaccination prevents you from getting the illness.

AO2 [4 marks]

Monoclonal antibodies

What are monoclonal antibodies?

- B-lymphocytes naturally produce several antibody types in response to a particular antigen. This mixture is called **polyclonal antibodies**.

- Antibodies that bind only to a particular antigen or part of an antigen are called **monoclonal antibodies**.

Hybridomas

- Producing monoclonal antibodies in quantity from B-lymphocytes alone is impossible because they cannot divide. This problem is solved by fusing them with a cancerous B-cell called a **myeloma**, which can divide. The fused cells are called **hybridomas**.

- Antibodies can be made that are specific to a certain antigen by the following process:
  - A mouse is genetically engineered to produce human antibodies.
  - It is injected with the antigen that triggers production of the required antibody.
  - If the immune response occurs, B-lymphocytes are removed.
  - The lymphocytes are fused with myeloma cells grown in culture to produce hybridomas. These cells are able to produce monoclonal antibodies and continuously divide.
  - Hybridomas are grown in culture and screened for antibodies specific to the antigen first injected into the mouse.
  - The monoclonal antibodies are then extracted.

EXAM TIP

There is quite a lot to remember here. You might find it useful to read through the information and draw out your own copy of the diagram. See if you can add labels to show what is happening at each stage without referring to the text. This will help you to remember the facts.

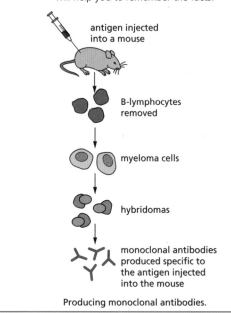

antigen injected into a mouse

B-lymphocytes removed

myeloma cells

hybridomas

monoclonal antibodies produced specific to the antigen injected into the mouse

Producing monoclonal antibodies.

Using monoclonal antibodies

- Pregnancy testing:
  - A pregnancy test kit consists of a dipstick impregnated with monoclonal antibodies that bind with the hormone **hCG (human chorionic gonadotrophin)**, which is present in the urine of a woman in the early stages of pregnancy.
  - The stick is dipped into a sample of urine: any hCG molecules present in the urine will bind to the antibodies at the end of the dipstick and travel up it to meet other antibodies to produce a colour change, indicating the woman is pregnant.
  - When there is no hCG in the urine, the antibodies combine with another band of different antibodies to produce a colour change that indicates the woman is not pregnant.

- Blood clots carry particular antigens. Specific monoclonal antibodies bind to the antigens. Markers on the antibodies enable doctors to locate the blood clots.

- Diagnosis and treatment of cancer:
  - Some types of cancer cell have different antigens at their surface compared with healthy cells.
  - Monoclonal antibodies which only bind to the antigens on the cancer cells are combined with anti-cancer drugs.
  - The advantage of using monoclonal antibodies is that they are cancer-cell specific. One of the problems with some other cancer treatments, such as drugs and radiotherapy, is that healthy cells are often killed as well as the cancerous cells.

Improve your grade

Monoclonal vs polyclonal

Higher: Explain the difference between polyclonal and monoclonal antibodies.   *AO2* [3 marks]

Microorganism growth and infection

Population growth

- Bacteria reproduce by dividing.

- Each generation is double the size of the previous generation – the increase is **exponential**.

- Exponential increase in a bacterial population only occurs when conditions for growth are ideal.

- Temperature, pH and the availability of resources such as nutrients and oxygen (depending on the species) are all factors which affect the rate of bacterial growth.

- The exponential growth slows as the increasing population uses up resources.

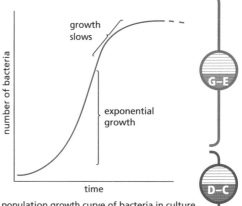

A population growth curve of bacteria in culture.

Growing microorganisms

- It is possible to culture (grow) bacteria in Petri dishes on jelly-like agar or in test-tubes with a liquid broth. Agar and broth are **growing media** which contain the nutrients and other substances bacteria need to grow.

- You can investigate how changing conditions, such as using different nutrient solutions, temperature or pH, affects the growth of bacteria.

- **Resazurin dye** can be used to measure the growth. Substances produced by the bacteria cause the dye to change colour so the faster the colour change, the faster the growth of the bacteria.

Remember!
To make sure your results are reliable you should use control variables. This means making sure that you keep constant all conditions other than the one you're investigating.

Louis Pasteur and aseptic techniques

- Louis Pasteur (1822–95) attempted to settle the question of why food went 'bad' with evidence from experiments.

- He put meat broth into glass flasks with S-shaped curves. He then boiled the contents of the flasks to kill any microorganisms.

- On cooling, the flasks' contents were not contaminated by microorganisms because the swan-necked design trapped them. As a result, the air reaching the meat broth was sterile, and the broth did not go bad.

- When the flask was tilted, the microorganisms fell into the meat broth and it soon turned bad.

- Pasteur's ideas that microorganisms are killed by heat and that procedures preventing contamination are possible, are the basis of the **aseptic techniques** we still use today.

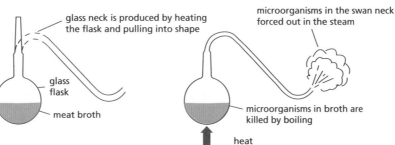

Pasteur's swan-necked flask experiments demonstrated that microorganisms are in the air.

How science works

You should be able to:

- interpret results from experiments on bacterial growth (including using Resazurin dye)

- use a bacterial growth curve to explain how the population is changing.

Improve your grade

Bacterial growth experiment

Foundation: Design an experiment to determine how temperature affects the growth of bacteria.

AO3 [5 marks]

Plants, defences and food supply

Pests and pathogens

- Pests are the plants, fungi and animals that destroy crops and livestock, or prevent land from being used for farming. They have a negative impact on human food supply.
- Plant pests (**weeds**) compete with crop plants for soil, water, light and nutrients.
- Fungal pests cause disease. For example, **blight** is a disease of potatoes.
- Animal pests are mostly **herbivorous** insects which eat the crops.
- Insect pests spread plant diseases. As greenfly suck the sap of plants, viruses pass through their mouthparts into the sap.
- Growers can use pesticides to kill pests.

> ### EXAM TIP
> You should be able to explain why weeds growing in amongst crops reduce the amount of crops grown (the yield). The crops need a good supply of water and light for photosynthesis and minerals from the soil to build tissue (biomass). The crops would have to share these resources with the weeds.

Plant defences

- Plants can produce chemicals that kill, paralyse or deter their attackers.
- **Alkaloids** such as caffeine, nicotine and quinine have different **pharmacological** effects, these include disrupting the transmission of nerve impulses causing paralysis, weakening cell structures or inhibiting protein synthesis. Almost all produce a bitter taste which deters animals from eating the plants.
- **Cyanogens** are stored in non-poisonous form in the vacuoles of plant cells. Eating breaks open the plant cells, releasing the cyanogens within. Enzymes in the cytoplasm cells catalyse the conversion of the cyanogens to poisonous hydrogen cyanide, which blocks cellular respiration. The animal eating the plant dies.
- **Phenolics** such as **tannins** and flavonoids make it difficult for herbivores to digest the plant material. The animals starve and die.
- **Terpenoids** such as taxol and citronella repel insects.
- Producing defensive chemicals costs plants resources and energy.
- Plants reduce these costs by:
  - only producing defensive chemicals when under attack
  - concentrating chemicals at the site of attack.

- Many of the chemicals that plants produce to defend themselves affect the **metabolism** of the cells of the herbivores eating them.

Pharmaceuticals

- We can use many of the chemicals that plants make to defend themselves to produce pharmaceuticals that treat human diseases and relieve their symptoms.
- Treating MRSA: honey contains **antibacterials** and can be used to keep wounds clear of infection.
- Treating malaria: quinine, from the bark and leaves of the *Cinchona* tree, is used to treat malaria. The drug lowers body temperature and kills the *Plasmodium* parasites which cause the disease.
- Relieving pain: aspirin is a derivative of salicylic acid, originally made from willow tree bark. It reduces pain, fever, swelling in joints and other tissues and the formation of blood clots.

Remember!
Malaria is a disease caused by the parasite *Plasmodium*, carried by mosquitoes.

◉ Improve your grade

Does honey contain antibacterials?

Higher: A scientist wanted to test the hypothesis that Manuka honey contains antibacterials. She spread a culture of bacteria over nutrient agar and added paper discs, one that had been soaked in distilled water, and one in Manuka honey. She then incubated the dish for three days. Her results are shown in the diagram. Explain what they show.

AO3 [3 marks]

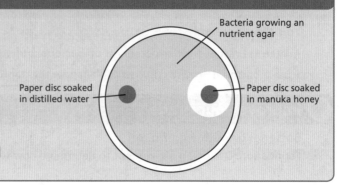

Rhythms of life

What are rhythms?

- Some environmental changes occur regularly and continuously: they have a rhythm. One example is the changing seasons.

- Organisms respond rhythmically in step with these predictable changes. For example, woodland plants respond to the seasonal changes in the intensity of light reaching the woodland floor. There is a lot of light in the winter and early spring, when there are few leaves on the trees, and little light in the summer, when the leaves are fully open and form a **canopy**.

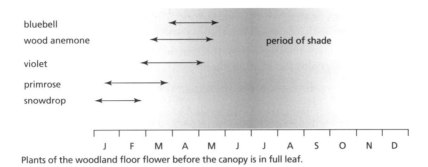

Plants of the woodland floor flower before the canopy is in full leaf.

- Plants of the woodland floor need to grow in the periods where there is plenty of light reaching them.

- The increase in the hours of daylight and light intensity are the trigger for the **overwintering** seeds of different plant species to:
  - *germinate* – the seeds sprout shoots and roots
  - *grow* and mature into plants producing flowers
  - *reproduce* and form new seeds.

G–E

Photoperiodicity in plants

- The period of light/dark is called the **photoperiod**. This ratio changes throughout the seasons. For example, in the UK the number of daylight hours is longer in the summer than in winter.

- The ratio of the period of light to dark needed to cause flowering is called the **critical period**. This is different for each plant species.

- The flowering response of plants falls into three categories:
  - long-day plants – flower in response to the long period of light of summer days
  - short-day plants – flower in response to the shorter period of light of spring or autumn days
  - day-neutral plants – flowering is unaffected by the period of light.

- Manipulating the photoperiod allows commercial plant growers to guarantee supplies of flowers out of season.

D–C

Circadian rhythms

- Many biological rhythms approximate to a 24-hour (**circadian**) cycle.

- Experiments show that circadian rhythms continue even when environmental conditions, such as light and temperature, stay constant. A rhythm that persists in this way is called **free running**.

- The rhythm is driven from within cells and not by environmental changes. Nevertheless, environmental cues 'set' the clock so that the rhythms run 'on time'.

- Sleep is an example of a circadian rhythm. Jet lag or shift work can affect this.

- Scientists think that **biological clocks** within cells drive circadian rhythms. Research suggests that switching genes 'on' and 'off' at the right time sets up a rhythm of transcription and protein synthesis.

- Many hormones and all enzymes are proteins. The rhythm of their secretion is often circadian, and supports this theory.

B–A*

> **Remember!**
> Circadian rhythms are those which happen in a 24-hour cycle (one day)

Improve your grade

Flowers for Christmas

Foundation: Describe how a plant grower could manipulate a long-day plant to flower in the winter to be used for a Christmas display.   *AO2* [2 marks]

Innate behaviour

What is innate behaviour?

G–E

- **Innate behaviour** is instinctive, automatic and predictable. It is inherited from parents.
- The faster an individual reacts, the better its chances of survival.

D–C

- The ethologist Tinbergen investigated the innate reaction of herring gull chicks to the red spot on their parent's beak.
- The chicks peck at their parent's beak when they want food. Tinbergen found that the chick pecks the beak less when the spot is covered.
- He also used model adult herring gull heads made of wood, where each beak except one had differently coloured spots, including red.
- Chicks pecked the red-spotted model beak more often than the unspotted beak.
- The models with beaks spotted with other colours were pecked more often than the unspotted beak but less often than the red-spotted beak.
- Male robins are fiercely territorial. The red breast is a warning to rival males.
- A robin will behave aggressively to a model robin painted with a red breast and even a ball of cotton wool soaked in red ink and attached to a piece of wire. This shows the behaviour is innate.

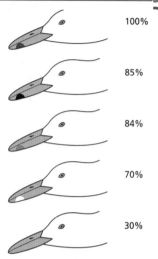

100%

85%

84%

70%

30%

Pecking response: percentage of herring gull chicks responding to model beaks, each spotted with a different colour.

Using choice chambers

B–A*

- You can use a **choice chamber** to investigate the innate responses of woodlice to dry/wet and light/dark conditions.
- Each section of the choice chamber has a different environment. You can place a group of woodlice into the middle and watch to see if they move.
- You will find that the woodlice move to conditions that they find favourable. This is an example of innate behaviour.
- The results show that woodlice prefer dark/damp conditions. This is because in dry conditions they quickly lose water from the body and die.

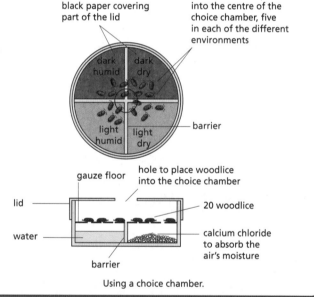

black paper covering part of the lid

20 woodlice are put into the centre of the choice chamber, five in each of the different environments

dark humid | dark dry
light humid | light dry

barrier

hole to place woodlice into the choice chamber

gauze floor

lid

20 woodlice

water

calcium chloride to absorb the air's moisture

barrier

Using a choice chamber.

How science works

You should be able to:

- carry out investigations looking into innate behaviour, e.g. using choice chambers
- interpret data collected from animal behaviour investigations.

Improve your grade

Innate behaviour
Foundation: Explain what is meant by the term 'innate behaviour'.

AO2 [2 marks]

Imprinting and habituation

Imprinting

- Ducklings and goslings follow the first moving thing that they see (usually their mother). This is called **imprinting**.
- The ethologist Lorenz studied this. He made sure that he was the first thing the ducklings saw when they hatched. They responded to him as if he were their mother.
- Imprinting only develops early in an animal's life during the **sensitive period**.
- The sensitive period depends on the species: the first 48 hours for a duckling and between 3 and 10 weeks for a dog.
- Imprinting on parents improves the chances of the young animals surviving, because their parents protect them and supply them with food.
- Imprinting can affect the social behaviour of adults. For example, goslings that have imprinted on ducks might attempt to mate with them later in life.

Habituation

- At first, putting models of hawks and owls around an airport and playing recordings of the distress calls of birds keeps birds away.
- After a while, however, the birds learn that there is no danger from a model hawk or that a distress call does not mean there is a predator about. They start to come back to the airport, where they pose a danger to aircraft.
- This form of learning is called **habituation**. The birds get used to a stimulus, see no danger and no longer respond to the stimulus.
- The snail's tentacles help it to test the direction in which it is moving. Each one contains touch-sensitive receptors. Touch its tentacles and a snail withdraws them into its head.
- You can investigate habituation by repeatedly touching a snail's tentacles gently, using a clean glass rod. The more times the tentacles are touched the less the snail responds to the stimulus.
- It learns that there is nothing really in its way, so that eventually it doesn't change direction, despite repeated gentle touching of its tentacles.

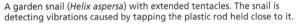

A garden snail (*Helix aspersa*) with extended tentacles. The snail is detecting vibrations caused by tapping the plastic rod held close to it.

- Imprinting and habituation are very important in animal training. Guide dog puppies are kept with their mother and siblings up until they are 6 weeks old to give them time to be socialised with other dogs, so avoiding problems later in life.
- At 6 weeks the puppies are put into private homes, which ensures that they have time to habituate by being exposed to many day-to-day situations, from vacuum cleaners to traffic noise.

Remember!
Imprinting is an innate behaviour, whereas habituation is a learned behaviour.

Guide dogs are given time to habituate while they are puppies.

Improve your grade

Imprinting
Foundation: Explain why imprinting on their mother helps ducklings to survive.

AO2 [2 marks]

Conditioning

What is conditioning?

- When behaviour changes in the light of experience, we say that the behaviour is learned.

- For example, a kitten will only show interest in food when it sees the food, tastes it and eats it. Seeing food and tasting it are **primary stimuli**.

- Later the animal learns to associate non-food stimuli with food. For example, a move by its owner to where the food is kept. Non-food associations are **secondary stimuli**.

- The secondary stimulus is not directly linked to the primary stimulus, but the association is learned. In this instance, the cat's behaviour is an example of **conditioning**.

G–E

Training animals

- Ivan Pavlov scientifically studied conditioned responses.

- When he placed food in a dog's mouth, Pavlov noticed that the flow of saliva increased. He also saw that the dog smelling his hand had the same effect. This was before food was placed in the dog's mouth. The dog's production of saliva increased even more when food followed Pavlov's personal smell.

- After a time Pavlov's personal smell alone produced the same response in the dog as if it had been given food. The dog had learned to associate a non-food secondary stimulus (Pavlov's personal smell) with food.

D–C

- Pavlov used the term 'conditioned' to describe the dog's response. **Classical conditioning** refers to this process.

- Conditioning can also be the result of trial and error learning. Reward (getting the response right) or punishment (getting the response wrong) are key to this type of learning.

- The process is called **operant conditioning**. An example is the promise of a treat for doing your homework.

> **Remember!**
> There are two types of conditioning: classical and operant.

- Operant conditioning plays an important role in animal training:

- A trained police horse will not be startled by gunfire or crowds of noisy people, etc. Negative reinforcers (events which the animal dislikes and which are removed immediately after the animal displays the wanted behaviour) are effective at conditioning their behaviour. For example, relaxing a restraint reinforces the wanted behaviour.

B–A*

Training helps police horses remain calm in noisy environments.

- Sniffer dogs are trained to search for the smells given off by money, drugs, explosives, human remains and much else. Dogs usually respond best to positive reinforcement, such as food, praise and stroking, and this helps to condition their behaviour.

- Dolphins can be trained to do tricks. The dolphin follows its trainer's signals and correct behaviour is immediately reinforced by rewarding with food or praise.

Improve your grade

Clicker training

Higher: You can train a puppy using a clicker. As soon as the puppy displays the behaviour you want, press the clicker (which makes a clicking sound) and then give the puppy a treat. After a while you will not need to give a treat after every click. Explain why. *AO2* [2 marks]

Courtship and mating strategies

Courtship behaviour

- **Courtship behaviour** is the mechanism used by animals, usually the male, to attempt to attract and secure a mate to reproduce with and create offspring.

- One example is the zigzag dance which male stickleback fish use to attract a female.

- Courtship behaviour:
  - establishes territory
  - drives away rival males
  - through advertising an individual's qualities, attracts females
  - enables males and females to recognise individuals of the same species as potential partners
  - helps to synchronise sexual behaviour between partners
  - encourages parental care by individuals of species who look after their offspring.

Mating strategies

- **Sexual reproduction** involves mating and the mixing of genes.

- Some species are **monogamous**, which means they mate with only one partner. This is common among birds.

- Many other species are **polygamous**, which means they mate with more than one partner.

- Polygamy usually means one male mates with several females.

- In some species males fight to establish who has the right to mate with the females. The winner benefits by passing on his genes through as many females as possible. The females benefit because they mate with the males with the 'best' genes.

> **Remember!**
> Courtship behaviour is important as it ensures that the individuals with the 'best' genes reproduce to pass on these genes and the characteristics that make them successful.

- The behaviour between a male and female sometimes forms bonds between the pair, helping to keep them together. Grey wolves are an example: the male and female usually mate for life.

- Cooperative hunting behaviour reinforces this **pair bonding**.

- Monogamy often occurs in species where pair bonding helps to motivate cooperation between the male and female to raise their offspring.

- The male bird helps the female to incubate eggs and to feed the young after hatching. Most birds do not mate for life but for a season. Others, like doves, robins or swans, may stay together over several seasons or even for life.

Grey wolves bond in pairs.

- Polygamy occurs in species which do not form strong pair bonds between male and female. Only one parent is involved in raising offspring. In mammals, males are usually the absent parent because young develop within the female and are nursed by her.

Improve your grade

Leopard mating strategy

Foundation: Male and female leopards will form pair bonds during the mating season and hunt together. They may stay together a short time after the cubs are born. Give two advantages of this mating strategy.

AO2 [2 marks]

Parental care

What is parental care?

- Many fish, amphibians and reptiles simply lay their eggs and leave them to hatch.

- Some species, however, look after their eggs until they hatch and may care for the young afterwards.

- In birds and mammals parental behaviour is highly evolved.

- Most birds build nests and have to incubate their eggs, keeping them at the correct temperature until they hatch. Feeding the chicks takes so much time and effort that it is common for male birds to help.

- Parental behaviour is triggered by the behaviour in the young:
  - Baby birds in the nest open their mouths wide and make 'begging' sounds. Parents respond by favouring the noisiest chick.
  - The bigger chicks get more food than the smaller ones. This produces some fit offspring who are more likely to pass on their genes. The weaker chicks may die or be pushed from the nest by the others.

A meadow pipit feeding a young cuckoo in its nest.

- Feeding and protecting offspring, and helping offspring to learn how to interact with individuals of the same species, avoid predators and catch prey are all part of parental care.

- Species where matings produce numerous offspring are usually polygamous. Parental care is minimal. Many animals that breed in this way do not look after their young at all, e.g. species of fish like cod.

- Species where matings produce relatively few offspring are usually monogamous and parental care of offspring is common, e.g. most species of bird.

- Parental care often involves risks. Caring for their young can make the parents more vulnerable to predator attack as they have to protect their babies. The parents may also be weakened themselves through finding it difficult to source sufficient food, or in the case of nursing mothers be malnourished through milk production.

- However, this **parental investment** is worth the risks, as parental care increases the survival chances of offspring and also increases the chances of parental genes passing to the next generation.

Evolution of parental care

- Parental care is a successful evolutionary strategy.

- Variation within a species is the mechanism of evolution by natural selection. If variation depends on parental genes passing from generation to generation, then parental care maximises the chances of this happening.

- This is particularly so in species where parents produce relatively few offspring, and is probably why special behaviours for rearing young have evolved in mammals and birds.

- In species where females each produce hundreds of thousands of eggs, only two offspring per pair of parents need survive for parental genes to transfer to the next generation. In fact, parental care in these circumstances would not be an advantage. Overpopulation would increase competition between individuals and lead to possible extinction.

> **Remember!**
> An evolutionary strategy is a behaviour that increases the chances that an individual's genes will be passed on to future generations.

Improve your grade

Evolutionary strategy

Higher: Birds will often only feed the noisiest, biggest chicks. The other chicks may die. Explain why this makes sense as an evolutionary strategy.

AO2 [3 marks]

Animal communication

Visual signals

- Communication is a form of behaviour that influences the actions of other individuals.

- Animals communicate with one another by releasing chemicals called pheromones, making sounds and giving visual signals.

- Animal behaviour has evolved to ensure survival. By communicating, animals can improve their chances of survival. For example:
  - by establishing territorial rights to provide them with food and shelter
  - by finding a mate to ensure that they can reproduce
  - by warning members of their group of potential threat.

- Pulling faces is a visual signal. It is a way of communicating our emotions to other people.

- Your feelings and intentions are signalled by the way you hold yourself (posture). This is called body language.

Remember!
Facial expression and body language mean different things in different species. For example, the open mouth grin of a chimpanzee shows fear, not happiness like it does in humans. A wagging tail in a cat signals annoyance. By contrast, when a dog wags its tail it is signalling happiness.

Sound signals

- In most species of birds it is the male that sings, often to warn other males away from its territory. A large territory will provide plenty of food to feed chicks.

- They may also use it to attract a female. In some species, males and females take it in turns to sing; this behaviour helps to strengthen their bond.

Male birds sing to warn off other males and to attract females.

- Other animals also use sounds to communicate:
  - Many species of monkey communicate by sound, as it is particularly useful in their forest habitat.
  - Frogs often attract mates with characteristic calls.
  - Whales make sounds called 'whale song', which is used for complex levels of communication.

Chemical signals

- A male cheetah when urinating on a tree is also releasing pheromones at the same time.

- The signal in the smell is understood by other male cheetahs to mean 'keep out of this territory as it belongs to another male'.

- Male silk moths are attracted to a female silk moth because of a pheromone she releases. The female is signalling that she is ready to mate.

- Once a male detects a female's pheromone trail, he follows its concentration gradient. This becomes stronger and stronger as the male approaches.

Male cheetahs urinate against trees to mark territory.

Improve your grade

Bird communication
Foundation: State two reasons why birds sing.

AO2 [2 marks]

Plant communication and co-evolution

Plant chemical use

- Communication happens when messages from senders are understood by receivers.

- In the plant world messages are molecules of different chemicals, senders are the plants producing the chemicals and receivers are other plants, animals, fungi or bacteria.

- Receivers may interpret the meanings in messenger molecules as invitations, warnings or stress depending on the type of chemical released and the receiver.

- Plants release chemicals in response to damage and other stress stimuli.

- Some of these chemicals attract parasites that in turn attack the organism that is damaging the plant. For example, when tobacco budworm caterpillars feed on tobacco plants, the plants send a signal to a species of wasp that lays its eggs in the caterpillars, which kills them.

- The message in the molecules is often quite specific. Only a particular receiver will understand it.

> **Remember!**
> Plants can communicate in other ways, including the use of brightly coloured petals and scents to attract pollinating insects.

- Some of the chemicals that plants produce and use for communication form vapours when released.

- These chemicals are volatile and they are called **volatile organic compounds (VOCs)**. Once airborne, these molecules quickly spread.

- Ethene is a VOC that affects the growth of plants. In one study, tobacco plants were genetically engineered to be insensitive to ethene. As a result they grew more vigorously than their non-engineered neighbours.

- Scientists have shown that VOCs released from the leaves of clipped sagebrush bushes reduces the insect damage of nearby wild tobacco plants. The sagebrush VOCs seem to increase the chemical defence levels in the tobacco plants, making them a less attractive food source to insects.

What is co-evolution?

- In co-evolution, each species exerts selection pressures on the other, and benefits from the others' adaptations that evolve as a result.

- The evolution of flowers and the insects that pollinate them is an example.

- Flower adaptations include: petals that are brightly coloured, scented and secrete sugar-rich nectar; anthers and stigmas that are positioned so that insects are likely to brush against them; pollen grains that are large and sticky.

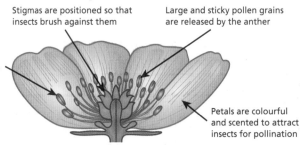

Stigmas are positioned so that insects brush against them

Large and sticky pollen grains are released by the anther

Pollen is produced in the anther (top part of the stamen). Insects brush against this

Petals are colourful and scented to attract insects for pollination

Flower adaptations enable pollination by insects.

- Adaptations of pollinating insects include: antennae that detect flower scent; eyes that detect colour; body hairs and other structures that collect pollen.

- Both species benefit:
  - the plant because the bee transfers its flowers' pollen to the stigmas of the flowers of another plant
  - the bee because it eats some of the pollen, and sucks up the sugar-rich nectar.

- Plants getting eaten is another selection pressure that promotes the evolution of adaptations.

- For example, milkweed produces poisonous chemicals that deter feeding. However, adaptations enable the metabolism of some insects (for example, monarch butterflies) to detoxify this. The monarch accumulates the milkweed's poisons in its own tissues. This co-evolved adaptation with milkweed deters any potential predator from feeding on the butterfly.

Improve your grade

Plant and animal communication

Foundation: Discuss differences and similarities in the ways plants and animals communicate.

AO2 [5 marks]

Human evolution

Understanding early human behaviour

- Because chimpanzees and gorillas are probably our closest living relatives, studying their social behaviour may enable us to glimpse the behaviour of our early human ancestors.

- An ethologist, Jane Goodall, studied chimpanzees and noticed the following:
  - They use twigs as tools to help them find food.
  - They form social groups and work together to hunt monkeys.
  - Males are larger than females and usually dominate them. In return, females and their young are protected and receive food.

- In Rwanda, Dian Fossey saw that gorillas also form social groups and use tools, although less frequently.

- She observed that the more powerful a male gorilla is, the more a female wants to mate with him, gaining protection for herself and her young.

G–E

Fossil evidence

- Fossil evidence suggests that our human ancestors probably diverged from chimpanzee ancestors about 5 mya (million years ago).

- The evolution of a large brain is an important trend in human evolution. So too is **bipedalism** (the ability to walk on two legs).

- Ardi is the fossil remains of a pre-human ancestor and is 4.4 mya old. Ardi was small-brained; walked upright; could move among the branches of trees; lacked the specialisation that chimpanzees have for hanging from branches, climbing vertically and knuckle walking, and had human-like teeth.

- Lucy lived 3.2 mya. The evidence suggests that she was shorter than Ardi, but like Ardi was small-brained. However, her legs and feet were more human-like, showing that she walked fully upright.

- The fossilised remains of 'Turkana boy' have been dated to 1.6 mya. He was much bigger-brained than Ardi or Lucy. The fossil's long legs and narrow pelvis suggest that he might have been an even better walker than modern humans.

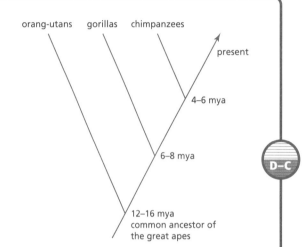

Humans and the great apes share common ancestry. *Homo sapiens* (humans) appeared about 200 kya (thousand years ago).

D–C

- Ardi (*Ardipithecus ramidus*) lived after the divergence from our most recent common ancestor shared with chimpanzees.

- She gives clues as to what the ancestor looked like – and that was *not* chimp-like. This probably means that the most recent **common ancestor** of humans and chimpanzees wasn't either.

> **Remember!**
> Humans did not evolve from apes. We share common ancestors with them. Out of all the apes, we have most features (and DNA) in common with chimpanzees because we evolved from a single common ancestor.

- The remains found near Ardi suggest that her habitat was moist woodland, very different from the present hot and arid environment of the region where she was found. So one theory is that climate change forced these early primates onto the savannah, where bipedalism rather than tree-dwelling was an advantage.

- *Australopithecus afarensis* (Lucy) adapted to be able to walk more efficiently and use tools. Her brain started to develop in size, perhaps because better tools led to a better diet. A bigger brain allowing more complex and precise tool-making skills would give an advantage.

- It seems that *Homo erectus* led the movement of our near ancestors out of Africa. They were similar to modern humans in size and stature and may possibly have had the ability to speak.

B–A*

Improve your grade

Evolution of bipedalism

Higher: Explain how climate change may have triggered the evolution of bipedalism in our ancestors.

AO2 [3 marks]

Stone tool technology

Stone tools developed over time

G–E

- A stone tool enables the user to do jobs that would not be possible without the tool, e.g. cutting up food, scraping skins and shaping wood.
- The first simple step in making a stone tool is to strike flakes from a stone (the core) with another stone (the hammer).
- Chimpanzees will strike a stone and produce a flake. However, judging where best to next hit the core with the hammer to produce a suitable tool requires greater intelligence.

- **Oldowan** refers to the earliest recorded stone tools from 2.6–1.5 mya. They were made by hitting a stone core to produce flakes which were used as cutting tools.

- The oldest specimens come from Africa. This evidence suggests that our early ancestors (probably *Homo erectus*) took their Oldowan technology with them as they migrated out of Africa and spread throughout the world.

- **Acheulean** tools were the result of a more sophisticated technology. Both sides of the core stone were struck to produce a cutting edge. The core was the tool, not the flakes.

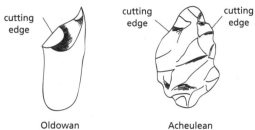

Oldowan and Acheulean tools compared.

- The tool was shaped and finished and different types of tool were produced, each type designed for a particular job.

- From about 300 kya (thousand years ago) **Mousterian** tools were being used. Their production required many stages.

D–C

- Types of tool included cutting tools, pointed tools designed to be tied to the end of a stick and scrapers for processing animal skins.
- The timeline here shows which *Homo* species used which tools.

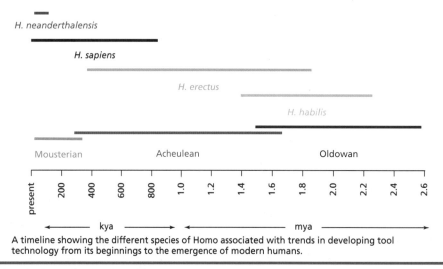

A timeline showing the different species of Homo associated with trends in developing tool technology from its beginnings to the emergence of modern humans.

How are stone tools dated?

B–A*

- Relative methods indicate whether rocks are older or younger than something else. For example, older stone tools are usually more deeply buried.

- Absolute methods give a date to rocks within a range of years. Stone tools sandwiched between two lava flows, for example, can be dated by dating the rocks.

- **Radiometric dating** depends on the known constant rate of decay of the radioactive isotopes in the rocks.

> **Remember!**
> Half-life means the time taken for half of the radioactive element in a sample of rock to decay.

Improve your grade

Radiometric dating

Higher: Carbon-14 is a radioactive isotope with a half-life of 5730 years. A sample of fossilised bone contains one eighth of its original carbon-14. Use radiometric dating to work out its age.   *AO3* [2 marks]

Human migration

Human migration and climate change

- A drying and cooler climate in eastern Africa 2.5 mya meant that our tree-dwelling ancestors lost much of their food supply as forests gave way to grassland.

- Individuals who could walk and run had an advantage over those adapted to tree-climbing.

- *Homo erectus* evolved as the first of the *Homo* genus to walk fully upright, and migrated out of Africa.

- Human migration out of Africa followed the sequence shown on the map below:

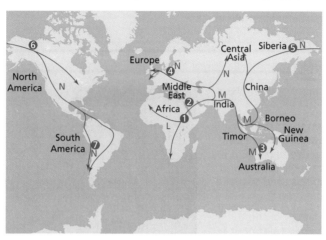

Human migration patterns out of Africa. The letters L, M and N refer to genetic markers described later.

- **1** 200 kya: *H. sapiens* appears. Our ancestors spread through Africa over the next 100 000 years.
- **2** 85 kya: A group and their descendants follow the coast of the Arabian Peninsula into India and on to China.
- **3** 70 kya: Groups cross by boat into Australia and New Guinea.
- **4** 50 kya: Groups move through the Middle East and into Europe.
- **5** 40 kya: Migrants from China move through central Asia, and into Siberia.
- **6** 23 kya: Their descendants pass from Siberia into North America.
- **7** 15 kya: Migration continues southwards into South America.

- Climate change made human migration easier or more difficult depending on date and location. For example, falls in the sea level due to the last ice age connected land masses that are separated today.

Mitochondrial DNA

- All of the **mitochondrial DNA (mtDNA)** inherited by offspring is contributed by mothers and not fathers, so follows a direct line of descent unchanged (except for mutations) from mother to offspring.

- mtDNA is less likely to degrade over time than nuclear DNA. It can still be extracted from fossils tens of thousands of years old. This means that it is very abundant.

- mtDNA mutates about 20 times faster than nuclear DNA. After several generations, each mutation becomes a **genetic marker** carried by most people in the region where it arose. Scientists can date the markers, since the age of fossils can be determined using radiometric techniques.

- Comparing the mtDNA sequences of people from different parts of the world identifies the number of markers in each population. The main markers are labelled L, M and N (see the map).

- The predominance of L in Africa and its relative rarity elsewhere suggest that L is the oldest mtDNA human marker and almost certainly identifies our most recent H. sapiens common ancestor: **African Eve**.

- Markers M and N are relatively rare in Africa. Also they appeared after L. This supports the idea that all non-Africans have their origins in Eve's descendants.

Remember!

Mitochondrial DNA is DNA found in mitochondria. Offspring inherit all of their mtDNA from their mother because during fertilisation only the nucleus of the sperm enters the egg, the rest of the sperm (containing the mitochondria) is left behind.

Improve your grade

Human migration and the ice age

Foundation: Explain how the last ice age made it possible for our ancestors to migrate across the world.

AO2 [2 marks]

Biotechnology

What is biotechnology?

- The term **biotechnology** refers to using plant cells, animal cells and microorganisms to produce useful **biomolecules** and then, perhaps, modify them chemically to make them even more useful.

- A biomolecule is any molecule produced by a living organism, e.g. vitamins, enzymes and various sugars.

- We use microorganisms to produce food mainly through **fermentation reactions**:
  - yeasts to make wine, beer and bread
  - moulds to flavour cheese
  - bacteria to make yogurt, cheese and vinegar.

- Genetic engineering, a type of biotechnology, means using genes and manipulating cells genetically.

Plant-based drugs

- Drugs sourced from plants are examples of biomolecules.

- People have long known that the bark and leaves of the willow tree relieve pain and reduce fever. The active ingredient in the liquid made from these is **salicin**, and salicylic acid made from it is used to make **aspirin**, a painkiller.

- Chewing the bark and leaves of the *Cinchona* tree is an effective treatment for malaria. The active ingredient is **quinine**. It reduces fever and kills the parasite that causes malaria.

- **Taxol**, which is extracted from the bark of the Pacific yew tree, kills cancer cells by stopping cell division. It has an effect on healthy cells, but affects cancer cells even more.

The bark and leaves of willow trees contain salicin.

- So great was the demand that the Pacific yew tree soon became an endangered species. Fortunately the leaves of the European yew tree were found to be the source of a similar taxol-like substance. Since the tree quickly replaces its leaves, there is no risk of it becoming endangered by the harvesting of its leaves. Chemists modified the substance to form a semi-synthetic version of taxol called **paclitaxel**.

> **Remember!**
>
> Using biotechnology is not a modern invention. People have been using fermentation to make food, and using biomolecules from plants as medicines, for thousands of years.

- Most drugs have unwanted side-effects on the user because of their **toxicity**.

- Paclitaxel may be combined with other substances which help to deliver the drug to where it is needed, which means it only affects the cancer cells. For example:
  - DHA is short for a type of fatty acid easily absorbed by cancer cells. Paclitaxel combined with DHA is not toxic until it enters cancer cells. Then the bond between the DHA/paclitaxel combination breaks and paclitaxel does its work.
  - Combining paclitaxel with the amino acid glutamate: cancer cells take up more of the glutamate/paclitaxel combination than healthy cells, reducing side-effects.
  - Combining paclitaxel with particular monoclonal antibodies that target specific types of cancer cell. Accurate targeting of cancer cells reduces the effects on healthy cells.

How science works

You should be able to:

- describe the uses of technological developments, including using biomolecules as medicines

- discuss their benefits, drawbacks and risks.

Improve your grade

Plant-based drugs

Foundation: State two drugs that are extracted from plants and describe their use. *AO2 [4 marks]*

Fermenters

Fermenters

- A **fermenter** is a container used to cultivate microorganisms for the production of biomolecules.
- They are used in waste treatment and for the production of antibiotics and of food (yogurt, cheese, soy sauce).

- Conditions inside industrial fermenters can affect microorganism growth rate.

- Aseptic techniques must be used. Superheated steam is pumped through, killing microorganisms that might spoil the product.
- Nutrients (substances that microorganisms need in order to multiply and grow) make up the culture medium.
- pH of the nutrient solution is controlled by adding acid or alkali to it. Optimum (best) pH depends on the microorganism cultured.
- If oxygenation is necessary sterile air is fed into the bottom of the fermenter through a perforated metal disc called a sparger. Air bubbles rise through the nutrient solution.
- Motorised paddles stir the fermenter's contents to ensure even distribution of nutrients, microorganisms, gases in solution and heat.
- Optimum temperature is maintained by a cooling system. Heat released by the motorised paddles and fermentation reactions is quickly dispersed by a water jacket.

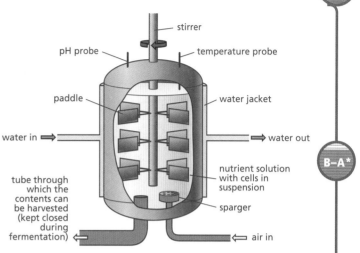

An industrial-scale fermenter.

Investigating yeast

- Home winemaking using **yeast** (a single-celled fungus) acting on fruit juice is an example of fermentation technology on a small scale.

- You can investigate the effect on the growth of yeast of different factors, such as pH, temperature, type of sugar, and species of yeast.
- Write down a hypothesis about your investigation. Next, identify the factors to be investigated. Design the experiment using the apparatus available in the laboratory. Work out how to measure the rate of the fermentation reactions, changing one factor at a time while keeping all other factors constant.

Remember!

The reaction used to make alcohol by yeast is called fermentation: sugar (glucose) → ethanol + carbon dioxide. It is a type of anaerobic respiration (requires no oxygen).

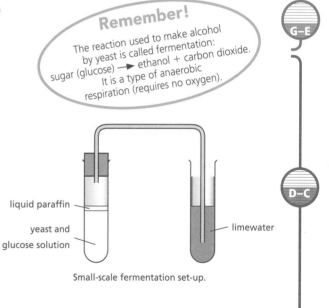

Small-scale fermentation set-up.

EXAM TIP

When designing investigations such as this, consider how you will gather your evidence. In the equipment shown you could measure the rate of fermentation by counting the number of bubbles of carbon dioxide produced or the time taken for the limewater to go cloudy – which would produce the most accurate data?

How science works

You should be able to:

- plan to answer a scientific question such as 'what factors affect the growth of yeast?'
- evaluate methods of data collection and consider their validity and reliability as evidence.

Improve your grade

Industrial fermentation

Higher: Explain why it is important to maintain a suitable temperature when carrying out fermentation on an industrial scale.

AO2 [4 marks]

Eating microorganisms

Mycoprotein

G–E

- Eating microorganisms produced by biotechnology may help us to feed the world's growing population.
- **Mycoprotein** is protein from fungus.

D–C

- The commercial product called Quorn is mycoprotein. It is made from the fungus *Fusarium sp.* It contains nearly 50% protein and less than 12% fat, and has a high vitamin and mineral content.
- Its nutritional value is similar to that of meat but it contains zero cholesterol and is high in fibre.

Remember!

Growing mycoprotein is classed as biotechnology because it is a biomolecule produced by a living organism (in this case, fungus).

Quorn with vegetables. Quorn is often used as a meat substitute.

B–A*

- The microorganisms used to produce mycoproteins are grown in large quantities in huge fermenters filled with nutrient solution.
- Nutrients used to grow mycoprotein microorganisms are often by-products sourced from other industrial processes, including pulp from fruit processing and agricultural waste (corn, wheat or rice starch, for example).
- Continuous culture is used. Nutrients are replaced in the fermenter as they are used up, and temperature and pH are carefully controlled.
- The conditions inside a fermenter are ideal for the rapid asexual reproduction of the microorganisms used to produce mycoproteins.

Microorganisms versus farming

D–C

- There are many advantages of using microorganisms for food.
- Cell division in microorganisms occurs every 20–30 minutes, meaning that they double their mass within hours. The crops and livestock that we eat take weeks or months to grow.
- Microorganisms are easier to work with than crops and animals, which can contract diseases or have difficult or unpredictable problems.
- Unlike crops, the production process is independent of the climate as it takes place in large fermentation tanks.
- The tanks take up little space compared with a farm.
- Microorganisms can feed on by-products from other industrial processes.

EXAM TIP

You might be asked to compare using microorganisms and farming for food. Remember to consider all the economical, social, environmental and ethical factors.

How science works

You should be able to:

- evaluate the use of microorganisms for food including ethical issues, and discuss the social, economic and environmental effects of such decisions.

Improve your grade

Mycoprotein

Foundation: David wants to cook a stir-fry but he can't decide whether to use mycoprotein or meat. Describe the health benefits of using mycoprotein rather than meat.   *AO2* [3 marks]

Making yogurt

Making yogurt

- Yogurt is made by adding a starter culture of lactic acid bacteria to warm **sterilised** milk.

- The bacteria produce enzymes which catalyse reactions that ferment the **lactose** to **lactic acid**. The milk becomes acidic and **coagulates** (solidifies) to form yogurt.

- When cool, the yogurt may be flavoured or have fruit added to it.

- The yogurt is placed in pots which are then sealed and sold.

Yogurt has become a mass consumer product.

G–E

- Factors that might affect yogurt-making include:
  - Temperature: different enzymes are active at different (optimum) temperatures.
  - Milk quality: for example, skimmed, semi-skimmed, full fat (whole), or lactose-free milk.

D–C

- The bacteria used to make yogurt are *Lactobacillus bulgaricus* and *Streptococcus thermophilus*.

- Their enzymes catalyse chemical reactions that ferment the lactose to lactic acid. This happens under anaerobic conditions.

- During fermentation, the numbers of bacteria increase, converting more and more lactose to lactic acid, which lowers the pH of the milk.

- The increasing concentration of lactic acid causes the milk to coagulate.

Remember!
Fermentation is a type of anaerobic respiration carried out by some microorganisms.

B–A*

Investigating yogurt making

- An experiment into factors that affect yogurt-making can be carried out using apparatus available in the lab.

- One method to measure the quality of the yogurt made is to measure thickness (viscosity) by timing how long it takes for a ball to sink to the bottom of a measuring cylinder full of yogurt.

EXAM TIP

You could be asked to comment on the quality of evidence from an investigation like this. Remember, valid evidence comes from controlling variables and reducing errors. Results of an investigation are considered reliable if readings are repeated and the repeats are similar.

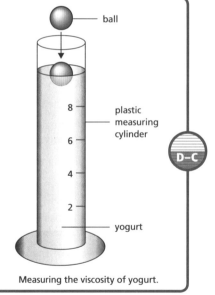

ball

8

plastic measuring cylinder

6

D–C

4

2

yogurt

Measuring the viscosity of yogurt.

How science works

You should be able to:

- plan an investigation to show the effect of different factors on yogurt making

- evaluate methods of data collection and consider their validity and reliability as evidence.

Improve your grade

Yogurt investigation

Foundation: As milk turns into yogurt it thickens (becomes more viscous). Outline the plan for an investigation into how the type of milk used affects yogurt production. *AO2* [4 marks]

Using enzyme technology

Enzyme technology

- Enzymes are useful industrial catalysts because:
  - only a particular reaction is catalysed by an enzyme, making it easier to collect and purify the end product
  - enzyme activity is high at moderate temperatures, saving energy costs
  - only small amounts of enzyme are needed
  - the enzyme is not used up in the reaction.
- Enzymes are used in food production, detergents, brewing and the pharmaceutical industry.

> **Remember!**
> Catalysts are substances which speed up the rate of a reaction without being used up in the reaction themselves. Enzymes are catalysts found in living things.

- **Chymosin** is an enzyme essential to cheese-making. It catalyses reactions that cause the proteins in milk (**curds**) to coagulate and separate from the liquid (**whey**).
- Chymosin used to be obtained from the stomach tissue of slaughtered calves but today most is made using genetically modified (GM) bacteria. GM-produced chymosin contains fewer impurities so it is more predictable.
- To make the soft centre in chocolates, manufacturers add **invertase** (sucrase) to a sucrose filling and store the mixture for several days at about 18°C. The enzyme catalyses the reaction, which converts solid sucrose into liquid glucose and fructose.
- **Biological washing powders** contain enzymes:
  - proteases break down proteins to amino acids
  - lipases break down fats and oils to glycerol and fatty acids
  - carbohydrases (such as amylase) break down polysaccharides (for example starch) into sugars.
- Including enzymes in washing powders means that washing is most effective at low temperatures so:
  - less energy is used to heat the water, saving costs and carbon emissions
  - the dye in coloured clothing is less likely to wash out of the fabric
  - the clothes are less likely to shrink.

Investigating enzymes

- Immobilised enzymes are protected, helping them to resist changes in temperature and pH. This allows industrial processes to be designed to maximise the activity of enzymes without damaging them.
- Immobilisation also means that enzymes are more easily recovered and reused so do not contaminate the end product.
- Lactase catalyses the reaction that breaks down lactose sugar (found in milk) to glucose and galactose.
- In some people, the cells lining the wall of the intestine do not produce lactase – they are lactose intolerant. Bacteria in the intestine feed on the undigested lactose, making these people feel unwell.
- Lactose-free milk is made using immobilised lactase which is bonded to insoluble and unreactive alginate beads.
- Food production depends on enzymes produced by different species of bacteria or fungi.
- For example, glucose isomerase is produced by the bacterium *Bacillus coagulans*. The enzyme converts glucose into fructose, which is sweeter. Fructose syrups are used to sweeten foods.
- Different species of the bacterium *Acetobacter* produce oxidase enzymes used in vitamin C synthesis.

How science works

You should be able to:

- investigate the use of immobilised lactase to produce lactose-free milk.

Improve your grade

Producing lactose-free milk

Higher: Milk contains lactose. This can be removed, turning the milk lactose-free, by adding the enzyme lactase. Outline the advantages of using immobilised lactase over just adding a solution of lactase to the milk.   *AO2* [4 marks]

Recombinant DNA technology

What is recombinant DNA?

- **Genes** are sections of DNA whose **base** sequences are the codes to synthesise the chains of amino acids which form **proteins**.

- Useful genes can be transferred from the cells of one type of organism to the cells of almost any other type: human to bacteria, for example.

- The host cells are the cells into which the genes are transferred. The organism with host cells is **genetically modified (GM)**.

- To do this the gene must be combined with another piece of DNA called a **vector**, which can be a virus or a **plasmid** (a circular piece of DNA found in bacteria).

- The combination of useful gene with vector DNA is called **recombinant DNA**. We say that the molecule has been **genetically engineered**.

B–A*

Enzymes and DNA technology

- **Restriction enzymes** can be used to cut out useful genes from longer lengths of DNA. They cut the DNA within a **recognition site** to form short, single-stranded lengths of exposed bases called **sticky ends**.

- The same restriction enzyme is used to cut the vector DNA into which the useful gene is to be inserted. This ensures that the exposed bases of the sticky ends of the useful gene are **complementary** to the bases of the sticky ends of the vectors and the gene can be successfully inserted.

- **Ligase** enzymes catalyse the bonding process that rejoins the DNA strands.

Remember!

Each recognition site is a short sequence of bases specific to each restriction enzyme. For example, the recognition site for EcoRI is GAATTC. This is where the enzyme will cut.

B–A*

vector — GAATTC / CTTAAG
sticky end of the vector (plasmid)
complementary sequence of bases
useful gene — AATTC / TTAAG
sticky end of the useful gene

How the useful section of a gene is inserted into the DNA vector.

Making genetically engineered insulin

- A person with Type 1 diabetes needs to inject insulin to regulate the concentration of glucose in their blood as their pancreas does not produce enough insulin.

- Nowadays this insulin is obtained from GM bacteria. The stages in the process are shown in the figure here.

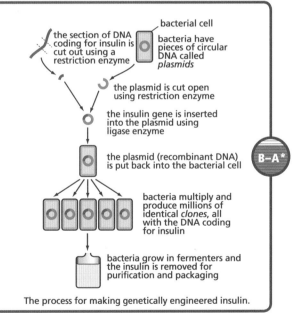

the section of DNA coding for insulin is cut out using a restriction enzyme

bacterial cell
bacteria have pieces of circular DNA called *plasmids*

the plasmid is cut open using restriction enzyme

the insulin gene is inserted into the plasmid using ligase enzyme

the plasmid (recombinant DNA) is put back into the bacterial cell

bacteria multiply and produce millions of identical *clones*, all with the DNA coding for insulin

bacteria grow in fermenters and the insulin is removed for purification and packaging

The process for making genetically engineered insulin.

B–A*

How science works

You should be able to:

- explain how genetic engineering has brought benefits to the lives of people with Type 1 diabetes.

Improve your grade

Genetically engineered insulin

Higher: In the past, people with Type 1 diabetes used insulin extracted from the pancreases of dead animals. Now human insulin is made using GM bacteria. Describe the benefits of this technological development.

AO2 [3 marks]

Producing transgenic plants

Creating transgenic plants

G–E

- Plants that have been genetically modified (GM) to create plants with beneficial characteristics obtained from the genes of other organisms are called transgenic plants.
- Crops can be modified advantageously to:
  - resist herbicides, so that weeds can be killed but not the crop
  - grow in places where rainfall is low
  - resist the microorganisms causing crop diseases
  - produce substances that kill their own insect pests.
  - improve the quality of food, e.g. the introduction of flavonoids in purple tomatoes.
- Growing GM crops increases the amount of food produced. This is particularly important in developing countries where harsh climate and poor soil can make growing crops difficult and food is sometimes in short supply.

D–C

- A method of creating a transgenic plant is by using a common soil bacterium called *Agrobacterium tumefaciens* as a **vector**:
  - *Agrobacterium*'s plasmid is called the Ti plasmid.
  - Ti means 'tumour inducing'. It causes the cells of a plant infected with *Agrobacterium* to multiply more quickly than usual.
  - A tumour-like mass of solid tissue (a **crown gall**) develops, small bits of which can be used to grow plants.
  - The cells of each of these plants carry a genetically engineered Ti plasmid.

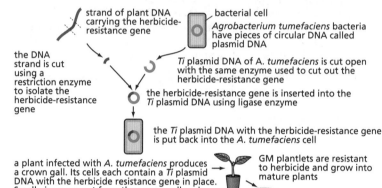

strand of plant DNA carrying the herbicide-resistance gene

bacterial cell
Agrobacterium tumefaciens bacteria have pieces of circular DNA called plasmid DNA

the DNA strand is cut using a restriction enzyme to isolate the herbicide-resistance gene

Ti plasmid DNA of A. *tumefaciens* is cut open with the same enzyme used to cut out the herbicide-resistance gene

the herbicide-resistance gene is inserted into the *Ti* plasmid DNA using ligase enzyme

the *Ti* plasmid DNA with the herbicide-resistance gene is put back into the A. *tumefaciens* cell

a plant infected with A. *tumefaciens* produces a crown gall. Its cells each contain a *Ti* plasmid DNA with the herbicide resistance gene in place. Small pieces are cut from the crown gall and cultured. Each grows into a plantlet. Each plantlet is a genetically modified version of the original

GM plantlets are resistant to herbicide and grow into mature plants

Genetically modifying crop plants with a herbicide resistance gene helps farmers to control weeds more efficiently.

Bacterial insecticides

B–A*

- **Insecticides** are used to protect crops. However, they also kill other wildlife, are harmful to humans and are costly to use.
- The soil bacterium *Bacillus thuringiensis* produces a toxin called **Bt insecticidal crystal protein** (Bt ICP), which kills a variety of crop pests.
- Transgenic crop plants which contain the Bt ICP gene can be produced using the method shown above. They can produce their own Bt ICP toxin and resist insect attack.
- Advantages of Bt-modified crops include:
  - Bt ICP is selective: different versions of the toxin kill different insect species and only those species (not beneficial species).
  - Bt ICP is harmless to other animals, including humans.
  - Harmful, chemical insecticides do not need to be used.
- A disadvantage is the appearance of Bt-resistant strains of pest species.

> ### EXAM TIP
> If a question asks you to evaluate a technology such as Bt crops, you should mention both the advantages and disadvantages.

How science works

You should be able to:

- discuss the benefits and risks of growing transgenic crop plants.

Improve your grade

Increasing food production

Foundation: Explain how growing transgenic plants may help increase food production in developing countries.
AO2 [3 marks]

Food security and production

What is food security?

- The world needs to produce more food for an increasing population. However, there are limiting factors, including a reduction in topsoil in which to grow crops because of soil erosion and less groundwater to irrigate crops because of climate change.

- **Food security** will only exist when everyone in the world is able to obtain enough food which is safe to eat and nutritionally balanced. Achieving food security depends on:
  - farmers consistently growing enough food
  - people having the means to obtain enough food
  - people's knowledge of basic nutrition and healthy eating.

G–E

Increasing food production

- Because of advances in plant breeding, irrigation methods and the use of pesticides and fertilisers, farmers are producing more food than ever before.

- Plant breeding programmes produce 'new crop' varieties with advantageous characteristics, such as high yield and insect resistance. Two varieties with desired characteristics are cross-bred to produce a new hybrid variety which is then reproduced asexually.

- Pesticides are the chemicals used to kill **pests**, and so assist in increasing crop yield.

- There are concerns that pesticide residues may contaminate food supplies and harm the environment, so farmers are encouraged to use pest-resistant varieties of plants and to adopt natural methods of controlling pests, such as companion planting or the use of beneficial organisms.

- Crop plants have been genetically modified to be resistant to herbicides, kill the insects eating them and grow where there is little rainfall.

- Genetic modifications can also increase plant growth. For example, by transferring *Rhizobium* into cereal plants, we add the genes responsible for nitrogen fixation. Like **leguminous** plants, the cereals can now make their own nitrates (fertiliser).

- Genetic modification produces plants with the desired characteristics more quickly than conventional breeding programmes.

- Despite their advantages, fears about damage to the environment and people's health have led some countries to ban growing GM crops.

Genetically modified crops.

Remember!
There is a difficult balance to be struck between producing enough food for the current population and making sure the environment and resources are protected so future generations also have food security. This is called acting in a sustainable way.

D–C

- Grain production has nearly doubled in the past 40 years, but the amount available to each person as food has fallen. There are a number of possible reasons for this including:
  - The increasing demand for meat in newly prosperous developing countries means that grain is bought for animal feed.
  - Population growth means higher demand and higher prices.
  - The increasing production of biofuels means that arable land is given over to growing crops to make biofuels rather than crops for food.

B–A*

How science works

You should be able to:

- discuss the social, economic and environmental effects of decisions surrounding food security.

Improve your grade

Food security
Foundation: Explain what is meant by the term 'food security'.   *AO2* [2 marks]

Biofuels

Why use biofuels?

- **Biofuels** are produced from **renewable** organic materials such as plant **biomass** (the organic material making up an organism's body). The stored energy is released when the biofuel is burnt.

- Ethanol is an important biofuel. It is obtained by fermentation of sugar by yeast and then distillation.

- Biogas is a biofuel produced by the anaerobic fermentation of plant material and organic wastes. **Methane** is an example.

Brazil produces ethanol-based biofuel using sugar cane.

- The advantages of biofuels compared with fossil fuels are:
  - Supply: biofuels are a renewable resource.
  - Clean burning: burning biofuels does not produce the pollutants sulfur dioxide and nitrogen oxides which combine with water vapour to produce **acid rain**.
  - Conservation: substituting fossil fuels with biofuels helps supplies of fossil fuels to last longer.
  - Greenhouse gases: burning both fossil fuels and biofuels releases carbon dioxide, a **greenhouse gas**. The difference is that the carbon dioxide released into the atmosphere by burning biofuels is only replacing the carbon dioxide absorbed during photosynthesis by the plants used to produce the biofuels in the first place. There is no net increase in the amount of carbon dioxide in the atmosphere, biofuels are **carbon neutral**.

- One disadvantage is that using land for growing biofuel crops means that less land is used for crop production, reducing food supply.

Remember!

Burning fossil fuels releases carbon dioxide that has been locked away for millions of years. This release increases the concentration of carbon dioxide in the atmosphere, which may contribute to global warming.

Burning biofuels produces fewer pollutants than burning coal in this power station.

Life-cycle analysis

- Life-cycle analysis allows us to calculate the impact of human activity on the environment.

- In the case of producing ethanol-based fuel, the analysis lists the processes (the life cycle) of producing biofuel and the contribution each part of the process makes to the release of carbon dioxide.

- Some scientists claim that burning the biofuels still releases the equivalent of less carbon dioxide compared with fossil fuels. However, other scientists using similar analyses claim that biofuels release more.

How science works

You should be able to:

- discuss the social, economic and environmental effects of decisions surrounding the use of biofuels.

Improve your grade

Air pollution

Foundation: Explain how using ethanol as a car fuel, rather than petrol, affects air pollution.

AO2 [3 marks]

B3 Summary

Reactions in cells produce waste products.

Urea, excess water and salts are removed from the blood by the kidneys.

Kidney failure is treated by dialysis, where a machine does this job instead.

The sex of offspring is determined at fertilisation; there is a 50% chance of a boy or a girl.

Sex-linked genetic disorders are carried on the sex chromosomes.

Conditions such as temperature affect the growth of microorganisms.

Microbiologist Louis Pasteur was the first to provide evidence that microorganisms caused decay. This led to the development of aseptic techniques.

The menstrual cycle is controlled by hormones.

Treatments using artificial hormones are available to help with infertility, for example IVF.

Control systems

Immunisation helps protect the body against infectious diseases.

Monoclonal antibodies are those which can only bind to one antigen. They have uses in medicine, including cancer treatments.

Biological rhythms that happen over 24 hours are called circadian, responses to changes in day length are photoperiodic.

Pest attack on plants has an impact on human food supply.

Some plants can defend themselves by producing toxic substances.

Courtship rituals, mating strategies and parental care are all important evolutionary strategies involved in reproduction. They ensure that genes from the best adapted organisms get passed on to future generations.

Communication is a form of behaviour that influences the actions of other individuals.

Animals communicate through sounds, facial expressions, body language and chemicals called pheromones.

Communication can take place between plant species and between animals and plants.

There are different types of behaviour: innate, learned, habituation, imprinting and conditioning (classical and operant).

Animals' behaviour can be exploited in order to train them.

Behaviour

Evidence for human evolution comes from fossils and stone tools.

Early humans migrated out of Africa to settle in all parts of the world.

Mitochondrial DNA is useful for tracking human migration and evolution.

Biotechnology refers to the way scientists and engineers use plant cells, animal cells and microorganisms to produce useful biomolecules such as food (mycoprotein and yogurt), enzymes and medicines.

Microorganisms can be grown in fermenters, where conditions are controlled in order to maximise the growth rate.

There are advantages of using microorganisms for food production. They are fast growing, easy to work with, can be grown in all climates and in a small amount of space.

Insulin for people with diabetes can be made using recombinant DNA technology where the human insulin gene is inserted into the DNA of bacteria.

Transgenic plants can increase food production because they can be grown in harsh climates. However, there are concerns with growing them.

Enzymes are useful industrial catalysts. They are used in the manufacture of cheese (chymosin), to make soft-centred sweets (invertase), in biological washing powders (proteases, lipases, carbohydrases) and to make lactose-free milk (lactase).

Biotechnology

Biofuels are fuels made from biomass, like ethanol made from the fermentation of sugar cane. There are advantages and disadvantages with their use.

B1 Improve your grade Influences on life

Page 4 Naming new species

Higher: Scientists exploring an area of the South American rainforests discovered several species of frog. They gave each a new binomial name.

Explain why classifying organisms in this way is important. *AO1 [3 marks]*

It identifies new species.

Answer grade: C. The answer only gives one reason. For full marks, mention two other reasons why classification is important. For example, it enables scientists who speak different languages to communicate about the frogs, it prevents confusion about different names for them, and it shows that this area of rainforest has an increased biodiversity as new species have been found there.

Page 5 Polar bear adaptations

Foundation: Explain how the fur of the polar bear is a good adaptation for surviving in the Arctic. *AO2 [4 marks]*

It is thick, which keeps it warm and because it is white it is camouflaged.

Answer grade: D/E. This answer lists the functions of the fur but does not explain *how* they would enable the bear to survive in the Arctic. To raise this to a grade C, explain that the thick fur acts as insulation by trapping air. You should also explain why the polar bear needs to be camouflaged (to hide from its prey so it can hunt effectively). Many students believe that a polar bear's thick fur keeps it warm because it stops the cold from the outside reaching the bear's skin. In fact, the reverse is true – the fur stops heat from the polar bear escaping. Remember – heat always travels from where the temperature is higher to where it is lower.

Page 6 Human evolution

Higher: Scientists believe that humans evolved from ape-like animals. Millions of years ago the Earth became drier and forests were replaced by grasslands. Before this change all apes walked on four feet. Afterwards, populations of apes emerged that walked upright on two feet and were able to see further across the grassland.

Use your knowledge of natural selection to explain why apes evolved in this way. *AO1 [3 marks]*

The apes that stood upright could see predators coming and so could run away and not get eaten. They then survived to pass on their genes to offspring which also walked upright.

Answer grade: B. The answer correctly identifies two points about natural selection. However, in order to achieve full marks you should mention that the apes show variation: some were more upright than others. You should also include the fact that the apes passed on their genes to their offspring through reproduction.

Page 7 Hair-colour inheritance

Foundation: Katy has red hair. Both her parents have brown hair. Explain how Katy inherited red hair, even though her parents do not have it. *AO2 [3 marks]*

Katy got the gene for red hair from her parents.

Answer grade: E. To achieve full marks, explain why Katy's parents do not have red hair. The red-hair allele must be recessive. Her parents both have the red-hair allele but their other allele (brown hair) masks it. Katy received two red-hair alleles from her parents during fertilisation, so Katy has two red-hair alleles (her genotype) and so therefore has red hair (her phenotype). Notice that red hair is referred to as an allele in these comments, not a gene. The red-hair allele is a type of hair-colour gene. Always use the correct terminology.

Page 8 Mendel's experiments

Foundation: Mendel discovered that the colour of pea flowers was controlled by a single gene. The red allele (R) was dominant, and the white allele (r) was recessive. He crossed a pure-breeding red-flowered plant with a pure-breeding white-flowered plant. What would be the genotype and phenotype of the pea plants that were produced? Use a genetic diagram to help you. *AO2 [4 marks]*

Cross: RR × rr		
	R	R
r	Rr	Rr
r	Rr	Rr

Answer grade: D. The Punnett square is correctly drawn and the correct genotypes of both parents and offspring are shown. However, the question asks for the phenotype of the offspring, which the Punnett square alone does not show. For full marks, include a genetic diagram with this information. In answering this type of question, it is important to understand the difference between genotype and phenotype. Here, the genotype of the offspring is Rr. This shows the alleles of the offspring. The phenotype is the physical characteristic. In this case, all the offspring would have red flowers.

Page 9 Sickle cell disease inheritance

Higher: Ben carries the mutated gene for sickle cell disease in his sperm. Janet is neither affected by the disease, nor is she a carrier of it.

What is the probability of their children having sickle cell disease? Show how you worked out your answer. *AO2 [3 marks]*

		Ben	
		D	d
Janet	d	Dd	dd
	d	Dd	dd

Probability of children having it is 2 in 4.

Answer grade: C. This would only achieve one of the three available marks. Ben's genotype of Dd is correctly identified, as he is a carrier of the allele, but sickle cell allele is recessive. This means that Janet would have the genotype DD. This would result in none of the children having the disease. Therefore, the probability is zero.

Page 10 Cooling down

Foundation: Sandeep is running a marathon. When he gets too hot he begins to sweat. Explain how sweating cools the body down. *AO2* [2 marks]

It evaporates.

Answer grade: E. Only 1 mark would be awarded here for mentioning evaporation. In order to bring this answer up to a C grade, you need to explain how the sweat evaporating will decrease body temperature. Many students believe that sweating cools down the body simply because having water on the skin makes you cooler. Remember, there is more to it than that: the sweat evaporates from the skin. To do this it needs heat energy, which it takes from the skin. This lowers the temperature of the skin and cools you down.

Page 11 Paralysis

Foundation: An injury that results in a broken spine may cause a person to be paralysed. Explain why. *AO1* [3 marks]

The nerves in the spine might be broken.

Answer grade: E. This answer only makes one suggestion and thus only achieves 1 of the 3 possible marks. To gain full marks, explain that the spinal cord is part of the central nervous system and contains many nerves that send messages from the brain to all parts of the body. When these impulses meet the muscles, they contract. If the nerves in the spinal cord are broken then impulses cannot cross them, so muscles will not respond.

Page 12 Synapses

Higher: Explain how an impulse travels over a synapse. *AO1* [3 marks]

Chemicals are released into the synapse and travel across it.

Answer grade: C. There is not enough detail in this answer to earn more than 1 of the 3 marks available. For an A grade, you need to describe every step in the process, e.g. the impulse reaches the end of the neurone, which triggers the release of chemicals called neurotransmitters into the synapse. This diffuses across the synapse and stimulates a new impulse in the next neurone.

Page 13 Calculating BMI

Higher: Susan is a normal-sized adult woman. She is 1.6 m tall and has a mass of 82 kg. Work out her BMI by using this equation:

BMI (kg/m²) = mass (kg) / height (m)²

Use the graph to explain how much of a risk Susan has of developing Type 2 diabetes. *AO3* [2 marks]

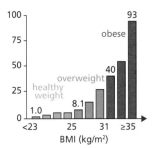

Her BMI is 32. She is obese so therefore has an increased risk of developing Type 2 diabetes.

Answer grade: B. The answer 32 has been calculated correctly, as has the fact that her risk of developing Type 2 diabetes is increased. However, the units for BMI have not been included (kg/m²) so a mark has been lost here. It is also good practice to include the working for any calculations you do.

Page 14 Weedkiller

Higher: Explain how plant hormones can be used as weedkillers that kill weeds only, without affecting the crops. *AO1* [3 marks]

The herbicide contains plant hormones that stimulate the growth of plant stems. Because the rate of root growth does not keep pace with the stem, the roots are not able to absorb enough water to support the growing plant and it dies.

Answer grade: C. This would fail to achieve anything higher than a C grade, as the answer has not explained why weedkillers only affect the weeds. For full marks, explain that weeds are usually broad-leaved and absorb more herbicide than narrow-leaved crop plants.

Page 15 Drink driving

Foundation: Explain why it is dangerous to drink alcohol and drive. *AO1* [3 marks]

Alcohol slows down your reaction times.

Answer grade: E. This answer would gain only 1 of the 3 available marks because it is incomplete. For full marks, explain why slow reaction times would be dangerous to a driver. Including scientific words in your answer would also show evidence of a C grade level of understanding. For example, mentioning that alcohol is a depressant. Recall also that even a small amount of alcohol can affect reaction times, but how much a person is affected depends on their age, body mass and gender (whether they are male or female).

Page 16 Ethical concerns

Higher: Jon and Margaret are both on the liver transplant waiting list. Jon is a 36-year-old father of three. He has cirrhosis caused by alcohol abuse. The cause of Margaret's liver failure is unknown. She is 83 years old. Doctors have to decide who receives the next available liver.

Choose who this should be and argue your case. *AO2* [5 marks]

Jon because even though he has abused alcohol in the past, he is young and has a family to support. With help he can overcome his alcohol addiction and go on to lead a healthy life.

Answer grade: C. This answer puts forward several good reasons why Jon should receive the liver. However, to achieve the full marks available and an A grade you should demonstrate an awareness of Margaret's case, too. Having outlined both cases, a conclusion should be drawn.

Page 17 Malaria prevention

Higher: The spread of malaria can be prevented cheaply and easily by covering beds with mosquito nets. Explain how this technique works. *AO2* [3 marks]

Mosquitoes cannot get through the net to bite the person so the malaria cannot be passed on.

Answer grade: B. A bit more detail is needed to achieve full marks. Remember – it is only an *Anopheles* mosquito carrying the malaria pathogen that needs to be prevented from biting the person. Try to include as much scientific vocabulary as you can, for example the terms vector, host and protozoa. Remember, the vector is the animal carrying the pathogen. The vector cannot get the disease. The host is the animal that the pathogen is passed on to and is susceptible to the disease, e.g. a human.

Page 18 Interdependence

Foundation: Plants and humans are interdependent.

Explain what this statement means, giving an example. *AO1* [2 marks]

Being interdependent means that plants and animals need each other for survival. An example is that animals eat plants.

Answer grade: E. This answer shows an understanding of the term interdependent, but has not applied it to an example. Not all animals eat plants. Lions eat plant-eaters (herbivores), but without plants there would be no prey for them to eat. Plants are at the start of every food chain.

Page 19 Metal recycling

Higher: Evaluate the use of metal recycling as an alternative to landfill. *AO3* [4 marks]

Metals are extracted from ores, which are non-renewable so our supplies of metal are running out. If we put metal in landfills it is lost forever, but if we recycle metal then we can use it again and we will not run out. Also, we are running out of space to put landfills and metal is non-biodegradable so it will stay in the ground.

Answer grade: B. This answer has covered nearly all the major points so would achieve a B grade. To push it up to an A, mention the chances of water pollution from burying metal in the ground. Also, discuss the drawbacks of recycling – such as the energy required to collect, sort and melt down the recycled metal – to present a balanced evaluation.

Page 20 Pond pollution

Foundation: A farmer grows wheat on his field. He notices that the water in a small pond next to the field has turned green and the fish have all died.

Explain what has happened. *AO2* [5 marks]

Chemicals from fertiliser have run off into the pond. This has caused the rapid growth of plants and algae which use up all the oxygen in the water, so the fish will die as they have no oxygen.

Answer grade: D. Two correct explanations have been given, but there is also a mistake in the answer – it is not the plants that use up oxygen in the water. To push this up to a C grade, explain that the bacteria use up the oxygen, not the plants. When the plants die they get decomposed by the bacteria. It is the bacteria that use up the oxygen in the water and cause other organisms in the pond to die.

Page 21 Carbon dioxide levels

Foundation: Scientists around the world are monitoring the amount of carbon dioxide in the atmosphere and collecting data such as that shown in the graph below.

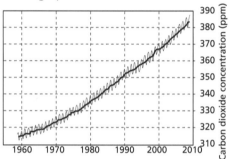

Describe the trend in the graph and suggest a reason for it. *AO3* [3 marks]

The graph shows that the amount of carbon dioxide in the atmosphere has increased since 1960. This is because we have more cars on the roads.

Answer grade: D. The trend has been described correctly, but the reason is not fully explained. The answer should explain that cars burn fossil fuels (petrol) in the engine, which releases carbon dioxide. You could also mention that it is not just cars that release carbon dioxide. Other vehicles such as lorries, trains and aeroplanes do, too. Also the burning of fossil fuels in power stations and deforestation by burning forests releases a lot of carbon dioxide.

Page 23 Looking at cells

Foundation: The image below shows some cells as seen down a microscope.

Are these animal or plant cells? Explain how you decided. *AO2* [2 marks]

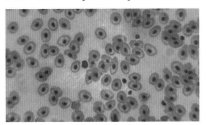

Animal cells because they have a nucleus.

Answer grade: E. The correct cell has been identified but the reason given is not sufficient – all cells have a nucleus. For full marks the answer should mention that this cell has no chloroplasts, vacuole or cell wall so therefore cannot be a plant cell. Remember, plant cells have both a cell membrane and a cell wall.

Page 24 Cell division

Higher: Why must the two strands in the DNA molecule separate during cell division? *AO2* [2 marks]

So each cell has one DNA strand.

Answer grade: U. This answer is incorrect and would not achieve any marks. To gain both marks available, explain that the strands need to separate in order to create two new DNA molecules. The DNA in cells consists of two complementary strands with their nucleotides held together by weak hydrogen bonds. When a cell is about to divide, these bonds break and the strands separate to enable new nucleotides to join up with each strand. This results in two new DNA molecules being formed – one for each cell.

Page 25 GM protest

Foundation: Fifty people turned up to protest on a piece of land that was growing GM wheat.

Outline the concerns they have. *AO1* [3 marks]

They don't think it is natural and are worried that it could harm the health of the people who eat it.

Answer grade: D. This answer gives two reasons and would therefore achieve only 2 of the 3 available marks. To improve to a C grade, give another reason why the people might be protesting. Remember, one of the things that concerns people the most about GM crops is that they will be able to breed with normal crops that are nearby (cross-pollination). This could cause changes – for example, the crop could produce a toxin in its leaves, which could spread to other plants, where it may disrupt food chains.

Page 26 Zygote to foetus

Foundation: Explain why mitosis is an essential process in the formation of a baby from a fertilised egg. *AO1* [3 marks]

Mitosis is needed to produce the egg and sperm cells that join to form the fertilised egg.

Answer grade: U. This answer is incorrect as the terms mitosis and meiosis have been mixed up, and would thus gain no marks. The correct answer should state that a fertilised egg is one cell (called a zygote), which will divide by mitosis to form the many cells that make up a baby. Remember that meiosis is the process that produces gametes (sex cells). An easy way to remember is that meiosis contains an 'e' for egg and an 's' for sperm.

Page 27 Cloning Daisy

Foundation: Daisy the cow produces the most milk in her herd. Her farmer is considering using her eggs for embryo transplants.

Explain to him why cloning her might be an even better idea. *AO2* [3 marks]

If you clone her then you will get another cow exactly like her who will produce lots of milk.

Answer grade: D. The answer is correct but is not detailed enough. To push this up to a C grade, explain why in this case cloning is better than embryo transplants. Embryo transplants involve using the eggs from the animal with desired characteristics and fertilising them with sperm from a male animal. The resulting embryos will have a mix of genes from both parents, and not necessarily the desired ones that you were trying to achieve. Cloning animals will produce offspring that are *identical* to the parent.

Page 28 Future applications of the HGP

Higher: In the future we may be able to use an individual's genome to calculate the likelihood of them developing diseases such as cancer.

Evaluate this potential application of the Human Genome Project. *AO2* [4 marks]

If a person's genome shows they might get a disease, they might not be able to get a job because the employer might be worried about them getting ill and taking time off work. But, it might be useful to know this as you can be told what symptoms to look out for and be able to get treatment quickly before the disease gets too bad.

Answer grade: B. This is a good answer, which discusses both the potential benefits and drawbacks to this technology. However, a little more detail would help to push this up to an A grade – for example, another benefit might be that doctors may be able to help with treatment such as stem cell therapy before the disease develops at all. Remember that when a question asks you to 'evaluate' something, it is asking you to provide both sides of the story – in this case both the benefits and drawbacks of this new technology. Try to get the word 'but' into the answer.

Page 29 Sickle cell mutation

Higher: Haemoglobin is a protein that is found in red blood cells. Sickle cell disease is a genetic illness where the red blood cells have a distorted shape. It is caused by a mutation in the gene for haemoglobin that converts a GAG codon into a GTG.

Explain how this causes a change in the shape of the haemoglobin molecule. AO1 [4 marks]

The change in the DNA will result in the wrong amino acids being put into the haemoglobin protein, which will affect its shape.

Answer grade: C. Although this answer is correct, there is not enough detail to gain higher than a C grade. To improve this, explain your understanding of the process of protein synthesis. For example, how could the change in the base bring about the wrong order of amino acids in the protein?

Page 30 Sex cell mutation

Foundation: A mutation occurs in the DNA of an organism's sperm cells.

Explain how this mutation will be passed to its offspring. AO1 [2 marks]

The mutation will be passed onto offspring by fertilisation.

Answer grade: D. Fertilisation has been mentioned as the process by which the mutation is passed on, but the answer lacks detail. For full marks, explain that if there is a mutation present in the DNA inside the nucleus of a sex cell then it will be present in the DNA of the zygote formed. As this one cell will undergo mitosis to form the organism, this mutation will be present in the nucleus of every cell in the adult organism.

Page 31 Understanding enzymes

Higher: Biological washing tablets contain enzymes that help break down stains found on clothes. Mark's clothes were very dirty so he decided to wash them at a much higher temperature than recommended on the instructions. The stains did not come off his clothes.

Use your understanding of enzymes to explain why. AO2 [3 marks]

The high temperature killed the enzymes so they did not work and did not break down the stains on the clothes.

Answer grade: U. This answer would not get any marks, as the science is incorrect. Enzymes cannot die as they are not living! At high temperatures, they change shape, or denature. The answer should have included this information and explained why denaturing makes enzymes less effective.

Page 32 The race

Foundation: You take part in a race. At first you sprint off feeling full of energy. However, half way through your legs start to ache and you have to stop. Explain why this happened. AO1 [3 marks]

My heart could not beat fast enough and my lungs could not breathe fast enough to get oxygen to my leg muscles, so they could not carry out respiration and make energy for my leg muscles to work.

Answer grade: E. This answer correctly states that the lungs and heart could not work fast enough to get the required levels of oxygen to the leg muscles, but respiration would not stop – anaerobic respiration would take over instead. The answer should explain this and then go on to link this to why the leg muscles would start to feel sore. Some of the energy stored in glucose is released without oxygen, a product of which is lactic acid, which is the chemical that makes the legs ache.

Page 33 Stroke volume

Higher: Ben is a professional runner. Through training he has been able to increase the stroke volume of his heart.

Explain how this enables Ben to run faster. AO2 [5 marks]

Increasing stroke volume will also increase cardiac output. This means that more blood is being pumped by the heart and so more oxygen and glucose are able to get to his respiring muscle cells in his legs. This will increase the rate of respiration, enabling him to release more energy.

Answer grade: B. This is a good answer that would achieve 4 marks out of a possible 5. What is missing is an explanation of why an increased rate of respiration will allow Ben to run faster. If muscle cells are able to release energy quickly, they will not just be able to contract more quickly, but more strongly as well.

Page 34 Weed removal

Foundation: Suzanne has weeds growing in her flowerbeds and notices that her plants are not growing. Explain why this is. AO2 [3 marks]

The weeds are taking water from the plants which they need to grow.

Answer grade: E. To improve the grade, this answer needs to explain how a lack of water leads to a low rate of photosynthesis, which will lead to poor growth. It should also mention that weeds will cover the plants, which reduces the amount of light reaching their leaves. This will also affect the rate of photosynthesis in the plants.

Page 35 Preserving fish

Foundation: Covering fish with salt and leaving it causes the fish to dry out and become hard.

Use osmosis to explain why this happens.
AO2 [3 marks]

The salt sucks the water out of the fish by osmosis so it dries out.

> **Answer grade: E.** This answer would gain 1 mark for offering a basic explanation. However, it does not use the process of osmosis to explain what is happening. You must be able to apply osmosis to many different situations. In this case, the salt surrounding the fish will have a much lower water concentration than the fish cells. This means that there is a net movement of water out of the fish cells into the salt by osmosis. This will cause the fish to lose water and become dry.

Page 36 Growth chart

Higher: Adam is four years old and has a mass of 13 kg.

Use the growth chart below to comment on his mass. *AO3* [3 marks]

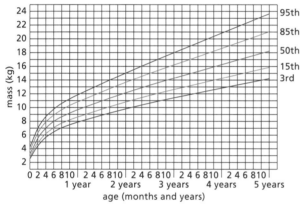

A growth chart for mass of boys aged up to 5 years
(Source: WHO Child Growth Standards)

He is underweight.

> **Answer grade: C.** The answer is correct, but does not give enough information to score higher than a C grade. To bring it up to A* standard, percentiles need to be explained. A four-year-old with a mass of 13 kg is on the 3rd percentile. This means that their mass is equal to or greater than 3% of children of the same age; 97% of children at that age are heavier than that child, so Adam is below average mass for a four-year-old.

Page 37 The heart

Foundation: Why is the heart classed as an organ?
AO1 [2 marks]

It is made up of lots of different types of cell.

> **Answer grade D.** In order to achieve full marks, the answer needs to explain what we mean by an 'organ'. Organs are made up of different types of tissue and have a particular function. For example, the function of the heart is to pump blood. It contains cardiac muscle tissue that can contract and relax, as well as nervous tissue and ligaments to hold the different tissues in place.

Page 38 Capillaries

Higher: Capillaries are blood vessels that are very thin (0.005 mm in diameter) and whose walls are only one cell thick.

Explain how these features enable them to carry out their function. *AO2* [4 marks]

Being so thin they can reach all parts of the body, so all cells are close to a capillary. This also increases the pressure in a capillary bed so tissue fluid is forced out. Because they are one cell thick, the substances they carry can easily pass out.

> **Answer grade: B.** This answer gives functions for each of the features described in the question, but it lacks detail and does not show a thorough understanding of the science. For full marks, explain that the pressure in the capillary bed is a result of the blood being at high pressure in the artery that supplies the bed with blood, and the narrow diameter of the capillary. Remember, at capillary beds there is an exchange of substances from the blood to the tissues, and waste products from the tissues to the blood.

Page 39 Enzyme experiment

Foundation: Dipesh mixed some starch with amylase in a beaker and left the mixture in a water bath at 37 °C. After 30 minutes he tested the mixture to see if there was any starch present.

Predict what Dipesh will find and give a reason for your answer. *AO3* [3 marks]

There would be no starch because the amylase is a carbohydrase enzyme, which helps breaks down starch.

> **Answer grade: C/D.** This is almost a complete answer, but it would have better to add that the starch would have been broken down into maltose and glucose. Remember that enzymes are only *catalysts* in the breaking down of food. The starch would eventually break down by itself, it would just take a lot longer.

Page 40 Probiotics vs prebiotics

Higher: Explain why some people believe that prebiotics are more likely to affect the health of the gut than probiotics. *AO1* [5 marks]

Probiotics contain live bacteria, which need to get to the intestines to have an effect. This means they have to survive storage and their journey through the digestive system. They also have to compete with the bacteria already present in the gut. Prebiotics contain sugar (food) for the 'good' bacteria in the gut, so this is more likely to get to the bacteria and have an effect.

> **Answer grade: A.** This answer contains all the information needed so would achieve an A grade. To bring it up to an A* standard, more detail could be added, for example, stating that acid in the stomach may kill the bacteria in probiotics.

Page 42 Osmoregulation

Higher: Describe the role of the kidney in regulating the water content of the blood (osmoregulation).

AO2 [3 marks]

In the nephrons in the kidney, water is reabsorbed into the blood. If the water balance of the body is low, more water will be reabsorbed.

Answer grade: C. This answer is correct but lacks detail. To raise it to an A/A* you should first explain that in the glomerulus of the nephron all the water is filtered out of the blood and into the Bowman's capsule. Then, at the convoluted tubules glucose is reabsorbed back into the blood, and water is reabsorbed at the loop of Henlé and the collecting duct. The amount that is reabsorbed is controlled by a hormone. Any excess water that is not reabsorbed forms urine, which leaves the kidney via the ureters.

Page 43 Dialysis

Higher: Explain how dialysis is designed to maximise the rate of diffusion of urea from the blood.

AO2 [4 marks]

The dialysis fluid does not contain any urea. This means that there is more urea in the patient's blood than the dialysis fluid so the urea passes from the blood, across the permeable membrane and into the dialysis fluid.

Answer grade: C. This answer would achieve 2 marks. To gain the extra 2 marks and get an A grade you need to mention another way that dialysis maximises diffusion: it maintains a high concentration gradient by quickly removing the dialysis fluid into which the urea has diffused. Also, to achieve higher grades you must demonstrate that you can use the correct terminology, so in this answer that means using the terms diffusion, concentration and diffusion gradient correctly.

Page 44 Oestrogen

Foundation: State two functions of oestrogen in the menstrual cycle. *AO2 [2 marks]*

Oestrogen builds up the lining of the uterus.

Answer grade: E. This answer gives only one function of oestrogen. The other function of oestrogen is that it stimulates the development of egg-containing follicles in the ovaries.

Page 45 Sperm cell adaptation

Foundation: Explain how a sperm cell is adapted to its function. *AO2 [4 marks]*

It has a tail, an acrosome and many mitochondria.

Answer grade: E. This answer describes the adaptations of a sperm cell but does not explain how these help it to perform its function, so as a result will only achieve 2 of the 4 marks available. To bring this up to full marks and a C grade you should explain that the tail helps the sperm to swim to the egg so it can be fertilised. The mitochondria carry out respiration to supply the tail with energy and the acrosome contains enzymes to digest the egg cell membrane so the nucleus of the sperm can enter the egg and fuse with its nucleus during fertilisation. You could also mention that the sperm is haploid, so it forms a diploid zygote when it fertilises the haploid egg.

Page 46 The inheritance of colour blindness

Higher: A red–green colour blind man and a woman who is a carrier of the allele have children. What is the probability of them having a girl with red–green colour blindness? Use a genetic diagram to help you to answer. *AO2 [4 marks]*

The probability would be 50%

		Mother	
		X^B	X^b
Father	X^b	$X^B X^b$	$X^b X^b$
	Y	$X^B Y$	$X^b Y$

Answer grade: B. The genetic diagram that the student has drawn is correct so that would earn them 3 marks out of the 4. However, they did not work out the probability correctly and doing so would bring this up to a perfect answer and an A*. Only the genotype $X^b X^b$ would be a girl who is colour blind, which is 1 in 4, or 25%.

Page 47 How immunisation works

Foundation: Explain how having the whooping cough vaccination prevents you from getting the illness. *AO2 [4 marks]*

The body starts to make antibodies which recognise the whooping cough pathogen. Then, if you get the disease your body will remember how to fight it.

Answer grade: D. The answer contains two scientific words (antibodies and pathogen) but if you are aiming for a C grade, it is important to use as many as you can in your answer. So you can say that the B-lymphocytes make antibodies against the weakened pathogen in the vaccine. If the person gets infected by the pathogen at a later date then memory lymphocytes are able to produce antibodies quickly before the pathogen has a chance to multiply and make the person ill.

Page 48 Monoclonal vs polyclonal

Higher: Explain the difference between polyclonal and monoclonal antibodies. *AO2 [3 marks]*

Polyclonal antibodies are a mixture, monoclonal antibodies are all the same.

Answer grade: C. You would achieve 2 marks for this answer. To aim for A* standard you need to explain scientific concepts in a lot more detail. The missing mark would be achieved by stating that monoclonal antibodies are specific to only one type of antigen (or one region of an antigen), whereas in a mixture of polyclonal antibodies there are antibodies specific to a range of antigens (or regions of antigens).

Page 49 Bacterial growth experiment

Foundation: Design an experiment to determine how temperature affects the growth of bacteria.

AO3 [5 marks]

Put the same amount of bacteria into five test tubes containing the same type of nutrient broth. Leave the mixtures at different temperatures, e.g. 10°C, 20°C, 30°C, 40°C and 50°C. Measure the growth of bacteria in each solution.

Answer grade: E. This answer achieves 2 marks out of a possible 5. The student mentioned 2 uses of control variables (using the same amount of bacteria at the start and the same type of nutrient broth), but could also have mentioned using the same volume of broth and checking that the pH is constant in each. Also, they did not mention how to measure the growth of the bacteria. Using resazurin dye and timing the colour change is a good method.

Page 50 Does honey contain antibacterials?

Higher: A scientist wanted to test the hypothesis that Manuka honey contains antibacterials. She spread a culture of bacteria over nutrient agar and added paper discs, one that had been soaked in distilled water, and one in Manuka honey. She then incubated the dish for three days. Her results are shown in the diagram. Explain what they show. *AO3 [3 marks]*

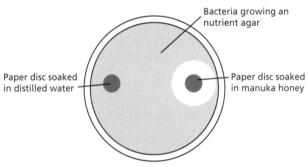

Bacteria growing an nutrient agar

Paper disc soaked in distilled water

Paper disc soaked in manuka honey

The Manuka honey has killed the bacteria so it shows it contains antibacterials.

Answer grade: C. This answer will achieve 1 mark and a C grade. To bring it up to an A/A* standard it needs to compare the effect of the honey against the distilled water (the control). Also, the results don't show that the honey killed the bacteria; just that it stopped it from growing. The clear area is called a 'zone of inhibition'.

Page 51 Flowers for Christmas

Foundation: Describe how a plant grower could manipulate a long-day plant to flower in the winter to be used for a Christmas display. *AO2 [2 marks]*

The grower would have to keep the plant warm so it thinks it is the summer and then it would flower.

Answer grade: U. This answer is incorrect so would not achieve any marks. The important thing to remember is that a long-day plant will flower in response to days with long periods of light and short periods of dark (so in the summer). To make it flower, the grower would have to grow the plant inside and use artificial lights to give the plant the impression of this long day length, even though outside it is winter.

Page 52 Innate behaviour

Foundation: Explain what is meant by the term 'innate behaviour'. *AO2 [2 marks]*

Innate behaviour is behaviour that you are born with.

Answer grade: E. This answer is correct but lacks detail. It would achieve 1 mark. To achieve maximum marks the answer should state that innate behaviours are instinctive, automatic and predictable: they follow a fixed pattern.

Page 53 Imprinting

Foundation: Explain why imprinting on their mother helps ducklings to survive. *AO2 [2 marks]*

They follow their mother around so don't get lost.

Answer grade: E. This answer states what imprinting is so would achieve 1 mark, but the reason why it is important is not really correct. To bring it up to a grade C level, it needs to state that in following their mother around the ducklings are protected against predators and will be supplied with food by their mother.

Page 54 Clicker training

Higher: You can train a puppy using a clicker. As soon as the puppy displays the behaviour you want, press the clicker (which makes a clicking sound) and then give the puppy a treat. After a while you will not need to give a treat after every click. Explain why. *AO2 [2 marks]*

The puppy knows that it has carried out the proper behaviour because of the sound.

Answer grade: C. This answer has given 1 correct statement so would be awarded 1 mark. To make sure you are answering questions to A/A* standard make sure you put in as much information as you can and use lots of scientific terminology. For example, in this answer the student could have explained that the puppy has learnt to associate the treat (the primary stimulus) with the sound of the clicker (secondary stimulus). This is called classical conditioning.

Page 55 Leopard mating strategy

Foundation: Male and female leopards will form pair bonds during the mating season and hunt together. They may stay together a short time after the cubs are born. Give two advantages of this mating strategy. *AO2 [2 marks]*

If they hunt in pairs they will be able to catch more food, which means more food for them and their offspring.

Answer grade: E. This answer has given 1 correct advantage so would be awarded 1 mark. To get a grade C another advantage needs to be stated. This could be that if the male stays with the female after the cubs are born then he can offer extra protection from animals that may prey on the cubs; the male and female can also share the task of hunting for food so one can stay with the cubs whilst the other is hunting. Both of these strategies will increase the chances of the cubs surviving to adulthood.

Page 56 Evolutionary strategy

Higher: Birds will often only feed the noisiest, biggest chicks. The other chicks may die. Explain why this makes sense as an evolutionary strategy. *AO2* [3 marks]

The parents couldn't get enough food to feed all the chicks. If they did this then they might all die.

Answer grade: C. This answer would achieve 1 mark. To get full marks and an A/A*, more detail has to be added. You could add that if all the chicks died then the parents' genes would not be passed on to future generations. Also, in just feeding the biggest chicks they are selecting the ones that have the 'best' genes and who would be more likely to survive to adulthood and pass on their genes to their offspring, hence passing down genes from their parents.

Page 57 Bird communication

Foundation: State two reasons why birds sing.
AO2 [2 marks]

To attract a mate so they can reproduce.

Answer grade: E. Only one reason is given so this would only be awarded 1 mark. The other reason which should have been stated is to warn other males away from their territory. The bigger a territory a male bird has, the larger the area it can gather food from, so the more food its chicks will have when it breeds.

Page 58 Plant and animal communication

Foundation: Discuss differences and similarities in the ways plants and animals communicate. *AO2* [5 marks]

Plants and animals both use visual and chemical communication but only animals use sound to communicate.

Answer grade: E. This answer states the similarities and differences but only achieves 2 marks. The question asks for a discussion. This, and the number of marks available, should give you a clue that a little more detail is needed and so examples should be used. You could say that both plants and animals use colour to communicate visually. For example, brightly coloured petals in flowers to communicate with pollinating insects and some poisonous animals use bright warning colours to deter predators. However, only animals use facial expression and body language. These comparisons can also be made for chemical communication in plants and animals to complete the answer.

Page 59 Evolution of bipedalism

Higher: Explain how climate change may have triggered the evolution of bipedalism in our ancestors.
AO2 [3 marks]

Climate change caused the environment to get drier, which meant that there were fewer trees. Our ancestors could be spotted more easily by predators so they had to run faster to escape.

Answer grade: C. The answer correctly describes the environmental change: that it got hotter and drier so the woodland changed to grassland. However, the effect this had on natural selection is not correct so it would only achieve 1 mark. In fact, the animals that could walk more upright had an advantage because they could spot predators (and prey) from further away. This meant they would survive to pass on the genes for walking upright.

Page 60 Radiometric dating

Higher: Carbon-14 is a radioactive isotope with a half-life of 5 730 years. A sample of fossilised bone contains one eighth of its original carbon-14. Use radiometric dating to work out its age. *AO3* [2 marks]

$5\,730 \times 8 = 45\,840$ *years old*

Answer grade: U. The calculation has been done incorrectly so the answer would not score any marks. It takes 5 730 years for the amount of carbon-14 to half. This means it will take another 5 730 years to half again (so become a quarter of its original amount). In another 5 730 years it will half again to one eighth the original amount so the correct calculation is $5\,730 \times 3 = 17\,190$ years old.

Page 61 Human migration and the ice age

Foundation: Explain how the last ice age made it possible for our ancestors to migrate across the world.
AO2 [2 marks]

The sea in between land froze so they could walk across it to reach new land masses.

Answer grade: E. The answer is correct in stating that our ancestors migrated to new land masses by crossing places where they would have been sea so would be awarded 1 mark. However, the sea did not freeze. During the Ice Age water was trapped in the polar ice caps, so sea levels were much lower and land masses that are separated by sea today would have been connected by dry land.

Page 62 Plant-based drugs

Foundation: State two drugs that are extracted from plants and describe their use. *AO2* [4 marks]

Aspirin comes from willow trees. Quinine is used to treat malaria.

Answer grade: D. This answer is not complete so would achieve 2 marks out of 4. It should mention that aspirin is a derivative of salicylic acid, originally made from willow tree bark, and it is a painkiller. Also, to make the answer more complete it would be good to add how quinine treats malaria: it reduces fever and kills the parasite that causes the disease.

Page 63 Industrial fermentation

Higher: Explain why it is important to maintain a suitable temperature when carrying out fermentation on an industrial scale. *AO2* [4 marks]

If the temperature gets too high then fermentation will slow down.

Answer grade: C. Whenever you are aiming for an A/A* answer try and include as much information as you can. This answer is brief and, even though it is not incorrect, it would only achieve 1 mark. Keeping the fermenter at an optimum temperature is important as this is the temperature at which the rate of fermentation and production of the product is fastest (meaning more profit for the manufacturers). You should also explain why this is the case: too low and the rate of reaction is slow because molecules do not have enough kinetic energy to collide with enough force for the reaction to take place, too high and enzymes that catalyse the reaction inside the microorganisms will denature and no longer work.

Page 64 Mycoprotein

Foundation: David wants to cook a stir-fry but he can't decide whether to use mycoprotein or meat. Describe the health benefits of using mycoprotein rather than meat. *AO2 [3 marks]*

Mycoprotein is high in protein and low in fat.

Answer grade: E. This answer achieves 1 mark. The question is worth three marks so you should make three different points. Also, it asks you to describe the health benefits compared to meat. Therefore a suitable answer might be: 'Mycoprotein has a similar protein content to meat but a lower fat content. Also, mycoprotein contains fibre (which meat doesn't). Fibre is important in your diet because it helps peristalsis and reduces the risk of constipation. Mycoprotein has zero cholesterol (meat can be quite high in it). Keeping blood cholesterol levels low decreases the risk of heart disease.

Page 65 Yogurt investigation

Foundation: As milk turns into yogurt it thickens (becomes more viscous). Outline the plan for an investigation into how the type of milk used affects yogurt production. *AO2 [4 marks]*

Choose some different milks, e.g. cow milk, sheep milk and goat milk. Use the same volume of each and warm them up and then add the same amount of the same starter culture to each and keep in a warm place overnight. Then measure how viscous each one is.

Answer grade: D. This answer does well to explain the independent variable (type of milk used) and the control variables (volume of milk and starter culture). However, it does not achieve full marks as it fails to explain how the dependent variable (viscosity) is measured. You could time how long it takes a ball to fall to the bottom of a measuring cylinder full of each yogurt. The slower the ball falls, the more viscous the yogurt is.

Page 66 Producing lactose-free milk

Higher: Milk contains lactose. This can be removed, turning the milk lactose-free, by adding the enzyme lactase. Outline the advantages of using immobilised lactase over just adding a solution of lactase to the milk. *AO2 [4 marks]*

Using immobilised enzymes means that they can be used again and again, which reduces the cost of producing the milk.

Answer grade: C. This answer describes one advantage so would be awarded 2 marks. To get full marks more than one advantage should be mentioned. You could also say that if you just add the enzyme to the milk then it would contaminate the product because it would be difficult to remove.

Page 67 Genetically engineered insulin

Higher: In the past, people with Type 1 diabetes used insulin extracted from the pancreases of dead animals. Now human insulin is made using GM bacteria. Describe the benefits of this technological development. *AO2 [3 marks]*

Using genetic engineering to make human insulin means using bacteria grown in a fermenter so the production is quick and reliable.

Answer grade: C. This answer mentions one benefit of the new technology over the old and would be awarded one mark and a grade C. You could also mention that the process makes human insulin (rather than animal insulin) which is more effective and produces no side-effects. Also, there are no ethical issues surrounding the use of bacteria to make the insulin.

Page 68 Increasing food production

Foundation: Explain how growing transgenic plants may help increase food production in developing countries. *AO2 [3 marks]*

They can grow in places where rainfall is low.

Answer grade: E. This answer only contains 1 point so would be awarded 1 mark. Plants can also be modified to resist herbicides so weeds can be killed but not the crop. The removal of weeds increases crop growth because it removes competition from other plants. Also, they can be modified to produce their own insecticides to stop insects feeding on them and resist diseases (also increasing yield).

Page 69 Food security

Foundation: Explain what is meant by the term 'food security'. *AO2 [2 marks]*

Making sure that everyone in the world has enough food to eat.

Answer grade: D. This answer provides one valid point so achieves 1 mark out of a possible 2. The other point that should have been made was that the food should be safe to eat and nutritionally balanced.

Page 70 Air pollution

Foundation: Explain how using ethanol as a car fuel, rather than petrol, affects air pollution. *AO2 [3 marks]*

Using ethanol will decrease the amount of air pollution.

Answer grade: E. The question asks for an explanation, so more detail is required in the answer. This answer would achieve only 1 mark. You could say that burning ethanol releases no sulphur dioxide or nitrogen oxides, which go on to form acid rain. Also, ethanol is considered a carbon neutral fuel so burning it would not increase the amount of carbon dioxide in the atmosphere. Carbon dioxide is a greenhouse gas.

How Science Works

Data, evidence, theories and explanations

As part of your Science and Additional Science assessment, you will need to show that you have an understanding of the scientific process – How Science Works.

This involves examining how scientific data is collected and analysed. You will need to evaluate the data by providing evidence to test ideas and develop theories. Some explanations are developed using scientific theories, models and ideas. You should be aware that there are some questions that science cannot answer and some that science cannot address.

Practical and enquiry skills

You should be able to devise a plan that will answer a scientific question or solve a scientific problem. In doing so, you will need to collect data from both primary and secondary sources. Primary data will come from your own findings – often from an experimental procedure or investigation. While working with primary data, you will need to show that you can work safely and accurately, not only on your own but also with others.

Secondary data is found by research, often using ICT – but do not forget books, journals, magazines and newspapers are also sources. The data you collect will need to be evaluated for its validity and reliability as evidence.

Communication skills

You should be able to present your information in an appropriate, scientific manner. This may involve the use of mathematical language as well as using the correct scientific terminology and conventions. You should be able to develop an argument and come to a conclusion based on recall and analysis of scientific information. It is important to use both quantitative and qualitative arguments.

Applications and implications of science

Many of today's scientific and technological developments have both benefits and risks. The decisions that scientists make will almost certainly raise ethical, environmental, social or economic questions. Scientific ideas and explanations change as time passes and the standards and values of society change. It is the job of scientists to validate these changing ideas.

How science ideas change

From the information you have learnt, you will know that science is a process of developing, then testing theories and models. Scientists have been carrying out this work for many centuries and it is the results of their ideas and trials that has provided us with the knowledge we have today.

However, in the process of developing this knowledge, many ideas were put forward that seem quite absurd to us today.

In 1692, the British astronomer Edmund Halley (after whom Halley's Comet was named) suggested that the Earth consisted of four concentric spheres. He was trying to explain the magnetic field that surrounds the Earth and suggested that there was a shell of about 500 miles thick, two inner concentric shells and an inner core. Halley believed that these shells were separated by atmospheres, and each shell had magnetic poles with the spheres rotating at different speeds. The theory was an attempt to explain why unusual compass readings occurred. He also believed that each of these inner spheres, which was constantly lit by a luminous atmosphere, supported life.

Reliability of information

It is important to be able to spot when data or information is presented accurately and just because you see something online or in a newspaper, does not mean that it is accurate or true.

Think about what is wrong in this example from an online shopping catalogue. Look at the answer at the bottom of the page to check that your observations are correct.

From box to air in under two minutes!

Simply unroll the airship and, as the black surface attracts heat, watch it magically inflate.

Seal one end with the cord provided and fly your 8-metre, sausage-shaped kite.

• Good for all year round use.

• Folds away into box provided.

• A unique product – not for the faint hearted.

• Educational as well as fun!

Once the airship is filled with air, it is warmed by the heat of the sun.

The warm air inside the airship makes it float, like a full-sized hot-air balloon.

Answer

Black absorbs heat, it does not attract it.

Glossary

A

abuse non-medical use of drugs legally available only with a doctor's prescription 15

Acheulean a more developed stone-tool technology than that of the Oldowan but which initially overlapped with it 60

acid rain rain with a pH of 2–5, usually caused by the emission of pollutants such as the oxides of sulfur and nitrogen 20, 70

acquired characteristics non-hereditary or environmental changes in an organism 7

acquired immune deficiency syndrome (AIDS) the collection of diseases associated with HIV infection 17

acrosome pointed end of the sperm head containing enzymes which help the sperm to penetrate the egg membrane 45

active site part of an enzyme to which a substrate bonds 31

active transport movement of molecules through a cell membrane against the concentration gradient; this process requires energy 35

adaptation refers to characteristics that best suit the survival of an individual 5, 58

adapted suited to surviving in a particular environment 6

addiction being dependent (hooked) on drugs or any other habit-forming substance 15

aerobic respiration respiration that involves oxygen 32, 33, 35, 42

African Eve the most recent common human ancestor (*Homo sapiens*) 61

algae aquatic organisms capable of photosynthesis 19, 20

alkaloids naturally occurring, mostly bitter-tasting compounds derived from amino acids 50

alleles different versions of a gene which control a particular characteristic 7, 8, 9

amylase an enzyme that catalyses reactions that break down starch to the sugar maltose 31, 39

anaerobic respiration respiration without using oxygen 32

animal vector an organism that transmits pathogens from host to host – insects are common disease vectors 17

animalia the animal kingdom 4

Anopheles the mosquito genus that transmits the malarial protozoan; *Anopheles gambiae* is the most common species in Africa 17

antibacterials substances that prevent bacteria from multiplying but are toxic to ingest, e.g. antibacterial soap 17, 18, 50

antibiotic therapeutic drug acting to kill bacteria or prevent them from multiplying, which is taken into the body 17, 18, 40

antibodies proteins produced by a particular type of white blood cell (B-lymphocytes) that bind to substances on the surface of pathogens and destroy them 18, 47

antidiuretic hormone (ADH) hormone released from the pituitary gland and which affects the permeability of the walls of the collecting ducts of nephrons to water 43

antifungals substances that kill fungi 17

antigen any substance that stimulates the production of antibodies 47

antiseptics substances that prevent bacteria from multiplying on the body and other surfaces 17

arteries blood vessels that carry blood away from the heart 38

aseptic conditions that prevent bacteria contaminating surfaces and infecting wounds 49

aspirin a pain-killing drug derived from salicin, extracted from the willow tree 62

atmosphere the layer of gases surrounding a planet 21

atria chambers of the heart that receive blood from the veins 38

auto-immune disease a disease caused by the body's immune system attacking its own tissues and organs, e.g. Type I diabetes 13

auxin a plant hormone involved in plant growth 14

axon a long projection from a nerve fibre that conducts impulses away from the body of a nerve cell 11, 12

B

backbone a flexible rod running along the length of the body near to its upper surface; it supports the body 4

bacteria single-celled microorganisms which can either be free-living or parasites (they sometimes invade the body and cause disease); the cell does not contain a distinct nucleus 5, 17, 18, 19, 21, 23, 25, 37, 40

base part of a nucleotide unit of DNA which is adenine (A), thymine (T), guanine (G) or cytosine (C) 24, 28, 29, 30, 67

beta-carotene an orange-yellow pigment that human cells convert into vitamin A 25

bile a chemical produced by the liver which aids the digestion of fats by emulsifying fat droplets 39

binge drinking consumption of large amounts of alcohol in a short period of time 15

binomial system the method of giving an organism a two-part name consisting of genus and species 4

biodiversity the range of different living organisms in a habitat, e.g. a woodland or pond 4

biofuel fuel produced from renewable plant or animal material 70

biological clock probable mechanism of circadian rhythms related to periodic switching on and off of gene activity 51

biological washing powder washing powder containing enzymes that digest biological stains on clothes 66

biomass the amount of organic material of an organism (usually measured as dry mass); waste wood and other natural material which are burned in power stations 19, 69

biomolecule any molecule produced by a living organism 62

biotechnology processes used to produce useful biomolecules 62

bipedalism upright walking on two legs 59

blight a disease of potato plants caused by a fungus 50

body mass index (BMI) a measure of someone's mass in relation to their height, used as a guide to thinness or fatness – values over 30 indicate obesity 13

Bowman's capsule part of the nephron into which urea and other substances pass from the blood by ultrafiltration 42

Bt insecticidal crystal protein a toxin that kills insects; produced by the bacterium *Bacillus thuringiensis* 68

C

canopy unbroken layers of leaves of woodland trees, which reduce the amount of light reaching the woodland floor 51

capillaries small blood vessels that join arteries to veins 32, 38

capillary beds a dense network of capillaries 38

capillary vessels small blood vessels that join arteries to veins 32

carbohydrates Organic molecules composed of carbon, hydrogen and oxygen 13, 21, 36, 39

carbon monoxide a toxic gas formed during incomplete combustion 15

carbon neutral a product that releases as much carbon dioxide when burned as is absorbed making it 70

cardiac muscle the muscle found in the heart that squeezes and relaxes continuously 38

carrier an individual who has a mutation causing a genetic disorder but is not affected by it because the mutation is recessive 46

catalyst a substance added to a chemical reaction to alter the speed of the reaction; it is effective in small amounts and is unchanged at the end of the reaction 31

cell membrane a membrane surrounding the cell and through which substances pass in solution into and out of the cell 23

cell wall surrounds plant cells and some bacterial cells – the cell wall of plants consists of 40% cellulose; the bacterial cell wall does not contain cellulose 4, 23

cellulose large polysaccharides made by plants for cell walls 4, 23

chalk porous, fine-grained rock composed mainly of calcareous shells of microorganisms 21

chemosynthesis the chemical reactions in different species of bacteria which utilise hydrogen from sources other than water to reduce carbon dioxide, forming sugars 18

chlorophyll a pigment found in plants that is used in photosynthesis (gives green plants their colour) 4, 23, 34

chloroplast a structure in plant cells and algae that absorbs light energy – where photosynthesis takes place 23, 34

choice chamber apparatus that allows an animal to choose simultaneously between alternative courses of action 52

cholesterol fatty substances that can block blood vessels 40

chordata a phylum of animals that possess a rod for supporting the body 4

chromatids produced as a result of replication of a chromosome (DNA replication); they appear as a pair joined by a centromere under the high power of a light microscope 26

chromosomes thread-like structures in the cell nucleus that carry genetic information – each chromosome consists of DNA wound round a core of protein 7, 24, 26, 46

Glossary

chymosin enzyme which catalyses reactions involved in cheese making; causes proteins in milk (curds) to coagulate and separate from the liquid whey 66

circadian biological rhythms of activity that approximate to the daily cycle 51

classical conditioning a type of learning where a response elicited by an appropriate stimulus is also elicited by a neutral stimulus 54

clone an organism whose genetic information is identical to that of the organism from which it was created 26, 27

coagulates change of a liquid to a solid or a semi-solid state 65

codon triplet of base pairs in DNA which codes for one amino acid 24, 29, 30

collecting duct tube in the kidney nephron through which water is reabsorbed from the liquid passing through into the blood 42

colour blindness a sex-linked genetic disorder caused by a mutation on the X chromosome 46

common ancestor an individual from which organisms are directly descended 4, 6, 36, 59

competition rivalry between competitors for supplies of limited resources 6, 40

complementary base pairing bonding between the bases of each strand of a double-stranded DNA molecule – each base on one strand of DNA bonds with its complementary partner on the other strand; adenine always binds with thymine; guanine always bonds with cytosine 24, 67

concentration gradient the difference in concentration of a substance between regions where it is in high concentration and where it is lower concentration 32

conferences meetings where participants exchange and present new ideas for research 7

consumers organisms that feed on food already made 19

continuous variation a characteristic that varies continuously; shows a spread of values between extreme values of the characteristic in question, e.g. the height of people shows a range of values between short and tall 5

convoluted tubules lead into and from the loop of Henlé and where substances are selectively reabsorbed into the blood from the liquid passing through the nephron 42

courtship behaviour behaviour that occurs before sexual activity that leads to reproduction 55

cowpox a non-serious viral disease caught by people from cows 47

critical period ratio of the period of light to dark over 24 hours 51

cross-breeding mating (or plant equivalent) between two individuals, resulting in offspring 8

crown gall tumour-like growth of tissue produced when a plant is infected with *Agrobacterium tumefaciens* 68

culture a combination of microorganisms and all the substances they need to live and multiply; the substances may be in solution or part of a jelly-like material (e.g. agar) on which microorganisms grow 25

curds solid protein (casein) precipitated from milk in acid conditions 66

cuttings a piece of stem cut from a parent plant, which has the potential to develop roots and grow into a new plant 14, 27

cyanogens poisonous compounds containing cyanide 50

cystic fibrosis a recessive genetic disorder in which thick, sticky mucus is produced, affecting the lungs and digestive tract in particular 9

cytoplasm a jelly-like material that fills the cell, giving it shape 7, 23, 29

D

daughter cells the new cells produced when parent cells divide 26, 37

decompose the separation of a chemical compound into simpler compounds 20, 21, 36

decomposers fungi and bacteria whose feeding activities cause decomposition 21

decomposition the process resulting from the feeding activities of fungi and bacteria that release nutrients from dead organic matter into the environment 21

denatured refers to irreversible changes in the structure of proteins (including enzymes); the changes stop the proteins from working properly 31, 34

dendrites the fine branches at the end of axons and dendrons 11

dendron a long projection of a nerve fibre that conducts impulses to the nerve cell 11, 12

denitrifying bacteria bacteria that converts nitrates into nitrogen gas 21

deoxygenated blood blood where the oxyhaemoglobin has reverted to haemoglobin 37, 38

depressants substances that slow down responses 15

diabetes a disease where the body cannot control its sugar levels 13, 28

dialysis treatment where blood from a person with kidney failure passes through equipment which separates the blood from a solution of suitable salts by a partially permeable membrane 43

dialysis fluid a solution of salts equivalent in concentration and composition to the salts found in solution in blood 43

differentiation the process during which a stem cell (unspecialised) develops into a particular type of cell (specialised) 28, 36, 37

diffusion the spread of particles through random motion from regions of higher concentration to regions of lower concentration 32, 35

diploid refers to cells with two sets of chromosomes (one set from each parent) – most cells are diploid (except gametes) and the symbol 2n represents the diploid state 26

discontinuous variation a characteristic that only has a limited number of values, e.g. blood group, shoe size 5

DNA deoxyribonucleic acid – a molecule found in all body cells in the nucleus; its sequence determines how our bodies are made (e.g. whether we have straight or curly hair), and gives each one of us a unique genetic code 7, 23, 24, 25, 26, 28, 29, 30, 31

DNA polymerase an enzyme that catalyses reactions that join up nucleotides forming DNA 31

dominant refers to an allele which controls the development of a characteristic, even if it is present on only one of the chromosomes of a pair of chromosomes 7, 8

dominant characteristic any characteristic that appears in the heterozygote 8

donor a person who gives (donates) an organ 16

donor eggs eggs taken from a female animal and fertilised in the laboratory 27, 45

drug a substance from outside the body that affects chemical reactions inside the body 15

E

ecosystem a habitat and all the living things in it 35

ectoparasite a parasite that lives on the external surface of the host 18

electrons tiny negatively charged particles within an atom that orbit the nucleus – responsible for current in electrical circuits 23

embryo the early stages in the development of an organism, from the time of first cell division 27, 28, 37

embryonic stem cells undifferentiated cells that are able to develop (differentiate) into any type of body cell 28

emulsification the breaking down of fat into more manageable molecules 39

endocrine glands glands that release the substances produced (hormones) directly into the blood 13

endoparasite a parasite that lives inside the host's body 18

endotoxin a poison produced by a pathogen within the body 17

enzymes biological catalysts (usually proteins) produced by cells that control the rate of chemical reactions in cells 10, 18, 25, 31, 39, 66

ethene a gas which is a plant hormone 14

ethics the actions taken as a result of moral judgements 16, 27

eutrophication the processes that occur when water is enriched with nutrients (from fertilisers) which allow algae to grow and use up all the oxygen 20

evolution the process whereby organisms change through time – present-day living things are descended from organisms that were different from them 6, 36, 58, 59

excess post-exercise oxygen consumption (EPOC) additional oxygen required after a period of anaerobic respiration 32

excretion removal of wastes produced by cell metabolism 42

exponential rate of increase that is double the previous number 49

Glossary

F

family a group consisting of several generations (used in classification of living things) 4

feedback regulation of a process by the results (outcomes) of the process 10

fermentation reactions chemical reactions that produce biomolecules 62

fermenter a large vessel containing a liquid culture of microorganisms and all the substances (nutrients) they need to live and multiply 25, 63

fertile able to reproduce sexually 4

fertilisation the moment when the nucleus of a sperm fuses with the nucleus of an egg 7, 26, 27, 28, 30, 45

fibrin an insoluble protein involved in the clotting of blood 37

flaccid soft, droopy, lacking turgor 35

flagellum a whip-like extension of a cell that lashes from side to side, driving the cell through liquid 23

foetus a stage in the development of an organism when tissues and organs are forming; after the embryo stage 26, 37

follicle stimulating hormone (FSH) hormone released by the pituitary gland, stimulating the development of egg follicles at the start of the menstrual cycle 44

food web a flow chart to show how a number of living things get their food (more complicated than a food chain) 19

fossil fuels fuel (coal, natural gas, oil) formed from the compressed remains of plants and other organisms that lived long ago 20, 21

food security when everybody can obtain enough food which is nutritious and safe to eat 69

fossils the preserved remains of organisms that lived long ago 36

free running persistence of circadian rhythm in constant environmental conditions 51

functional foods any healthy foods claimed to have health-promoting or disease-preventing properties 40

fungi organisms which can break down complex organic substances (some are pathogens and harm the body) 4, 21

G

gall bladder a small, sac-like structure connected to the small intestine by the bile duct; it stores bile, which breaks down fats in partly digested food 39

gametes the male and female sex cells (sperm and eggs) 8, 26, 45

gene a section of DNA that codes for a particular characteristic, by controlling the production of a particular protein or part of a protein by cells 7, 8, 9, 24, 25, 28, 30, 67

genetic code all of the base sequences of the genes that enable cells to make proteins 24

genetic disorder an inherited disease that arises as the result of a mutated gene, passed on from parents to children 9

genetically engineered result of the process that produces recombinant DNA 67

genetic engineering techniques that make it possible to manipulate genes in the cells of organisms 16, 25

genetic marker a mutation used to identify a biological event 61

genetically modified (GM) a GM organism has had its DNA modified by the insertion of DNA from another species 25, 67

genome all of the DNA in each cell of an organism 28

genotype all of the genes of an organism 7

genus a group consisting of more than one species (used in classification of living things) 4

geotropism (or gravitropism) growth movement in response to the stimulus of gravity 14

glomerulus knot of capillary blood vessels associated with the Bowman's capsule 42

glucagon a hormone produced by the pancreas that promotes the conversion of glycogen to glucose 13

glycogen a type of carbohydrate whole molecule consists of many glucose units joined together 13

greenhouse gases gases that contribute to the greenhouse effect by preventing heat radiating from the atmosphere into space 70

growing media solids (agar) or liquid (broth) which contain all the nutrients and other substances microorganisms need to grow and multiply 49

H

habituation learned behaviour that decreases in response to the repeated application of the stimulus eliciting the behaviour in the first place 53

haemoglobin the chemical found in red blood cells which carried oxygen 9, 29, 37

haemophilia a sex-linked genetic disorder that causes a person's blood not to clot properly 46

hallucinogens substances that give a false sense of reality 15

haploid refers to cells with only one set of chromosomes – gametes are haploid; the symbol n represents the haploid state 26

heart rate the number of heartbeats every minute 33

heartbeat the two-tone sound of one complete contraction and relaxation of the heart 33

herbicides chemicals that kill plants – used to remove weeds (unwanted plants) from crops, gardens and public places 14, 25

herbivorous refers to animals that feed only on plants 50

herd effect the minimum percentage of a population that needs to be immunised so that the whole population is protected from infectious disease 47

heterozygous refers to the pair of alleles of a gene where the alleles are different 7, 8

HIV human immunodeficiency virus – the virus that causes AIDS 17

homeostasis self-adjusting mechanisms that allow the body to keep a constant internal environment 10, 13, 42

homeotherms animals that regulate their body temperature 4

homozygous refers to the pair of alleles of a gene where the alleles are the same 7, 8

hormones substances produced by animals and plants that regulate activities; in animals, hormones are produced by and released from endocrine tissue into the blood to act on target organs, and help to coordinate the body's responses to stimuli 10, 13, 14

host the individual infected with a pathogen transmitted by a vector; the organism on which a parasite lives (the parasite takes food from the host) 18

host mother a female animal whose uterus is used for the growth of embryos that are not its own 27

human chorionic gonadotropin (hCG) a hormone produced by a female in the early stages of pregnancy 48

Human Genome Project an international group of scientists aiming to map the human genome 28

hybridoma type of cell produced by the fusion of non-antibody-producing myeloma and healthy antibody producing B-lymphocytes 48

hybrids the offspring of parents which are not the same species 4, 5

hydrothermal vents cracks in the seabed where water is heated as a result of volcanic activity 5, 18

hypothalamus part of the brain that has several functions, such as acting as the link the nervous system to the endocrine system 10

I

immune response the body's recognition and defence against foreign antigens 47

immunisation receiving defence against pathogens 47

imprinting learning to identify a parent (or substitute) 53

in vitro fertilisation eggs fertilised outside the body in the laboratory 45

indicator species the presence or absence of these species indicates how polluted (or not) a particular environment is 20

infectious a disease that passes (is transmitted) from person to person 17

innate behaviour that is inherited 52

insecticides chemicals used to kill insects 68

insemination introduction of sperm into the female reproductive system 45

insoluble a substance that will not dissolve (something that will not dissolve in water may dissolve in other liquids) 31, 37, 39

insulin a hormone produced by the pancreas that promotes the conversion of glucose to glycogen 13

insulin insensitivity a condition in which target tissues (e.g. liver and muscles) do not respond to insulin 13

intensity the radiant power per unit area 34, 35

invertase enzyme which catalyses the reaction of sucrose into glucose and fructose; used to make soft centres in chocolates; also called sucrase 66

involuntary response an automatic response to a stimulus that you do not think about 12

K

key a chart of alternative statements that identifies organisms 5

kingdoms used in classification and refers to the largest grouping (except for domain) of organisms which have characteristics in common 4

L

lactose sugar found in milk 65

lactic acid formed during the fermentation of lactose in milk; causes the milk to coagulate into yogurt 65

leguminous plants whose roots carry nodules that contain nitrogen-fixing bacteria 18, 69

lichens a combination of fungi and algae – the relationship between the organisms is an example of mutualism 20

ligases enzymes that catalyse reactions that insert (paste in) pieces of DNA into lengths or loops of other DNA 25, 67

limewater an aqueous solution of calcium hydroxide; used to test for the presence of carbon dioxide 33

limiting factor a factor that limits a process 34

lineage known ancestry 7

locus the position of an allele on its chromosome 7

loop of Henlé U-shaped part of the nephron that helps to control the amount of water reabsorbed into the blood from the liquid passing through the nephron 42

luteinising hormone (LH) hormone released by the pituitary gland which completes the development of an egg follicle and stimulates its release 44

lymphocyte type of white blood cell that destroys viruses and bacteria that cause disease by the production of antibodies 47

M

mass the amount of matter inside an object, measured in kilograms 36

meiosis a type of division of the cell nucleus that results in four daughter cells, each with half the number of chromosomes (haploid) of the parent cell (diploid) 26, 46

menstruation breakdown of the lining of the uterus during the menstrual cycle 44

meristem the tissue in most plants where growth occurs 36

messenger RNA (mRNA) a molecule of RNA with the code for a protein 29

metabolism all of the chemical reactions taking place in a cell 19, 50

methane a biogas produced by the anaerobic fermentation of plant material and organic wastes 70

microorganisms single-celled organisms that are only just visible when using light microscope 17, 40, 64

mitochondria structures in cells just visible when using light microscope; where respiration occurs, releasing energy 23

mitochondrial DNA (mtDNA) the DNA content of a mitochondrion 61

mitosis a type of division of the cell nucleus that results in two daughter cells, each with the same number of chromosomes as the parent (usually 2n) 26, 37

monoclonal antibodies antibodies that only bind to a particular antigen or part of antigen 48

monogamous relationship where a male and female pair for the breeding season or even a lifetime 55

monohybrid refers to the inheritance of a single characteristic 8

morals deciding what is right or wrong 16

Mousterian a stone-tool technology that replaced Acheulean 60

MRSA methicillin-resistant *Staphylococcus aureus* 17

mucus a sticky material consisting of a mixture of substances produced by goblet cells 9, 18, 20

multicellular an organism made of many cells 4, 23

mutation a permanent change in the structure of a gene – the DNA within cells is altered (this happens in cancer) 7, 9, 13, 30

mutualism a relationship between individuals of different species where both benefit 18

mycoprotein fungus-based version of a single-cell protein (protein-rich food produced by microorganisms) 64

myeloma a cancerous type of B-lymphocyte which produces a single type of antibody and which continues to divide in culture 48

N

natural selection a process that results in the individuals of a population with characteristics suited to a particular environment surviving, reproducing and therefore passing on the genes controlling the characteristics to their offspring – natural selection is the mechanism of evolution 6, 36

negative feedback a mechanism where changes are reversed to achieve a stable level 43

negative tropism growth movement away from a particular stimulus 14

nephrons tubules which make up the kidney 42

nerve impulses electrical impulses that pass along a neurone 10, 11, 12, 37

neurone a nerve cell that carries nerve impulses 11, 12, 37

neurotransmitter a chemical released from the end of a neurone into a synapse and which stimulates the next neurone to trigger new nerve impulses 12, 15

nitrifying bacteria bacteria that convert ammonium compounds into nitrates 21

nitrogen-fixing bacteria bacteria that convert gaseous nitrogen into nitrogen-containing compounds 18, 21

non-renewable resources resources which are being used up more quickly than they can be replaced, e.g. fossil fuels; they will eventually run out 19

nucleotides the building block units that combine to form a strand of DNA; each nucleotide unit consists of the sugar deoxyribose, a base and a phosphate 24, 29

nucleus a distinct structure in the cytoplasm of cells that contains the genetic material 4, 23, 26, 29, 37

nutrients substances essential to maintaining living processes 21, 39

O

objective lens the lens in a microscope 23

Oldowan earliest type of stone-tool technology 60

operant conditioning a type of learning where a response is reinforced by either reward or punishment 54

order a group consisting of several families (used in classification of living things) 4

organ a collection of tissues joined in a structural unit to serve a common function 37

osmoregulation the control of an organism's fluid balance 10, 42

osmosis movement of water from a less concentrated solution to a more concentrated solution through a partially permeable membrane 35

overwintering refers to the seeds of plants which survive the harsh winter climate 51

oviparous animals that lay eggs, the embryo does not develop within the mother's body 4

oxygenated blood blood containing oxyhaemoglobin 37, 38

oxyhaemoglobin the result of oxygen binding to haemoglobin in red blood cells 37

P

paclitaxel semi-synthetic version of taxol 62

painkillers drugs that affect the nervous system, deadening pain 15, 62

pair bonding behaviour between a male and female of the same species that reinforces a relationship 55

pancreas the organ that produces the hormones insulin and glucagon (from endocrine tissue) and digestive enzymes (from exocrine tissue) 13, 39

parasitism a relationship between individuals of different species where one benefits (parasite) and the other is harmed (host) 18

parental investment the time and energy parents spend on rearing offspring 56

pathogens harmful organisms that invade the body and cause disease 17, 18

pedigree the known genetic line of descent from generation to generation 7, 9

peer review the process of evaluating the quality of research using anonymous review by experts in a particular field 7

pentadactyl limb the basic arrangement of five digits present in most vertebrates 36

pepsin an enzyme that catalyses reactions that break down protein to peptides (short-chain amino acids) 39

peptides short polymers of amino acids, generally 2–20 amino acid units in length 29

Glossary

percentile the value of a variable below which a certain percentage of observations fall 36

peristalsis the contraction and relaxation of muscles, which propagates in a wave down the muscular tube 39

pests organisms which compete with or harm humans e.g. insects which eat crops 69

pharmacogenomics the study of how variations in the human genome affect an individual's response to drugs; may lead to the development of drugs tailored to be the most effective according to an individual's genetic make-up 28

pharmacological relating to the action of drugs on the body 50

phenolics naturally occurring compounds in plants that contain benzene 50

phenotype all of the characteristics of an organism 7, 8

phloem columns of living cells in plant stems; carries dissolved glucose and other substances to all parts of the plant 35

photoperiod the period of light/dark over 24 hours 51

photosynthesis a process carried out by green plants where sunlight, carbon dioxide and water are used to produce glucose and oxygen 19, 21, 34

phototropism growth movement in response to the stimulus of light 14

physical properties properties that can be observed without changing the chemical composition of a substance, e.g. colour, density, melting point and boiling point 46, 67

pituitary gland an endocrine gland attached to the base of the brain near the hypothalamus 43

plant stanol esters substances found in food such as wheat and maize that reduce the absorption of harmful cholesterol 40

plantae the plant kingdom 4

plasmid DNA loops of DNA found in the cytoplasm of bacterial and yeast cells 23, 67

Plasmodium the protozoan genus that causes malaria – *Plasmodium falciparum* is the most dangerous species, *P. vivax* the least 17

poikilotherms animals that cannot regulate their body temperature 4

pollutants substances released into the environment that are harmful to health and wildlife 20

pollution the effects of pollutants which contaminate or destroy the environment 20

polyclonal antibodies a mixture of antibodies which bind to a range of different antigens or parts of antigens 48

polygamous relationship where an individual (usually male) mates with a number of opposite-sex partners (usually female) during the breeding season 55

polypeptides polymers of amino acids, generally 21–50 amino acid units in length 29

population organisms of the same species that live in the same geographical area 6, 19, 35

positive tropism growth movement towards a particular stimulus 14

prebiotics non-digestible food ingredients to stimulate growth of bacteria in the digestive system 40

predators animals that feed on other animals 19

prey an animal that is eaten by a predator 19

primary immune response response of the immune system to infection by a particular pathogen, virus or bacterium, for the first time 47

primary stimulus stimulus directly associated with the response elicited by the stimulus 54

prioritise to rank in order 16

probiotics live microorganisms thought to be beneficial to health 40

producers organisms that synthesise sugars (food) by photosynthesis or chemosynthesis 19

product the substance formed in a reaction 31

prokaryotes single-celled organisms that lack a distinct nucleus 4

proteins molecules made up of amino acids, more than 50 amino acids in length 7, 9, 18, 21, 24, 25, 29, 30, 31, 39, 67

protoctista single-celled organisms that have a distinct nucleus; also some simple multicellular (many-celled) organisms such as seaweed 4

pulse a ripple of blood as it is forced along the arteries by the beating heart 33

Punnett squares a type of genetic diagram that sets out the results of genetic crosses in the form of a table 8

pure-bred a characteristic of an organism that passes unchanged from generation to generation – the organism is homozygous for the characteristic in question 8

pyramid of biomass a diagram representing the biomass of the trophic levels of a community 19

Q

quinine treatment for malaria; originally extracted from the bark and leaves of the *Cinchona* tree 62

R

radiometric dating a method of dating fossils and artefacts by measuring the proportions of radioactive isotopes 60

rate of reaction the speed with which a chemical reaction takes place 31

reaction time the time taken to respond to a stimulus 15

receptor part of a neurone that detects stimuli and converts them into nerve impulses 11, 12

recessive refers to an allele which controls the development of a characteristic only if its dominant partner allele is not present 7, 8, 9

recessive characteristic an allele that does not develop a particular characteristic when present with a dominant allele 8

recipient a person who receives a donated organ 16

recognition site a short sequence of bases that is specifically cut by a particular restriction enzyme 67

recombinant DNA combination of a useful gene with vector DNA 67

recovery period the period during which lactic acid is removed and breathing and heart rates return to normal after exercise 32

recycling the reprocessing of materials to make new products 19

red blood cells blood cells which are adapted to carry oxygen 9, 15, 37

reflex arc the pathway taken by a nerve impulse from a receptor, through the nervous system, to an effector (does not go through the brain), bringing about a reflex response 12

reflex response an automatic action not controlled by the brain, made in response to a stimulus 12

rejection destruction of a donor organ because of the activity of the recipient's immune system 16

renewable resources energy resources that can be replenished at the same rate that they are used up, e.g. biofuels – they will not run out 19, 70

replication when organisms or cells make copies of themselves 26, 30

resazurin dye a dye that changes colour because of the substances produced by bacteria in a solution containing the dye 49

resistance refers to pathogens, e.g. bacteria, that are not affected by drugs that previously were effective treatments 17

resolving power the ability to see objects close together as separate from one another 23

resources the raw materials taken from the environment and used to run industry, homes and transport, and to manufacture goods 19

respiration the series of chemical reactions that oxidise (break down) glucose, releasing energy: in the presence of oxygen, glucose is oxidised to carbon dioxide and water 21, 32, 33

response the action taken as a result of a stimulus 12

restriction enzymes enzymes that catalyse reactions that cut strands of DNA into shorter pieces 25, 67

retina the covering of light-sensitive cells at the back of the eyeball 11

ribonucleic acid (RNA) a type of nucleic acid found in cells but not used to build chromosomes; some types of RNA are involved in protein synthesis 29, 30

ribosome a component of a cell that creates proteins from all amino acids and RNA representing the protein 29

ring species a connected geographical sequence of neighbouring species that can interbreed with one another; however, the two 'end' species of the sequence cannot interbreed 5

S

salicin chemical that acts as a painkiller; found in the bark and leaves of the willow tree 62

saprophytic feeding from dead organic matter 4

scavengers animals that feed on dead animals 19

Glossary

scientific journals periodic publications with articles contributed by scientists reporting on their new research 7

secondary immune response response of the immune system to subsequent infection by a pathogen that it has encountered before 47

secondary stimulus stimulus that elicits the same response as a particular primary stimulus, but is different from the primary stimulus 54

sedimentary rock rock formed by the sedimentation of material on riverbeds and ocean floors 36

seedling a germinating seed which is at a stage where shoots and roots are visibly deepening 14

sensitive period the time when imprinting develops in a young animal 53

sequence an arrangement in which things follow a pattern 24, 28, 30

sequencers machines that automatically determine (work out) the base sequences of DNA (or the amino acid sequence of proteins) 28

sexual reproduction the joining of genetic material from two organisms to produce offspring 55

sickle cell crisis the periods of pain experienced when sickled red blood cells clump together, restricting blood flow to the organs of the body; each crisis may last for days, weeks or months 9

sickle cell disease a recessive genetic disorder in which the shape of haemoglobin molecules is altered, so they absorb less oxygen 9

silent mutation a mutation that alters the base sequence of a codon but does not result in alteration of the sequence of amino acid units of the protein in question 30

smallpox a serious (often fatal) viral disease 47

speciation an evolutionary process that results in new species 6

species a group of individuals able to mate and reproduce offspring, which themselves are able to mate and reproduce 4, 5, 6, 18, 20

specific relating to a particular thing or event, e.g. a particular hormone affects only a particular target tissue 13, 31

starch large polysaccharides made by plants as a form of food storage 39

stem cells undifferentiated (unspecialised) cells that are able to develop (differentiate) into differentiated (specialised) cells 28

sterilised all microorganisms present on the surface or in a liquid have been eliminated 65

sticky ends short, single-stranded lengths of DNA at either end of a piece of double-stranded DNA 67

stimulants substances that speed up responses 15

stimulus a change in the environment that causes a response by stimulating receptor nerve cells, e.g. a hot surface 10, 12

stoma (plural stomata) a pore found in plants, used in gas exchange 34, 35

subcutaneous fat literally means 'fat under the skin' 13

substrate molecules at the start of a chemical reaction; the substance that an enzyme helps to react 31

surrogate mother a female who receives an embryo developed from a fertilised donor egg and who carries the embryo to the completion of pregnancy 45

synapse the gap between two adjacent neurons 12

T

tannins bitter-tasting phenolic compounds found in plants 50

target tissues tissues that respond to hormones 13

taxol a substance with anti-cancer properties, extracted from the yew tree 62

terpenoids naturally occurring lipid-based compounds found in plants 50

thermoregulation the processes than enable an animal to keep its body temperature constant 10

tissue culture the growth of fragments of tissue in a liquid or on gel, which provides all the substances needed for their development; conditions are sterile and controlled 27

tissue fluid a solution that bathes and surrounds the cells of multicellular animals 38

tissues groups of cells that work together and carry out a similar task, e.g. lung tissue 13, 14, 27, 28, 32, 37, 38

toxicity poisonous effect 62

transfer RNA (tRNA) a molecule of RNA that transports amino acids to ribosomes 29

transpiration the movement of water and mineral salts from roots to leaves in plants 35

transplantation tourism travelling to another country to buy organs 16

trophic literally means relating to feeding 19

tropism growth movement by plants in response to stimuli coming mainly from one direction 14

turgid rigid owing to high fluid content 23, 35

U

unicellular consisting of a single cell 4

urea nitrogenous waste substance produced by the liver 42

urine solution of urea and other substances produced by the kidneys and removed (excreted) from the body to the environment 42

V

vaccine injected into the body during vaccination (immunisation); contains harmless antigens and triggers the immune response in order to induce immunity 47

vacuole a fluid-filled space in the cytoplasm of cells – most plant cells have a permanent vacuole; if vacuoles are present in animal cells they are temporary 23

validated to establish the soundness of, or to corroborate, evidence 7

variation the difference in characteristics between species and the range of a characteristic individuals of the same species 5, 6, 7, 30

vasoconstriction narrowing of the lumen (internal space) of blood vessels in cold conditions – this reduces the flow of blood 10

vasodilation widening of the lumen (internal space) of blood vessels in hot conditions – this increases the flow of blood 10

vector (1) length of DNA which, when combined with a gene, enables that gene to be transferred into the cells of another species; (2) organism that transmits pathogens from host to host 67, 68

vegetative reproduction asexual reproduction from the vegetative parts of a plant: the roots, leaves and stem 27

veins blood vessels that carry blood back to the heart 38

ventricles chambers of the heart that pump blood into the arteries 38

vertebrates animals that have the characteristic of a backbone in common 4, 36

villi finger-like structures on the surface of the small intestine which give it a greater surface area for absorption 39

viruses very small infectious organisms that reproduce within the cells of living organisms and often cause disease; they consist of a protein layer surrounding a strand of nucleic acid 4, 17, 37

vitamin A a vitamin that is essential for growth and vision 25

volatile organic compound (VOC) a substance that gives off a vapour at ambient temperature 58

voluntary response a response to a stimulus that you think about and can control 12

W

wavelength the distance between neighbouring wave peaks or wave troughs 23

weeds plants growing where they are not wanted 50

whey the liquid left after protein has precipitated from milk 66

X

xenotransplantation transplantation of organs from another species 16

xylem columns of hollow, dead reinforced cells in plant stems; used for the transport of water and dissolved minerals from the roots to all part of the plant 35

Y

yeast single-celled fungus traditionally used to make bread and alcoholic drinks 63

Z

zygote a fertilised egg 26, 45

Exam tips

The key to successful revision is finding the method that suits you best. There is no right or wrong way to do it.

Before you begin, it is important to plan your revision carefully. If you have allocated enough time in advance, you can walk into the exam with confidence, knowing that you are fully prepared.

Start well before the date of the exam, not the day before!

It is worth preparing a revision timetable and trying to stick to it. Use it during the lead up to the exams and between each exam. Make sure you plan some time off too.

Different people revise in different ways and you will soon discover what works best for you.

Remember!

There is a difference between *learning* and *revising*.

When you revise, you are looking again at something you have already learned. Revising is a process that helps you to remember this information more clearly.

Learning is about finding out and understanding new information.

Some general points to think about when revising

- Find a quiet and comfortable space at home where you won't be disturbed. You will find you achieve more if the room is ventilated and has plenty of light.

- Take regular breaks. Some evidence suggests that revision is most effective when tackled in 30 to 40 minute slots. If you get bogged down at any point, take a break and go back to it later when you are feeling fresh. Try not to revise when you're feeling tired. If you do feel tired, take a break.

- Use your school notes, textbook and this Revision guide.

- Spend some time working through past papers to familiarise yourself with the exam format.

- Produce your own summaries of each module and then look at the summaries in this Revision guide at the end of each module.

- Draw mind maps covering the key information on each topic or module.

- Review the Grade booster checklists on pages 160–162.

- Set up revision cards containing condensed versions of your notes.

- Prioritise your revision of topics. You may want to leave more time to revise the topics you find most difficult.

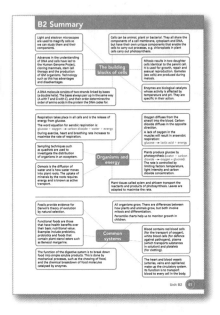

Workbook

The **Workbook** (pages 91–159) allows you to work at your own pace on some typical exam-style questions. You will find that the actual GCSE questions are more likely to test knowledge and understanding across topics. However, the aim of the Revision guide and Workbook is to guide you through each topic so that you can identify your areas of strength and weakness.

The Workbook also contains example questions that require longer answers (**Extended response questions**). You will find one question that is similar to these in each section of your written exam papers. The quality of your written communication will be assessed when you answer these questions in the exam, so practise writing longer answers, using sentences. The **Answers** to all the questions in the Workbook can be cut out for flexible practice and can be found on pages 163–176.

At the end of the Workbook there is a series of **Grade booster checklists** that you can use to tick off the topics when you are confident about them and understand certain key ideas. These Grade boosters give you an idea of the grade at which you are currently working.

Collins Workbook

NEW GCSE

Biology

Foundation and Higher

for Edexcel

Revision Guide +
Exam Practice Workbook

Author: Gemma Young

Classification and naming species

1 a Classify the following animals into their correct vertebrate group.

    i cane toad .... **[1 mark]**

    ii kangaroo .... **[1 mark]**

    iii basking shark .... **[1 mark]**

    iv penguin .... **[1 mark]**

    v python .... **[1 mark]**

b A tarantula does not belong to any of these groups. Explain why.

.... **[1 mark]**

2 Iguanas are reptiles that spend a large portion of the day basking on hot rocks in the Sun. Why do they need to do this?

....

....

.... **[2 marks]**

3 Plants are autotrophs.

a What does this mean?

.... **[1 mark]**

b What do the cells of plants contain that other cells do not?

.... **[2 marks]**

4 Lichen are compound organisms. This means that they are made up of fungi and algae cells. Explain why they are difficult to classify.

....

.... **[2 marks]**

5 The archaeopteryx was an animal that lived 150 million years ago. Archaeopteryx fossils show that it had feathers, a backbone that extended into its tail and dry scales on its face and claws. Explain why scientists classified it as a vertebrate, but found it difficult to classify it any further.

....

....

....

.... **[3 marks]**

6 a Tigers are a species of cat. What does the word 'species' mean?

.... **[1 mark]**

b The offspring of a male lion and a female tiger is called a liger. What do we call animals that are the offspring of two different species?

.... **[1 mark]**

7 a The brown rat has the two-part name *Rattus norvegicus*. Which part of this is its genus name?

.... **[1 mark]**

b The species name of the pacific rat is *exulans*. What is its two-part name?

.... **[1 mark]**

8 On an expedition to a rainforest, scientists discovered 50 different-looking spiders in one small area. Explain why the scientists must classify the spiders before they can make a judgement about the biodiversity of the spiders in that area.

....

.... **[2 marks]**

Identification, variation and adaptation

1 A group of students are pond-dipping. They are asked to comment on what species live in the pond. Suggest why a key would be useful to them.

....

.... **[1 mark]**

2 a Oak is a species of tree. Give two examples of variation seen in oak trees.

.... **[2 marks]**

b Animals also show variation. For each of the following examples, state whether it shows continuous or discontinuous variation.

i weight .... **[1 mark]**

ii blood group .... **[1 mark]**

iii length of limbs .... **[1 mark]**

c You measured the hand spans of the students in your year group and also asked them their eye colour. Describe which type of graphs you would use to display this data and explain your choices.

....

....

....

.... **[4 marks]**

3 The greenish warbler is a species of bird that lives in the regions surrounding the Himalayas. There are many subspecies of the bird. Most of the subspecies can interbreed, but two cannot. Explain why scientists think this may be an example of a ring species.

....

.... **[2 marks]**

4 Camels are well adapted to living in deserts. Explain how each of the features below enables a camel to survive in desert conditions.

a Fat stored in hump

.... **[1 mark]**

b Wide feet

.... **[1 mark]**

c Ability to close nostrils

.... **[1 mark]**

d Lemmings are small round animals that look like fat hamsters. They live in the Arctic. Explain how the size and shape of the lemming helps it survive the cold temperatures.

....

.... **[2 marks]**

e Another Arctic animal is the caribou. Its fur contains hollow hairs. How does this help keep it warm?

....

.... **[3 marks]**

5 Giant tube worms live around deep-sea hydrothermal vents, where temperatures can reach above 90 °C. They belong to the same phylum as earthworms. Explain why the two species would have some characteristics in common but many that are different.

....

....

.... **[3 marks]**

Evolution

1 a Snakes are found in habitats all over the world, including rainforests, deserts and even the sea. All species of snake on Earth evolved from a common ancestor but they all have different characteristics. Explain why.

.... **[1 mark]**

b Rattlesnakes are a group of venomous snakes that can be found in a range of habitats in America.

i Suggest one resource that rattlesnakes compete for.

.... **[1 mark]**

ii Some species of rattlesnake have become extinct. What does this mean?

.... **[1 mark]**

iii Suggest a reason why these species became extinct.

.... **[1 mark]**

c Rattlesnakes show variation in the colour of their skin. This ranges from pale brown to dark green. Most snakes found in the desert have pale skin. Use natural selection to explain why.

....

....

.... **[3 marks]**

d The end of a rattlesnake's tail (the rattle) is specially adapted to make a rattling noise when shaken. The snake does this to warn away predators. Rattlesnakes evolved from snakes that did not have this 'rattle'.

Suggest how this evolution occurred.

....

....

....

....

....

.... **[4 marks]**

2 In 1995, at least 15 iguanas survived a hurricane in their home of the Virgin Islands. They survived for a month on a raft of uprooted trees and landed on another island called Anguilla, which had no iguana population.

a Explain why the iguanas may have found it difficult to survive on Anguilla.

....

.... **[2 marks]**

b If they do survive, a new species of iguana may evolve. Explain how this will occur.

....

....

.... **[3 marks]**

Genes and variation

1 For each of these examples of variation, state whether they are inherited or environmental:

  a Eye colour .... **[1 mark]**

  b Hair length .... **[1 mark]**

  c Blood group .... **[1 mark]**

G–E

2 For each definition below, state whether it is a description of DNA, genes or chromosomes.

  a This long molecule is wound around proteins to form chromosomes. .... **[1 mark]**

  b Many of these are found on one chromosome. .... **[1 mark]**

  c These are arranged in pairs inside the nucleus of most cells. .... **[1 mark]**

3 Ryan and Chloe are both very tall. Their one-year-old son, Ethan, is also expected to be tall when he is older. Why is this?

....

....

                                                   [2 marks]

D–C

4 A comparison of the DNA of humans and chimpanzees show that these animals share 99% of their DNA. Explain how this is evidence for Darwin's theory of evolution.

....

....

                                                   [3 marks]

B–A*

5 Mia has alleles for both blood group O and blood group A.

  a Explain why she has two alleles.

....
[1 mark]

G–E

  b Is Mia heterozygous or homozygous for blood group?

....

                                                   [1 mark]

6 Mice have two alleles for fur colour, white and grey. A white mouse and a grey mouse mate. All of the babies have grey fur.

  a What is the phenotype of the babies?

....

                                                   [1 mark]

  b Which of the alleles is the most likely to be dominant?

....

                                                   [1 mark]

D–C

  c Explain why you think this.

....

....

                                                   [2 marks]

7 This family pedigree shows the Jones family. Family members with red hair are shaded grey.

  a What is the relationship between Mark and Holly?

.... **[1 mark]**

  b Explain why Holly has red hair when neither of her parents do.

....

....

....

                                   [3 marks]

Robert   Susan

Kirsty   Chris   Rosie   Daniel

Mark   Holly   Jacob

B–A*

Monohybrid inheritance

1 Mendel bred together pure-breeding plants with red flowers and pure-breeding plants with white flowers. He gathered the seeds and planted them. All of the first-generation offspring had red flowers.

a Which allele is dominant – the allele for red flowers or the allele for white flowers?

.... **[1 mark]**

b Mendel then bred together the offspring. What colour flowers would you expect this second generation to have?

.... **[1 mark]**

2 Scientists did not take much notice of Mendel's laws of monohybrid inheritance until 16 years after his death. Suggest a reason why.

.... **[1 mark]**

3 Use letters to represent the following genotypes.

a Homozygous dominant

.... **[1 mark]**

b Homozygous recessive

.... **[1 mark]**

c Heterozygous

.... **[1 mark]**

4 Complete the Punnett square opposite to show the likely offspring from one of Mendel's breeding experiments with the red- and white-flowered plants as discussed in Question 1.

Cross: Rr × rr		
Parental gametes	R	r
r		
r		

[2 marks]

5 What is the probability that offspring from the cross as shown in the Punnett square in Question 4 will:

a have red flowers .... **[1 mark]**

b have white flowers .... **[1 mark]**

c be heterozygous .... **[1 mark]**

d be homozygous dominant .... **[1 mark]**

e be homozygous recessive .... **[1 mark]**

6 Mendel then bred the red-flowered plants from this cross to produce a second generation.

a Draw a Punnett square to show this cross. **[2 marks]**

b What is the probability of offspring with white flowers?

.... **[1 mark]**

Genetic disorders

1 Harry is 19 years old. His sperm cells all carry a mutation.

a What is a mutation?

.... [1 mark]

b Harry's future children will also have this mutation. Why?

....

.... [1 mark]

2 Cystic fibrosis is an example of a genetic disorder. Those affected produce thick, sticky mucus, particularly in their lungs and digestive system.

a Explain what we mean by the term 'genetic disorder'.

.... [1 mark]

b Describe the main symptoms of cystic fibrosis.

....

.... [2 marks]

c Another genetic disorder, sickle cell disease, causes red blood cells to become sickle-shaped. Explain how the disorder can lead to organ damage.

....

....

....

.... [3 marks]

3 The diagram below is a pedigree analysis for sickle cell disease. A coloured shape indicates an affected individual.

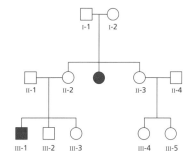

a What is the function of a pedigree analysis?

.... [1 mark]

b Which individuals *must* be a carrier of the sickle cell allele?

.... [1 mark]

c Draw a genetic diagram such as a Punnett square to show the cross between II-1 and II-2.

[2 marks]

d What is the probability that II-4 is a carrier of the sickle cell allele?

.... [1 mark]

Homeostasis and body temperature

G–E

1 Name two things that are kept constant inside the body.

.... [2 marks]

D–C

2 Jade is at the cinema. She drinks a litre of cola, has to go to the toilet and misses the end of the film.

a What change will happen to Jade's blood as she drinks the cola?

.... [1 mark]

b What is her kidneys' response to this stimulus?

.... [1 mark]

c Describe how this response is brought about by the brain.

....

.... [2 marks]

d Why is this response known as 'self-regulating'?

.... [1 mark]

B–A*

e This response in Jade's body is an example of negative feedback. What would the response have been if her brain gave positive feedback?

....

.... [2 marks]

G–E

3 James goes outside into the snow without a coat on. His body temperature starts to decrease.

a What is normal body temperature for a human?

.... [1 mark]

b James starts to shiver. How does this help to raise his body temperature?

.... [1 mark]

D–C

c Explain how James's body knows when to stop shivering.

....

....

....

.... [3 marks]

B–A*

d Vasoconstriction also takes place in James's body. Explain how this response is brought about and how it helps James to maintain a normal body temperature outside in the snow.

....

....

....

....

.... [4 marks]

Senses and the nervous system

1 a Which **two** parts of the body make up the central nervous system?

.... [2 marks]

b Name **two** sense organs.

.... [2 marks]

c How does information travel from sense organs to the brain?

.... [2 marks]

2 a In which sense organ would you find receptors for:

   i touch   .... [1 mark]

   ii light   .... [1 mark]

   iii vibrations   .... [1 mark]

   iv chemicals   .... [1 mark]

b Explain why the lips are the most sensitive part of the face.

.... [1 mark]

3 Raj is playing as a goalkeeper in a football game. The ball is heading towards him. Study this diagram of his eye.

a In which labelled part of his eye will receptors be stimulated?

.... [1 mark]

b Describe how this image reaches the brain.

....

....

....

....

.... [2 marks]

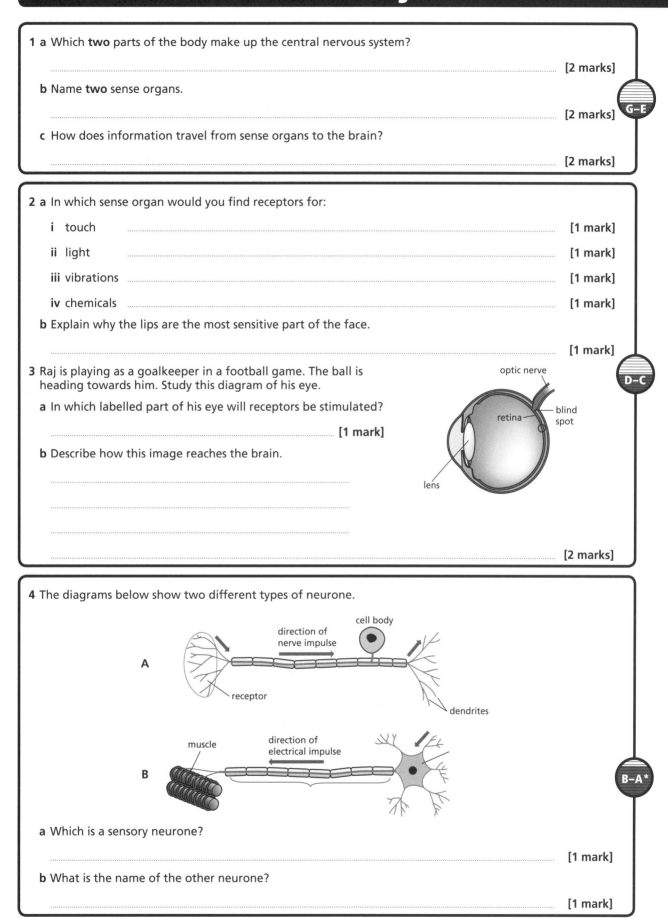

4 The diagrams below show two different types of neurone.

A — direction of nerve impulse — cell body — receptor — dendrites

B — muscle — direction of electrical impulse

a Which is a sensory neurone?

.... [1 mark]

b What is the name of the other neurone?

.... [1 mark]

Responses and coordination

1 For each of the following responses, say whether they are involuntary or voluntary.

  a Blinking

  .... [1 mark]

  b Pulling your hand away from a hot saucepan

  .... [1 mark]

  c Chewing a sandwich

  .... [1 mark]

2 For one of the involuntary responses in Question 1, explain how it protects the body.

  .... [1 mark]

G–E

3 A nerve impulse reaches a gap (synapse). Describe what happens in order for the impulse to start again in the next neurone in the chain.

→ direction of nerve impulses

....

.... [2 marks]

D–C

4 Reflex actions do not involve the brain.

  a How does this allow them to be fast?

  .... [1 mark]

  b Why do they need to be fast?

  ....

  .... [2 marks]

5 You touch a hot pan. Almost immediately, your arm moves away from the pan.

  Describe the sequence of events that occurs to bring this about.

  ....

  ....

  ....

  ....

  ....

  .... [5 marks]

B–A*

Hormones and diabetes

1 Testosterone is produced by the testes. It controls the development of male characteristics during puberty.

  a Which word in the sentence above is a hormone? .... [1 mark]

  b Which word is a gland? .... [1 mark]

  c Testosterone affects muscles situated all over the body. How does it reach them?

  .... [1 mark]

2 Padma has just eaten a chocolate bar, which causes her blood glucose level to rise. Her pancreas releases a hormone.

  a What is the hormone called? .... [1 mark]

  b What is its function?

  .... [1 mark]

3 The graph opposite shows changes in the blood glucose level of a person throughout a day.

Use the graph to state a time the following events occurred:

  a Food was eaten

  .... [1 mark]

  b The person exercised

  .... [2 marks]

  c Explain why this change happened in blood glucose levels when the person exercised.

  ....

  .... [2 marks]

  d Explain what happened in order for the blood glucose level to go back to 80 mg per 100 ml between 60 and 120 minutes.

  ....

  .... [3 marks]

  e What hormone was released at 300 minutes?

  .... [1 mark]

4 Emma has diabetes. Her body does not produce a certain hormone.

  a Name this hormone.

  .... [1 mark]

  b Which type of diabetes does Emma have?

  .... [1 mark]

  c In order to stay healthy Emma's body needs this hormone. How does she supply her body with it?

  .... [1 mark]

  d What would happen if she did not do this?

  ....

  .... [2 marks]

  e Emma inherited diabetes. Explain how.

  ....

  .... [2 marks]

Plant hormones

G–E

1 Tropisms can be positive or negative. Complete each of these statements with the correct word.

   a A shoot growing towards the light is .... phototropism. **[1 mark]**

   b A shoot growing away from gravity is .... gravitropism. **[1 mark]**

D–C

2 For each of the following examples of tropisms, explain how it helps the plant to survive.

   a Shoots growing towards the light.

   .... **[1 mark]**

   b Roots growing downwards into the soil.

   .... **[1 mark]**

B–A*

3 The picture opposite shows the shoot of a plant being exposed to light coming from one direction.

light

   a On which side of the shoot (A or B) is the light brightest?

   .... **[1 mark]**

   b Name the tropism that the plant is displaying.

   .... **[1 mark]**

A   B

   c On which side of the shoot (A or B) will the concentration of auxin be highest?

   .... **[1 mark]**

   d Explain how this causes the bending of the shoot.

   ....

   ....

   ....

   .... **[3 marks]**

B–A*

4 Plant growers may use rooting powder on their plant cuttings.

   a What is the function of rooting powder?

   .... **[1 mark]**

   b Why would a plant grower want to take cuttings?

   ....

   ....

   .... **[2 marks]**

D–C

5 In 1926, scientists found that a substance produced by a type of fungus increased the distance along a shoot between leaves. They called the substance gibberellin.

   a What evidence is there that gibberellin is a plant hormone?

   .... **[1 mark]**

B–A*

   b Scientists treated seedlings with different concentrations of gibberellin. Predict the results.

   ....

   .... **[1 mark]**

Drugs, smoking and alcohol abuse

1 State what type of drug each of the following is (painkiller, hallucinogen, stimulant or depressant).

 a Sleeping pills .... [1 mark]

 b Cocaine .... [1 mark]

 c Paracetamol .... [1 mark] **G–E**

 d Magic mushrooms .... [1 mark]

 e Nicotine .... [1 mark]

2 There are around 250,000 heroin addicts in the UK.

 a Explain why people become addicted to heroin.

 ....

 .... [2 marks] **D–C**

 b Why do many heroin addicts turn to crime?

 ....

 .... [2 marks]

3 A group of people were asked to carry out a reaction-time test before and after drinking a cup of coffee.

 a Predict what happened to their reaction times after drinking the coffee.

 .... [1 mark] **B–A***

 b Explain what effect caffeine has on the nervous system.

 ....

 .... [2 marks]

4 State the substance found in tobacco smoke that contributes to the following illnesses.

 a Lung cancer .... **[1 mark]**   **b** Heart disease .... [1 mark]

5 Why do many smokers constantly have a bad cough? **G–E**

 ....

 .... [2 marks]

6 Paul drinks four pints of beer in one night.

 a State one short-term effect of drinking this much alcohol.

 .... [1 mark]

 b Half a pint of beer contains one unit of alcohol. How many units has Paul drunk?

 .... [1 mark] **D–C**

 c Explain why frequently drinking this much alcohol could be dangerous to Paul's health.

 ....

 .... [2 marks]

7 Research data was collected about the causes of people dying from lung conditions.

 a The number of people dying from tuberculosis fell. Suggest why.

 .... [1 mark]

 b However, the number of people dying from lung cancer rose. Suggest why. **B–A***

 .... [1 mark]

 c This data could not, by itself, prove that smoking caused lung cancer. Why not?

 .... [1 mark]

Ethics of transplants

1 Maria has kidney failure. This means that both of her kidneys have stopped working.

   a Maria needs a kidney transplant. What does this mean?

   .... **[1 mark]**

   b Maria has a sister who has two healthy kidneys. Explain why she would be a first choice of donor.

   ....

   .... **[1 mark]**

2 Bernard needs a lung transplant. His brother comes to visit him and suggests he becomes a donor. Why is this not possible?

   .... **[1 mark]**

G–E

3 The search for alternative sources of human organs has raised many ethical issues.

   Suggest ethical arguments against buying organs from people in developing countries (transplantation tourism).

   ....

   ....

   .... **[2 marks]**

4 Another possible source of human organs are animal organs (xenotransplantation).

   a Why are pig organs considered the best for human transplants?

   .... **[1 mark]**

   b Explain why xenotransplantation is not currently used as an option for transplantation.

   .... **[1 mark]**

   c What technology may make xenotransplantation possible in the future?

   .... **[1 mark]**

   d Give **one** ethical argument against xenotransplantation.

   .... **[1 mark]**

D–C

5 At any one time there will be several people waiting for transplants.

   Explain why people have to wait.

   .... **[1 mark]**

6 Doctors have to decide which patient will be next to receive an organ. Discuss the factors that doctors will consider when making this difficult decision.

   ....

   ....

   ....

   ....

   .... **[3 marks]**

B–A*

Infectious diseases

1 Tuberculosis is an infection of the lungs caused by bacteria.

   a What word describes a microbe that causes disease?

.... [1 mark]

   b Tuberculosis is an infectious disease. What does this mean?

.... [1 mark]

   c Why do bacteria grow and multiply so well inside human lungs?

.... [1 mark]

G–E

2 Infectious diseases can be spread in many different ways. For each method below, state a disease that is spread in this way.

   a Through moisture droplets in the air .... [1 mark]

   b Eating or touching undercooked food .... [1 mark]

   c Sewage in drinking water .... [1 mark]

D–C

3 Some types of bacteria can cause diarrhoea, which can be fatal. Explain why.

....

....

....

.... [4 marks]

B–A*

4 Some insects can be vectors.

   a What does the term 'vector' mean?

.... [1 mark]

   b A person in an African village becomes ill with malaria. Describe how the disease gets passed to other people in the village.

....

....

....

.... [3 marks]

G–E

5 Britney falls over and cuts her knee. Her Mum puts antiseptic cream on the cut. Why?

....

.... [2 marks]

G–E

6 Ortis goes to his doctor with a bad cold. The doctor does not prescribe him any antibiotics. Why not?

....

.... [2 marks]

D–C

7 There is an outbreak of MRSA in a hospital ward. MRSA is an antibiotic-resistant bacteria.

   a Why is MRSA dangerous to the patients in the ward?

....

.... [2 marks]

   b How did resistance in MRSA arise?

....

....

....

.... [3 marks]

B–A*

Defences and interdependency

1 Why is it vital that skin heals itself after a cut?

....

.... [2 marks]

2 The human body produces many different chemicals that are used to defend against pathogens. For each of the following chemicals, state where in the body it is made.

a Lysozyme .... [1 mark]

b Sebum .... [1 mark]

c Hydrochloric acid .... [1 mark]

3 HIV is a virus that destroys white blood cells. Explain why people infected with HIV are at high risk of dying from infectious diseases.

....

.... [2 marks]

4 Many areas of tropical rainforest are destroyed each year. Explain why it is important that they are conserved to help in the fight against infectious diseases.

....

.... [2 marks]

5 a Aphids are tiny insects that feed on the sap of plants. Sap contains sugars that the plants make through photosynthesis and use as food. Is this an example of mutualism or parasitism? Explain the reason for your choice.

....

.... [2 marks]

b Aphids give the sap they collect to ant colonies. The ants defend the aphids against attacks from their predators, such as ladybirds. Is this an example of mutualism or parasitism? Explain the reason for your choice.

....

.... [2 marks]

6 A gardening technique called companion planting makes use of mutualism between plants. The image opposite shows an example called 'the three sisters' technique.

a The bean plant is leguminous. Describe the mutualism between it and nitrogen-fixing bacteria.

corn
has tall, sturdy structure

beans
are a climbing leguminous plant. Leaves are covered with prickly hairs.

squash
leaves cover the ground

....

....

....

....

.... [3 marks]

b Choose one other example of mutualism between two of the plants, and explain the relationship.

....

....

.... [2 marks]

Energy, biomass and population pressures

1 A food chain that exists in the ocean is: seaweed ⟶ limpet ⟶ octopus ⟶ seal

  a Choose the organism in the food chain that is an example of a:

    i producer ....   **ii** consumer ....   **[2 marks]**

  b A limpet is a herbivore. What does this mean?

    ....   **[1 mark]** **G–E**

  c Fill in the gaps in the following sentence.

    A seal is a ...., its prey is the ....   **[2 marks]**

  d Crabs feed on bits of dead plants and animals that fall to the ocean floor.

    What type of consumer are they? ....   **[1 mark]**

2 a Why are food webs a more accurate representation of feeding relationships than food chains?

  ....

  ....   **[2 marks]** **D–C**

  b Explain why food chains are rarely longer than five organisms.

    ....

    ....   **[2 marks]**

3 Sketch a pyramid of biomass for the food chain in Question 1. Label each level with the name of the organism only.   **B–A***

    [2 marks]

4 A population pyramid for Germany is shown opposite.

  a Compare the numbers of children and adults living in Germany.

    ....   **[1 mark]**

  b Is the population of Germany set to increase or decrease in the future? Use the pyramid to explain your prediction.   **G–E**

    ....

    ....   **[2 marks]**

Germany

Age: 80+, 75-79, 70-74, 65-69, 60-64, 55-59, 50-54, 45-49, 40-44, 35-39, 30-34, 25-29, 20-24, 15-19, 10-14, 5-9, 0-4

Males   Females

6 4 2 0 2 4 6
Percent of Population

5 Plastic is a resource made from the raw material crude oil.

  a Predict how the demand for plastics will change in the near future. Give a reason for your prediction.

    ....   **[2 marks]** **D–C**

  b Scientists are researching ways of making plastics from raw materials other than oil. Give a reason why this is a good idea.

    ....   **[1 mark]**

6 Adil has to sort out his rubbish into two bags. Paper, metal and some plastic goes into a recycling bag. The rest goes into a normal black refuse bag.

  a State the two places that the rubbish in the black bag could end up.

    ....   **[2 marks]** **B–A***

  b Adil thinks that recycling wastes energy as so much is used up collecting and sorting the contents of the recycling bag. Counteract his argument.

    ....

    ....   **[2 marks]**

Water and air pollution

1 Farmers use fertilisers to increase crop yield. These fertilisers may contain pollutants.

a Define the word 'pollutant'.

.... **[1 mark]**

b Name one pollutant that may be found in fertilisers.

.... **[1 mark]**

c These pollutants could enter drinking water. How?

....

.... **[2 marks]**

G–E

2 Ponds and rivers that have increased amounts of pollutants in their water will also contain higher than normal numbers of bacteria.

a Explain why.

....

....

.... **[3 marks]**

b Why is this a problem for animals living in the polluted water?

....

.... **[2 marks]**

D–C

3 A sample of water is taken from a river and is found to contain high numbers of bloodworms. Comment on the oxygen concentration in the water and link this to how polluted it is.

....

.... **[2 marks]**

B–A*

4 Acid rain or snow is a major environmental concern.

a Describe how burning fossil fuels can produce acid rain or snow.

....

.... **[2 marks]**

b State one way that acid rain damages the environment

.... **[2 marks]**

5 A scientist surveyed the distribution of lichens. She counted the number of different species that grew on trees at various distances from the centre of a polluted city. Her results are shown opposite.

Distance to the town centre (km)	0	1	2	3	4	5	6	7	8
Number of different species of lichen	0	1	2	4	4	5	8	10	13

a Describe the relationship between the number of species and the distance from the centre of the city.

.... **[1 mark]**

b What do these results show about the levels of sulfur dioxide in the air as you get further from the city centre? Explain how you know.

....

....

.... **[3 marks]**

D–C

6 Explain how cars in the UK can cause acid rain in Sweden.

....

....

.... **[3 marks]**

B–A*

Recycling carbon and nitrogen

1 Food for decomposers is dead plants and animals.

  a Name an organism that is a decomposer.

  .... **[1 mark]**

  b Without decomposers plants couldn't grow. Explain why.

  ....

  .... **[2 marks]**

G–E

2 This diagram of the carbon cycle shows how carbon is recycled around the Earth.

  Name the process missing in:

  A .... **[1 mark]**

  B .... **[1 mark]**

3 Animals need carbon in order to build tissue.

  a How do they get the carbon they need?

  .... **[1 mark]**

  b A carbon atom that makes up the muscle of an animal will one day return to the atmosphere. Explain how this will happen.

  ....

  ....

  .... **[3 marks]**

D–C

4 Both nitrifying and denitrifying bacteria live in the soil. Nitrifying bacteria require high levels of oxygen to survive. Denitrifying bacteria are anaerobic. This means they do not require oxygen and high levels will kill them.

  a Describe the role of nitrifying bacteria in the nitrogen cycle.

  ....

  .... **[2 marks]**

  b What do denitrifying bacteria do?

  .... **[1 mark]**

  c The soil beneath Sandra's lawn is very waterlogged. She notices that her grass goes yellow and does not grow well. Explain why.

  ....

  ....

  ....

  ....

  .... **[5 marks]**

B–A*

B1 Extended response question

*In the 1920s, Dutch biologist Frits Went investigated the development of cereal seedlings. He suggested that a substance – which he called auxin – regulated growth of the shoots. He carried out experiments to investigate the effects of auxin on shoot growth in response to light. One of the hypotheses that Went wanted to test was: **The tip of the shoot detects the direction of light**.

Write a plan that will enable you to test this hypothesis.

D–C

[6 marks]

Questions labelled with an **asterisk** (*) are ones where the quality of your written communication will be assessed. You should take particular care with your spelling, punctuation and grammar, as well as clarity of expression on these questions.

Seeing cells and cell components

1 Gareth wanted to see what one of his cheek cells looked like.

  a Why must he use a microscope to do this?

  .... [1 mark]

  b He used an objective lens with magnification ×20 and an eyepiece lens with magnification ×10. What is the total magnification he used to view the cells?

  .... [1 mark]

2 Give **two** advantages of using an electron microscope over a light microscope.

....

.... [2 marks]

3 Look at the diagram of a cell opposite.

  a Name the missing components (1 and 2).

  1..

  2.. **[2 marks]**

  b Is this an animal or a plant cell? Explain your decision.

  ....

  .... [2 marks]

4 The type and number of components of cells differ according to their function. Explain why:

  a Sperm cells have many mitochondria in their cytoplasm.

  ....

  .... [2 marks]

  b The cell walls of the cells in a plant stem are thicker than the walls of other plant cells.

  ....

  .... [2 marks]

  c Plant root cells have no chloroplasts but leaf cells have many.

  ....

  ....

  .... [3 marks]

5 A scientist studied a cell under a microscope and drew a diagram of what he saw. He labelled some of the components.

  Which component(s) is found:

  a In plant and animal cells?

  .... [1 mark]

  b In both plant and bacterial cells?

  .... [1 mark]

  c Is this a bacterial cell? Explain your decision.

  ....

  .... [2 marks]

DNA

1 a DNA has a double helix structure. What does this mean?

....

....

.... **[2 marks]**

b The bases of a single strand of DNA are AATGCTTA.
Write out the order of the bases in the other
complementary strand.

....

.... **[1 mark]**

c In a gene, a nucleotide with the base C changes into an A. Explain why this may affect the
protein made from this gene.

.... **[2 marks]**

2 Explain the purpose of each of the following stages in the DNA extraction process.

a Adding a detergent/salt solution to the cells.

....

.... **[2 marks]**

b Using a protein-denaturing enzyme.

....

.... **[2 marks]**

c Adding cold methanol.

....

.... **[2 marks]**

3 The hydrogen bonds holding the complementary base pairs together are weak.

Explain why this is important.

....

.... **[2 marks]**

4 Explain how the work of Franklin and Wilkins helped Watson and Crick to discover the
structure of DNA.

....

.... **[2 marks]**

5 Explain how genetic engineering relies on the fact that the genetic code is universal.

....

....

....

.... **[3 marks]**

G–E

D–C

B–A*

G–E

B–A*

Genetic engineering and GM organisms

1 Human insulin can be produced by bacteria grown in a fermenter.

a Why are these bacteria known as a GM organisms?

.... [1 mark]

b The culture inside the fermenter has to be maintained at a temperature of around 37 °C. Why?

....

.... [2 marks]

G–E

2 Bacteria are genetically engineered by following the procedure shown in the diagram below.

strand of DNA carrying a gene which enables
cells to produce useful proteins

bacterial cell

bacteria have pieces of circular DNA
called plasmid DNA

A

B

C

plasmid is put back
into the bacterial cell

bacteria multiply and produce millions of
identical clones, all with the DNA coding
for the required protein

bacteria grow in special tanks called fermenters.
The end product is removed from the fermenter

For each of the stages A, B and C, state what type of enzyme is used.

....

.... [3 marks]

D–C

3 State **one** benefit and **one** drawback of using genetically engineered insulin in the treatment of diabetes.

....

.... [2 marks]

B–A*

4 A type of GM cotton plant called Bt cotton produces a toxin in its leaves, which kills any insect pests that feed on it.

a Explain why farmers may want to grow Bt cotton instead of normal cotton.

....

.... [2 marks]

b State **one** reason why people may be worried about farmers growing Bt cotton.

.... [1 mark]

G–E

5 Vitamin A deficiency is believed to cause the death of around two million people a year in developing countries.

a How can the GM crop golden rice help people in these countries?

....

.... [2 marks]

b Some people are against golden rice being available for consumption. State **one** of their arguments.

....

.... [2 marks]

D–C

6 Scientists have developed GM wheat that is resistant to herbicides. Explain how growing herbicide-resistant wheat helps the farmers to make more profit.

....

....

.... [3 marks]

B–A*

Mitosis and meiosis

1 Mitosis is a type of cell division. Describe why:

a Mitosis results in two daughter cells.

.... [1 mark]

b The daughter cells are genetically identical to the parent cell.

.... [1 mark]

c Skin cells frequently undergo mitosis.

.... [1 mark]

G–E

2 Hydras are organisms that can carry out both asexual and sexual reproduction.

Which type of cell division:

a Is used to form offspring in asexual reproduction?

.... [1 mark]

b Forms gametes for sexual reproduction?

.... [1 mark]

D–C

3 An adult hydra cell has 30 chromosomes. The diagram opposite shows the stages that happen during mitosis.

a For each cell (1–3) state how many chromosomes are present.

.... [2 marks]

b The daughter cells are clones. What does this mean?

.... [1 mark]

c The daughter cells are diploid. What does this mean?

.... [1 mark]

4 When the hydra reproduces sexually it carries out meiosis.

a Why is meiosis needed in order for sexual reproduction to take place?

....

.... [2 marks]

The diagram opposite shows the stages that happen during this process.

b For each stage (1–7), state the number of chromosomes present in each cell.

....

....

.... [3 marks]

c Which cells are haploid? Why are haploid cells essential for successful sexual reproduction?

....

....

.... [3 marks]

d Each daughter cell is genetically different. Explain how this occurs.

....

.... [2 marks]

B–A*

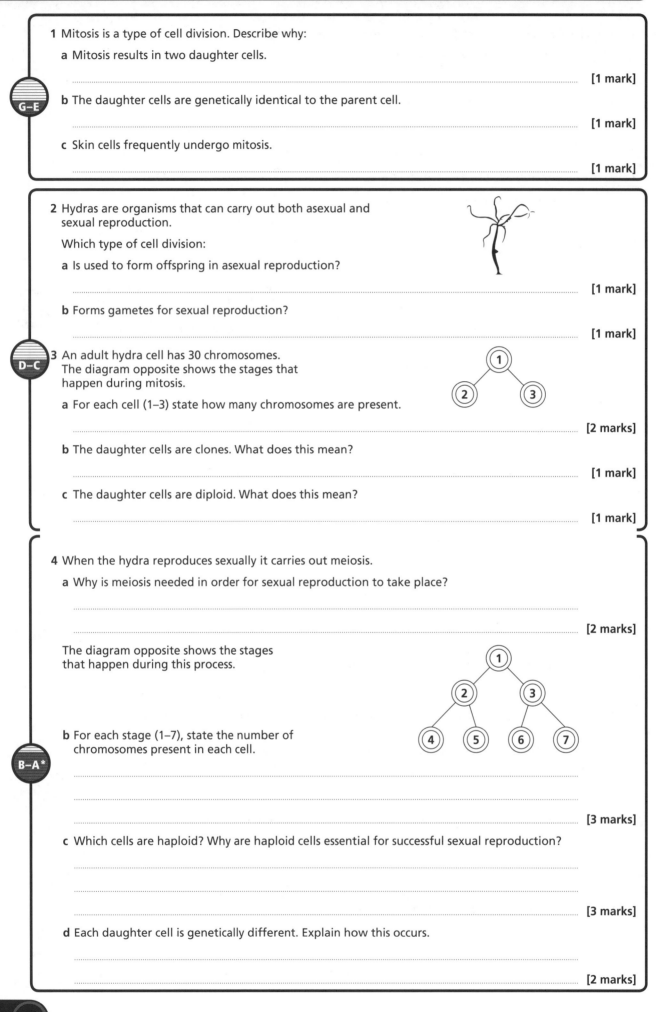

Cloning plants and animals

1 Susan has successfully bred an award-winning plant. She wants to clone it.

a What are clones?

.... [1 mark]

G–E

b Why does Susan want to clone her plant?

.... [1 mark]

c State **one** method she can use to clone her plant, and explain how to carry it out.

....

....

D–C

.... [3 marks]

2 An egg was taken from a cow and fertilised in the laboratory. The resulting embryo was split into individual cells and each cell put into the womb of a host mother.

a Explain why the host cow will give birth to more than one baby.

.... [1 mark]

b The babies will be clones. Why?

....

G–E

.... [2 marks]

c Why might a cattle farmer want to carry out this procedure?

....

.... [2 marks]

d Why might the farmer want to consider cloning rather than embryo transplants?

....

....

D–C

.... [2 marks]

3 The Pyrenean ibex, a form of wild mountain goat, was officially declared extinct in 2000, but scientists have preserved tissue samples and can use these to create clones.

D–C

a Give **one** risk of making clones of the ibex.

.... [1 mark]

b Outline the process that could be used to clone the ibex.

....

....

B–A*

....

.... [4 marks]

Stem cells and the human genome

1 Choose the correct words to complete the following statements about stem cells:

a Stem cells are cells that have the potential to do any job.

They are .... [1 mark]

b Stem cells then change into the different types of cell that have a specific job.

This is called .... [1 mark]

G–E

2 We can use stem cells to treat people whose tissues are damaged.

a Why are embryonic stem cells more useful than adult cells in stem cell therapy?

....

.... [2 marks]

b Some people feel that using embryonic stem cells is ethically wrong. Why do they think this?

....

.... [2 marks]

D–C

3 You see a website advertising a cure for blindness using stem cell therapy in a clinic in China.
Outline reasons why people should be cautious about going there for treatment.

....

....

....

.... [3 marks]

B–A*

4 Scientists are working on stem cell therapy using adult stem cells that have been programmed for reverse differentiation.

Explain the reasons why these stem cells would be suitable for stem cell therapy.

....

....

....

.... [3 marks]

5 a What was the primary aim of the Human Genome Project?

.... [1 mark]

b Many scientists from different countries worked together on the project. Why was this collaboration helpful?

....

.... [2 marks]

B–A*

c Scientists hope to use the results to work out the protein that each gene in the genome codes for. State **one** potential application for this information.

.... [1 mark]

Protein synthesis

1 The image below represents a protein molecule.

G–E

a What are the individual units called?

.... [1 mark]

b It would be accurate to call this molecule a peptide rather than a protein. Why?

....

.... [2 marks]

2 a State **two** differences between DNA and RNA.

....

.... [2 marks]

D–C

b What is the function of messenger RNA (mRNA)?

....

.... [2 marks]

3 The DNA sequence for a short section of a gene that codes for a protein used inside a cell is GGT GCT ACG TAG CCT AAT.

a Write the sequence of the mRNA that will be formed during transcription of this sequence.

.... [1 mark]

b What is the purpose of transcription?

....

....

.... [3 marks]

c Which of the following tRNAs is a carrier for the first amino acid in this part of the protein? Explain how you worked out your answer.

B–A*

1 C C T   2 G G U   3 C C A

....

.... [2 marks]

d A mutation causes the first A base in this DNA strand to turn into a G. Suggest how this could affect the cell.

....

....

....

.... [4 marks]

Mutations

1 Naima has a lung infection caused by bacteria multiplying inside them. A mutation occurs in the DNA of one of the bacteria. It results in the bacteria being resistant to the antibiotic penicillin.

a Is this mutation harmful or beneficial to the bacteria? Explain the reason for your answer.

....

.... [2 marks]

b Bacteria reproduce by mitosis. Explain why offspring of this bacteria will also carry the mutation.

.... [1 mark]

c Naima's doctor prescribes her some penicillin. Numbers of the mutant bacteria grow rapidly inside Naima's lungs, but the numbers of normal bacteria decrease. Explain why.

....

....

....

.... [4 marks]

2 The table opposite shows part of the DNA strand from a gene and two mutated versions.

Normal DNA base sequence	Mutation 1	Mutation 2	Mutation 3
T	T	T	T
T	T	T	T
A	A	G	A
A	A	A	A
G	G	A	G
C	C	G	C
C	C	C	T
C	C	C	C
C	T	C	C
T	G	C	T
G	A	T	G
A		G	A
		A	

a State the number of the mutation that is an example of:

i an insertion .... [1 mark]

ii a deletion .... [1 mark]

iii a substitution .... [1 mark]

b Explain why any of these mutations could affect the function of the protein that is coded for by this gene.

....

.... [2 marks]

3 The amino acid lysine (lys) is specified by the codons AAA and AAG. A mutation occurred in a gene as shown opposite.

Normal DNA base sequence	Mutated sequence
G	G
C	C
T	T
A	A
A	A
G	A
G	G
T	T
G	G
C	C
T	T
A	A

a Explain why the protein coded for by this gene is not affected by the mutation.

....

....

....

....

....

.... [3 marks]

b What type of mutation is this an example of?

.... [1 mark]

Enzymes

1 Amylase and pepsin are examples of enzymes that are found in the human digestive system.

  a Enzymes are biological catalysts. What does this mean?

.... [2 marks]

  b Why are enzymes needed for human digestion?

.... [2 marks] **G–E**

  c Pepsin is found in the stomach, which contains acid. Describe what the activity of pepsin will be like at pH 10. Give a reason for your answer.

....

.... [3 marks]

2 Pepsin catalyses the breakdown of proteins into amino acids. In this reaction what is the:

  a substrate? .... [1 mark]

  b product? .... [1 mark] **D–C**

  c Explain why the way enzymes work is sometimes referred to as the 'lock and key' hypothesis.

....

.... [2 marks]

3 Describe the role of **one** enzyme involved in protein synthesis and explain why an enzyme is needed.

....

.... [2 marks] **B–A***

4 The graph opposite shows the effect of temperature on an enzyme-controlled reaction.

  a Describe what is happening to the activity of the enzyme between –5 °C and 0 °C.

.... [1 mark]

  b What is the optimum temperature for this enzyme?

.... [1 mark] **G–E**

  c The enzyme was taken from a fish. Would you say the fish lived in warm or cold water? Give a reason for your answer.

....

.... [2 marks]

5 Kuba was investigating the action of the enzymes. He kept the concentration of enzyme the same but slowly increased the concentration of substrate, measuring the rate of reaction each time. All other factors, such as temperature, were kept constant.

  a At first he found that increasing the amount of substrate speeded up the rate of the reaction. Why?

....

.... [3 marks] **D–C**

  b Kuba then discovered that the rate of reaction stopped increasing, even though he was still increasing the concentration of substrate. Why?

.... [1 mark]

6 Amylase is an enzyme that breaks starch down into glucose. It has an optimum pH of around 8.

  Explain why starch is not broken down by amylase at pH 1.

....

.... **B–A***

.... [4 marks]

Respiring cells and diffusion

1 The table opposite compares the percentage by volume of inhaled and exhaled air in humans.

Gas	Inhaled air (%)	Exhaled air (%)
Nitrogen	78	78
Oxygen	21	16
Carbon dioxide	0.035	4
Other gases	about 1–2	about 1–2

a State the difference in the percentage of carbon dioxide between inhaled and exhaled air.

[1 mark]

b Why is the percentage of oxygen in exhaled air lower than in inhaled air?

[2 marks]

c Why is there no difference in the percentage of nitrogen?

[1 mark]

2 Lydia is out doing her weekly run.

a During the first 10 minutes she runs at a fast pace. What type of respiration are her leg muscle cells carrying out?

[1 mark]

b After 10 minutes she notices she has less energy and her legs start to ache. What type of respiration is being carried out now in her leg muscles?

[1 mark]

c Why did Lydia's leg muscles start to ache?

[1 mark]

d Why did she have less energy?

[1 mark]

e Lydia decides to rest after 20 minutes. She continues to breathe fast and her legs start to feel better. Explain why.

[2 marks]

3 A pot of fresh coffee is brewing in the kitchen. Use ideas about diffusion to explain why the smell travels throughout the house.

[3 marks]

4 Glucose molecules pass through the wall of the small intestine and enter blood capillaries via diffusion.

a Explain why this process is vital to human survival.

[3 marks]

b Where is the concentration of glucose highest: in the small intestine or the bloodstream? Explain why this is important.

[3 marks]

5 a Explain how a concentration gradient is maintained across the small intestine.

[3 marks]

b Why is it important that this concentration gradient is maintained?

[1 mark]

Effects of exercise

1 During exercise breathing rate increases, enabling more oxygen to enter the blood through the lungs.

a Why is more oxygen needed in the blood during exercise?

....

.... [3 marks]

b Give another reason why it is important that breathing rate increases during exercise.

.... [1 mark]

c Apart from the lungs, which other organ is important in increasing the amount of oxygen getting to exercising muscles?

.... [1 mark]

G–E

2 You are asked to carry out investigations into how exercise affects the body. For each of these questions, suggest a simple method to collect results and predict what they will show.

a How does exercise affect the amount of carbon dioxide exhaled in one breath?

....

....

.... [3 marks]

b How does exercise affect heart rate?

....

.... [2 marks]

D–C

3 Three people had breathing measurements taken.

a Use the following equation to fill in the missing values in the table.

$$\text{number of breaths in a minute (breathing rate)} \times \text{volume of air per breath} = \text{volume of air exchanged}$$

Person	Volume of air per breath (dm³)	Breathing rate (breaths per minute)	Volume of air exchanged per minute (dm³)
Tom	4.4	50	i
Vishram	0.5	ii	9
Chelsea	iii	20	6

[3 marks]

b Which person is:

i at rest?

.... [1 mark]

ii exercising?

.... [1 mark]

iii a young child?

.... [1 mark]

B–A*

4 Peter has a stroke volume of 0.07 l. His resting heart rate is 72 beats per minute.

Use the following equation to calculate his cardiac output.

cardiac output = stroke volume × heart rate

....

.... [3 marks]

Photosynthesis

G-E

1 An apple tree is a green plant that carries out photosynthesis.

a Why is photosynthesis an essential process for the tree?

.... **[2 marks]**

b The flowers of the tree are white. Can the petal cells carry out photosynthesis? Give a reason for your answer.

.... **[2 marks]**

D-C

2 Explain **one** way that a leaf is adapted for photosynthesis.

.... **[2 marks]**

3 Greenhouses are used to increase the rate of photosynthesis of the plants growing inside.

a Suggest how tomatoes grown inside a greenhouse would compare to those grown outside.

.... **[1 mark]**

G-E

b For each labelled part of the greenhouse, explain how it maximises the rate of photosynthesis of the plants growing inside.

i .... **[1 mark]**

ii .... **[1 mark]**

iii .... **[1 mark]**

i shades removed from ceiling
ii heater
iii automatic watering system

c Suggest one more addition that would maximise photosynthesis even more.

.... **[1 mark]**

D-C

4 An experiment was set up as shown in the diagram below. The lamp was moved towards the plant and the average number of bubbles of oxygen released by the plant per minute was counted and recorded at each distance. The results are shown in the table below.

Distance between the lamp and plant (cm)	Number of bubbles of oxygen released per minute
50	1
45	2
40	5
35	10
30	16
25	32
20	54
15	56
10	56
5	56

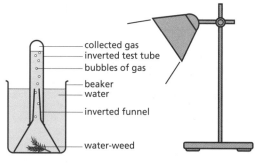

collected gas
inverted test tube
bubbles of gas
beaker
water
inverted funnel
water-weed

a Describe how you could prove that the collected gas was oxygen.

.... **[2 marks]**

b Use the results to describe how light intensity affects the rate of photosynthesis.

.... **[1 mark]**

c Explain why the number of bubbles does not increase any further once the lamp gets closer than 15 cm away.

....

.... **[2 marks]**

B-A*

d The switched-on lamp was left 5 cm away from the water-weed for a further 30 minutes. After this time, the number of bubbles released in one minute was counted again. The result was only 5 bubbles. Explain why.

....

.... **[3 marks]**

Transport in plants, osmosis and fieldwork

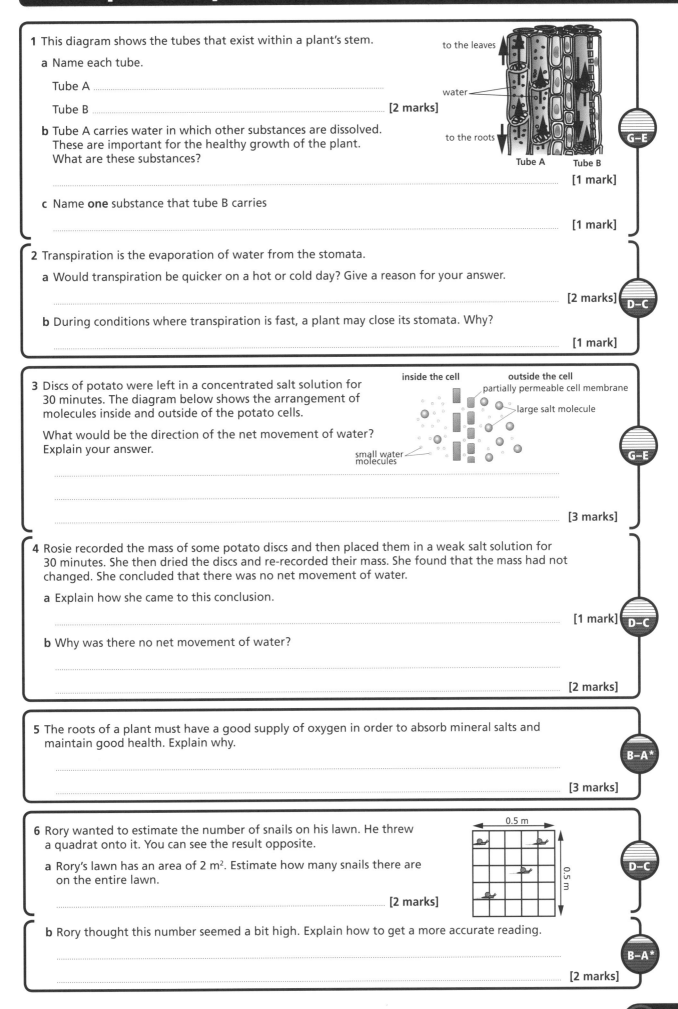

1 This diagram shows the tubes that exist within a plant's stem.

to the leaves

water

to the roots

Tube A   Tube B

  a Name each tube.

   Tube A ....

   Tube B .... **[2 marks]**

  b Tube A carries water in which other substances are dissolved.
    These are important for the healthy growth of the plant.
    What are these substances?

   ....
   [1 mark]

  c Name **one** substance that tube B carries

   ....
   [1 mark]

G–E

2 Transpiration is the evaporation of water from the stomata.

  a Would transpiration be quicker on a hot or cold day? Give a reason for your answer.

   ....
   [2 marks]

  b During conditions where transpiration is fast, a plant may close its stomata. Why?

   ....
   [1 mark]

D–C

3 Discs of potato were left in a concentrated salt solution for
  30 minutes. The diagram below shows the arrangement of
  molecules inside and outside of the potato cells.

  What would be the direction of the net movement of water?
  Explain your answer.

  inside the cell   outside the cell
  partially permeable cell membrane
  large salt molecule
  small water
  molecules

   ....
   ....
   ....
   [3 marks]

G–E

4 Rosie recorded the mass of some potato discs and then placed them in a weak salt solution for
  30 minutes. She then dried the discs and re-recorded their mass. She found that the mass had not
  changed. She concluded that there was no net movement of water.

  a Explain how she came to this conclusion.

   ....
   [1 mark]

  b Why was there no net movement of water?

   ....
   ....
   [2 marks]

D–C

5 The roots of a plant must have a good supply of oxygen in order to absorb mineral salts and
  maintain good health. Explain why.

   ....
   ....
   [3 marks]

B–A*

6 Rory wanted to estimate the number of snails on his lawn. He threw
  a quadrat onto it. You can see the result opposite.

  0.5 m
  0.5 m

  a Rory's lawn has an area of 2 m². Estimate how many snails there are
    on the entire lawn.

   .... **[2 marks]**

D–C

  b Rory thought this number seemed a bit high. Explain how to get a more accurate reading.

   ....
   ....
   [2 marks]

B–A*

Fossil record and growth

1 Amira found a fossil inside a lump of sedimentary rock.

a What is a fossil?

.... [1 mark]

G–E

b Why are fossils found in sedimentary rock?

....

....

.... [3 marks]

2 a What do we mean by 'gaps in the fossil record'?

....

.... [2 marks]

D–C

b Some people believe that the gaps in the fossil record are evidence that **disproves** Darwin's theory of natural selection. Give **one** way that scientists explain the gaps.

.... [1 mark]

3 The images opposite show the 'arm' limb of three different modern-day animals.

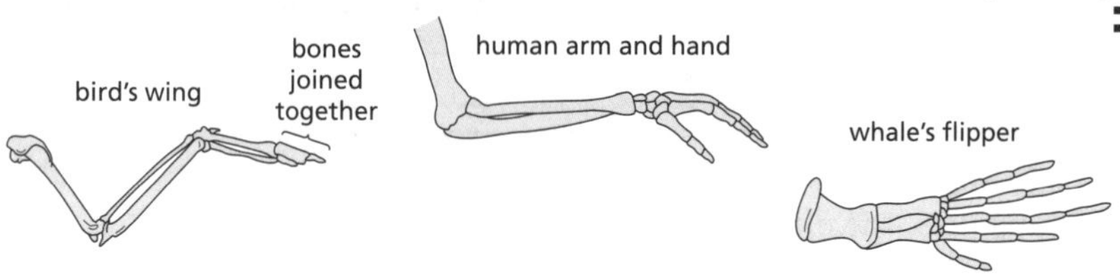

bird's wing   bones joined together   human arm and hand   whale's flipper

a What do these limbs have in common?

.... [1 mark]

B–A*

b Why are they all slightly different?

.... [1 mark]

c Explain how this is evidence for evolution.

....

.... [2 marks]

4 A sapling is a young tree. What will happen to the sapling's cells in order for it to grow?

G–E

.... [1 mark]

5 State **one** similarity and **one** difference between the growth of plants and animals.

D–C

....

.... [2 marks]

6 Use the growth chart opposite to answer the following questions.

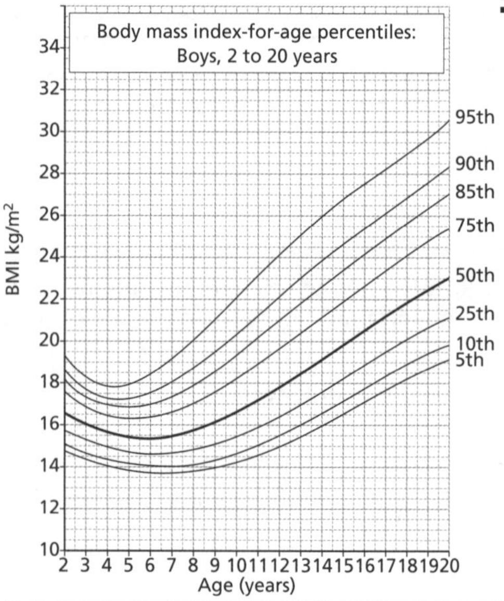

a What is the average BMI for a boy aged 15 years?

.... [1 mark]

b Matthew is 11 and has a BMI of 16 kg/m². Which percentile is he on?

.... [1 mark]

B–A*

c Explain what this means.

....

.... [1 mark]

Body mass index-for-age percentiles: Boys, 2 to 20 years

95th
90th
85th
75th
50th
25th
10th
5th

BMI kg/m²

Age (years)

Cells, tissues, organs and blood

1 Classify each of these as a cell, tissue or organ.

a Muscle .... [1 mark]

b Neurone .... [1 mark]

c Sperm .... [1 mark]

d Liver .... [1 mark]

G–E

e Skin .... [1 mark]

2 Match each of the organs below to the organ system it is part of.

a	ovary	1	digestive system
b	stomach	2	nervous system
c	heart	3	circulatory system
d	brain	4	reproductive system

[4 marks]

3 Most cells in the adult human body have undergone differentiation. What does this mean?

....

.... [2 marks]

4 For each of the following cells, give **one** way that it is adapted to carry out its function.

D–C

a Red blood cell.

....

.... [2 marks]

b Sperm cell.

.... [2 marks]

5 Why are patterns in gene activity vital in the process of differentiation?

....

B–A*

.... [3 marks]

6 Name these **two** blood cells.

a

b

a .... [1 mark]

G–E

b .... [1 mark]

c Name one other component of blood.

.... [1 mark]

7 Describe how red blood cells transport oxygen from the lungs to respiring tissues.

....

....

D–C

.... [3 marks]

8 Michael has cut his leg. In a few minutes a clot forms over the wound.

a Which component of the blood is responsible for the clot?

.... [1 mark]

B–A*

b Explain how the clot protects Michael's body.

....

.... [2 marks]

The heart and circulatory system

1 For each of the following parts of the heart, state its function.

   a Pulmonary artery.

   .... [1 mark]

   b Valves.

   .... [1 mark]

   c Vena cava.

   .... [1 mark]

2 Fill in the missing words to complete the order of the flow of blood through the heart.

   Vena cava ➝ right .... ➝ .... ventricle ➝ .... artery.   [3 marks]

3 Why is the wall of the left ventricle thicker than that of the right ventricle?

   ....

   ....

   .... [3 marks]

4 Explain why the human heart is known as a 'double pump'.

   ....

   .... [2 marks]

5 During one pumping cycle blood flows through each side of the heart.

   a Describe how blood enters the ventricles from the atria.

   ....

   .... [3 marks]

   b How is blood prevented from returning into the atria?

   .... [1 mark]

6 Name **three** types of blood vessel.

   .... [3 marks]

7 Name the types of blood vessel being described below.

   a Carries blood from tissues to the heart.

   .... [1 mark]

   b Has the largest diameter.

   .... [1 mark]

   c Carries blood at a high pressure.

   .... [1 mark]

   d Walls are only one cell thick.

   .... [1 mark]

8 Why do veins need valves?

   ....

   .... [2 marks]

9 What is the function of a 'capillary bed'?

   ....

   ....

   .... [3 marks]

G–E

D–C

B–A*

G–E

D–C

B–A*

The digestive system

1 Name the parts of the digestive system on the diagram.

a .... [1 mark]

b .... [1 mark]

c .... [1 mark]

2 Give a reason why:

a Food is chewed in the mouth.

.... [1 mark]

b Food is mixed with saliva in the mouth.

.... [1 mark]

3 What is the function of peristalsis?

.... [1 mark]

4 Janet has a gall stone blocking her bile duct.

a What is the function of the bile duct?

.... [2 marks]

b Predict how a blockage will affect Janet's health.

....

.... [3 marks]

5 What is the function of enzymes in digestion?

....

.... [3 marks]

6 A science class set up an experiment using the equipment opposite and left it for 30 minutes.

For each of these substances, predict if the class will detect it in the warm water surrounding the Visking tubing, giving a reason for your answer.

thread to attach
to support
warm water
mixture of protein,
starch and protease
Visking tubing

a Protein.

....

.... [2 marks]

b Amino acids.

....

....

.... [3 marks]

c Glucose.

....

.... [2 marks]

7 Explain how the structure of the villi of the small intestine is related to its function.

....

....

....

.... [4 marks]

Functional foods

G–E

1 Yakult is a drink that contains the bacteria *Lactobacillus*. The makers of Yakult claim that drinking it improves the health of the digestive system.

   a Why is Yakult classed as a functional food?

   .... [1 mark]

   b What type of functional food is Yakult?

   .... [1 mark]

D–C

2 Another type of functional food is prebiotics.

   a Explain how these increase the amount of 'good' bacteria in the alimentary canal.

   ....

   ....

   .... [3 marks]

   b Why does an increase in 'good' bacteria improve the health of the alimentary canal?

   ....

   .... [2 marks]

3 The margarine Benecol has added plant stanols.

   a What are the claimed health benefits of this functional food?

   .... [1 mark]

   b How believable are these claims? Explain your answer.

   ....

   ....

   .... [2 marks]

B–A*

4 Brainactive cereal bars are a functional food containing plant omega-3, which is a type of fat that may enhance concentration and learning in children.

   A study was carried out where a class of Year 5 children ate a Brainactive cereal bar before school every day for a month. At the end of the month their teacher was asked if she saw an improvement in the learning of each child. The teacher said that 75% of the children had an improvement.

   Brainactive cereal bars used this as evidence to make the claim that eating their cereal bars enhances learning in children. Evaluate this claim.

   ....

   ....

   ....

   ....

   .... [4 marks]

B2 Extended response question

*Homeostasis is used to keep human temperature at around 37 °C. Explain why it is dangerous for our body temperature to go much higher. Use what you know about enzymes in your answer.

[6 marks]

Questions labelled with an **asterisk** (*) are ones where the quality of your written communication will be assessed. You should take particular care with your spelling, punctuation and grammar, as well as clarity of expression on these questions.

Removing wastes

G–E

1 Urea is a waste substance produced by cell metabolism.

  a In which organ is made?

  .... [1 mark]

  b In which organ is removed from the blood?

  .... [1 mark]

2 What is meant by the term **excretion**?

....

.... [2 marks]

D–C

3 Match the part of the urinary system to its function: [4 marks]

Part	Function
Ureter	Tube which carries urine from the bladder to outside the body
	Takes filtered blood away from the kidneys
Kidney	Removes excess water, urea and other waste products from the blood
	Stores urine
Urethra	A tube that takes urine from the kidney to the bladder
Bladder	Takes blood to the kidneys where it is filtered

B–A*

4 Describe the process of filtration that occurs in the kidney nephrons.

....

....

....

.... [3 marks]

5 Reabsorption that happens in the kidney nephrons is termed selective. Explain why:

....

....

....

.... [3 marks]

Helping the kidneys to function

1 Raj has been diagnosed with short-term kidney failure caused by a blocked ureter.

  a His doctor advises him to eat less protein. Why is this?

  ....

  .... **[2 marks]** G–E

  b He needs surgery to remove the blockage. Why is it important this happens as soon as possible?

  .... **[1 mark]**

2 Name one benefit and one drawback to the patient of using dialysis to treat their kidney failure.

....

....

....

.... **[2 marks]**

3 Why is the concentration of glucose in the dialysis fluid kept the same as that of the blood?

....

.... **[2 marks]**

4 A kidney transplant is a cure for long-term kidney failure, so why are there so many people with this on dialysis?

....

.... **[1 mark]**

5 Beth spends a hot afternoon playing tennis and forgets to drink very much. Why does the urine she produce that evening have a low volume?

....

.... **[2 marks]**

6 Explain how the release of ADH from the pituitary gland decreases the volume of urine. B–A*

....

....

....

.... **[4 marks]**

Controlling the menstrual cycle

G–E

1 Read through the stages of the menstrual cycle and place the letters in the boxes to show the correct order of events. The first one has been done for you.

A An egg is released from the ovary.

B Menstruation begins.

C The uterus lining starts the build-up.

D The uterus lining is soft and thick.

[3 marks]

```
        ┌───┐
      ↗ │ B │ ↘
┌───┐   └───┘   ┌───┐
│   │           │   │
└───┘           └───┘
      ↖ ┌───┐ ↙
        │   │
        └───┘
```

2 In which organ in the female reproductive system does:

a An egg-containing follicle mature?

.... [1 mark]

b The embryo develop?

.... [1 mark]

D–C

3 Study the diagram and answer the questions below.

a Which hormones are represented by A and B?

.... [2 marks]

b Which event in the menstrual cycle is triggered by low levels of **both** hormones?

.... [1 mark]

c Which event in the menstrual cycle occurs around day 14?

.... [1 mark]

4 A type of contraceptive pill contains high levels of progesterone. Explain how it works.

....

....

.... [3 marks]

B–A* **5** The increased use of FSH as a fertility drug has increased the number of multiple births. Explain why.

....

....

....

.... [4 marks]

Sex cells and fertilisation

1 Choose the correct words to fill the gaps in this paragraph:

The animal male sex cell is called sperm and the female sex cell is called an ....

Sex cells are also called .... Each sex cell contains one set of ....

material. The joining of the nuclei of the male and female sex cell is called .... **[4 marks]**

G–E

2 The body cell of a pig contains 38 chromosomes. How many chromosomes are found in a:

a Pig sperm cell?

.... **[1 mark]**

b Pig zygote?

.... **[1 mark]**

D–C

3 Explain the function of the acrosome in the sperm cell.

....

.... **[2 marks]**

4 Some couples go to a clinic for fertility treatment.

a The man in couple A is found to have a very low sperm count. Suggest two possible solutions which might enable the couple to have a baby.

....

.... **[2 marks]**

b The woman in couple B does not have a uterus, although she does have healthy ovaries. Explain how using IVF and a surrogate mother could be used to help the couple to have a child that carries their own genes.

....

....

....

....

....

.... **[4 marks]**

B–A*

Sex and sex-linked genetic disorders

1 Below is an image of the chromosome pairs from a person. Pair 23 is shown as XY.

  a What do we call pair 23?

  ....

  .... **[1 mark]**

  b Are these chromosomes from a man or a woman?

  .... **[1 mark]**

2 Use the letters X and Y to fill in the gaps in this paragraph:

  During meiosis, the egg cells produced all carry one .... chromosome. However, 50%

  of sperm carry one .... chromosome and 50% carry one .... chromosome. **[3 marks]**

3 Claire is 3 months pregnant. She already has four sons so she is sure that this baby is also
a boy. Use a genetic diagram to show her why there is a 50% probability that this baby is a girl.

[4 marks]

4 Study this pedigree diagram which shows the inheritance of haemophilia in a family.

■ = male with haemophilia

□ = male without haemophilia

● = female with haemophilia

○ = female without haemophilia

  a Couple D and E wish to have another child. Draw a genetic diagram to show the possible
genotypes of this child.

[4 marks]

  b What is the probability of their having another child with haemophilia?

  .... **[1 mark]**

5 Explain why it is rare for a woman to suffer from haemophilia.

....

....

.... **[4 marks]**

Immunisation

G–E

1 Edward Jenner (1743–1823) was a country doctor who noticed that milkmaids often got cowpox but rarely got smallpox. He believed that getting cowpox protected you against getting smallpox.

a What was Jenner's observation?

.... [1 mark]

b What was his theory?

.... [1 mark]

c What evidence did he collect which proved his theory?

....

.... [2 marks]

2 A mother is unsure about giving her child the whooping cough vaccination because she is worried about possible side-effects. State two advantages of giving her child the vaccine.

....

.... [2 marks]

3 From the list below, choose the correct labels for A and B on the diagram.

.... [2 marks]

Antibodies   **Antibiotics**   **Antigens**

bacteria   A   B

4 Name the white blood cell which:

a Produces antibodies when a new pathogen is encountered.

.... [1 mark]

b Ingests pathogens.

.... [1 mark]

c Produces antibodies if a pathogen infects the body for a second time.

.... [1 mark]

D–C

5 You can become naturally immune to a pathogen by being infected. How does a vaccine make you immune without giving you the illness?

....

....

.... [2 marks]

6 Antibodies specific to the invading pathogen are produced during the immune response. Describe and explain the difference between the primary and secondary immune response.

....

....

....

.... [4 marks]

B–A*

Monoclonal antibodies

1 Antibodies are specific. What does this mean?

.... [1 mark]

2 Study the diagram of antibodies below.
Does this represent monoclonal or polyclonal antibodies?
How do you know?

.... [2 marks]

antigen binding site

3 Why are cancer (myeloma) cells used in the production of monoclonal antibodies?

....

....

.... [3 marks]

4 Scientists produce a sample of an antigen found on the surface of red blood cells.
Describe the steps used to make monoclonal antibodies that bind to this antigen.

....

....

....

....

....

....

....

.... [5 marks]

5 Discuss the benefits of using monoclonal antibodies to treat cancer over radiotherapy.

....

....

....

....

.... [3 marks]

Microorganism growth and infection

1 A species of bacteria divides once every hour.

   a If we start with one bacterium, how many will there be after 3 hours?

   .... **[1 mark]** G–E

   b What do we call growth like this, where the population doubles?

   .... **[1 mark]**

2 A species of bacteria called E. coli normally lives inside your intestines. Scientists grew a sample of E. coli in some liquid broth which contains nutrients needed for the bacteria to grow. They incubated the mixture at 37 °C and measured the number of bacteria every 20 minutes for 5 hours.

   a They could use resazurin dye to measure the population. Describe how they could do this.

   ....

   .... **[2 marks]**

   b Their results are shown below. Explain the shape of the graph.

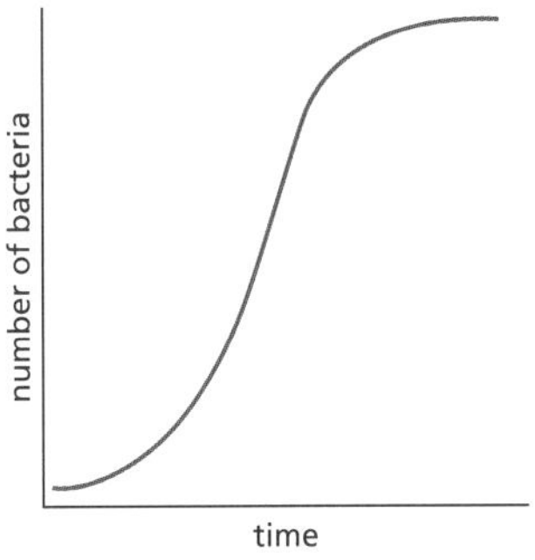

   ....

   ....

   ....

   ....

   .... **[2 marks]**

D–C

   c Add a line to the graph to predict the effect on growth of incubating the bacteria at 15 °C. **[2 marks]**

3 Chloe replicated some of Pasteur's experiments. She added some sterile nutrient broth to three different sterile glass flasks as shown below:

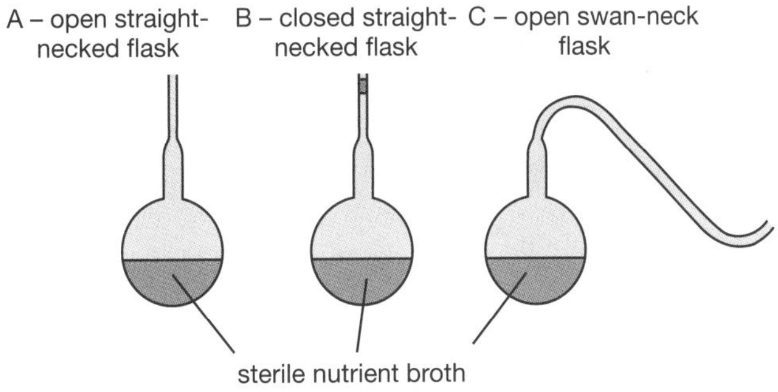

A – open straight-necked flask   B – closed straight-necked flask   C – open swan-neck flask

sterile nutrient broth

She left them all at room temperature for five days.

   a Explain why Chloe used sterile broth and flasks.

   ....

   .... **[2 marks]**

B–A*

   b Explain why the broth went cloudy in flask A but not in flasks B and C.

   ....

   ....

   .... **[3 marks]**

   c Chloe suggests that microorganism have got stuck in the bottom of the curve in the swan necked flask. Suggest how she could prove her hypothesis.

   ....

   .... **[2 marks]**

Plants, defences and food supply

1 There are many different types of pests that have an impact on human food supply.

a Draw lines to match the type of pest to the correct example.

Type of pest

| Herbivorous insect |

| Fungal disease |

| Insect that spreads disease |

| Weed |

Example

| Potato blight |

| Locust |

| Dandelion |

| Greenfly |

[3 marks]

b Slugs and snails feed on the leaves of carrots. Why does this affect the size of the carrots (which are the roots of the plant)?

....

....

....

[3 marks]

2 Acacia trees produce alkaloids in their leaves.

a How does this deter animals from eating them?

.... [1 mark]

b If a tree is being eaten it will release a gas to warn other nearby trees. The gas will diffuse away from the tree under attack. On detection of this gas, other trees will start to produce the alkaloid in their leaves. Explain how this mechanism allows the trees to conserve energy and resources.

....

....

....

....

[2 marks]

3 Explain why, in the past, chewing on willow bark was used to treat headaches.

....

....

[2 marks]

Rhythms of life

1 Study the diagram below and use it to answer the questions.

Name **one** environmental change on the forest floor that occurs predictably the same each year.

....

.... **[1 mark]**

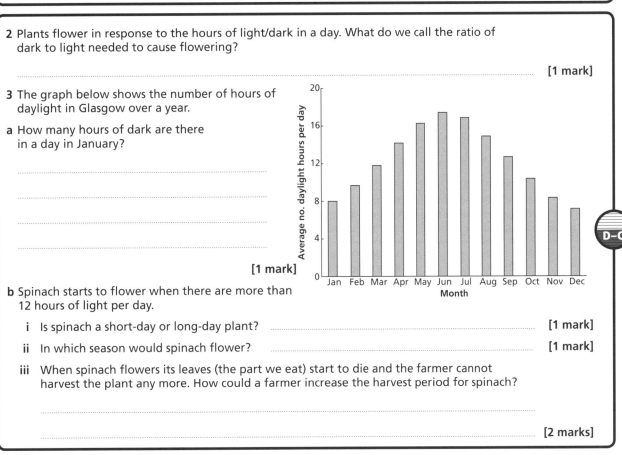

bluebell
wood anemone
violet
primrose
snowdrop
period of shade

J F M A M J J A S O N D

G–E

2 Plants flower in response to the hours of light/dark in a day. What do we call the ratio of dark to light needed to cause flowering?

.... **[1 mark]**

3 The graph below shows the number of hours of daylight in Glasgow over a year.

a How many hours of dark are there in a day in January?

....

....

....

.... **[1 mark]**

Average no. daylight hours per day

Month

D–C

b Spinach starts to flower when there are more than 12 hours of light per day.

　i　Is spinach a short-day or long-day plant? .... **[1 mark]**

　ii　In which season would spinach flower? .... **[1 mark]**

　iii　When spinach flowers its leaves (the part we eat) start to die and the farmer cannot harvest the plant any more. How could a farmer increase the harvest period for spinach?

....

.... **[2 marks]**

4 The production of many hormones and proteins follows a circadian rhythm.

　a What do we mean by a 'circadian rhythm'?

....

.... **[2 marks]**

　b Give another example of something controlled by a circadian rhythm in humans.

.... **[1 mark]**

5 Melatonin is a hormone produced by our bodies which controls how sleepy we feel.

　a Describe what this graph shows about its levels in the body over a 24-hour period.

....

....

....

.... **[3 marks]**

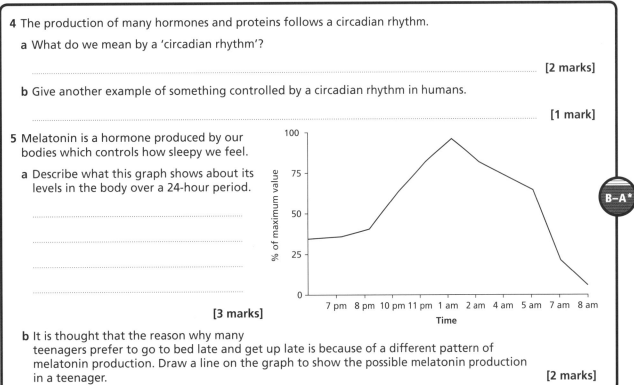

% of maximum value

7 pm 8 pm 10 pm 11 pm 1 am 2 am 4 am 5 am 7 am 8 am

Time

B–A*

　b It is thought that the reason why many teenagers prefer to go to bed late and get up late is because of a different pattern of melatonin production. Draw a line on the graph to show the possible melatonin production in a teenager. **[2 marks]**

Innate behaviour

1 Female turtles lay their eggs in nests on beaches and leave the eggs to hatch. The eggs hatch at night and as soon as the hatchlings emerge from the nests they head towards the sea.

a How do we know that the behaviour of the turtle hatchlings is innate?

.... [1 mark]

b How does this behaviour help the hatchlings to survive?

.... [1 mark]

c Scientists believe that the hatchlings know where the sea is because of the reflection of the moon on the surface. What stimulus are they responding to in their behaviour?

.... [1 mark]

2 Describe **one** innate behaviour displayed by a human newborn baby.

.... [1 mark]

3 Herring gull chicks peck at their parent's beaks. Explain how this innate behaviour helps them to survive.

.... [1 mark]

4 Niko Tinbergen carried out an experiment where he made wooden models of the head of an adult herring gull with different coloured spots on the beak. He displayed these to herring gull chicks and noted how many times the chicks pecked at the beaks. The results are shown below.

Colour of spot on model beak	Percentage of herring gull chicks responding to beak
None	30%
Blue	84%
White	70%
Red	100%
Black	85%

Use the data to decide whether the following statements are true or false:

a The chicks never pecked at the beak with no spot.

.... [1 mark]

b The data proves why herring gulls have red spots on their beak.

.... [1 mark]

c The data shows that herring gull chicks can distinguish between the colours black and blue.

.... [1 mark]

5 Triboliums are small beetles that can sometimes be found in packets of flour in kitchen cupboards.

Suzanne used a choice chamber to investigate the innate behaviour of triboliums. One half was kept dry and the other half was kept damp. She added 10 triboliums and left them for 10 minutes. Her results are shown below:

Conditions	Number of triboliums after 5 minutes	Number of triboliums after 10 minutes
Dry	6	9
Damp	4	1

a State **two** control variables that Suzanne should use in this investigation.

.... [2 marks]

b State what these results show about the behaviour of triboliums.

.... [1 mark]

c How could Suzanne make her results more reliable?

.... [1 mark]

Imprinting and habituation

1 Write the missing words into the paragraph below:

Ducklings and goslings follow the first moving thing that they see (usually their parent).

This is called .... It is a type of .... behaviour. This behaviour

will only develop during the .... period. It improves the chances of the young

animals to survive, because the parent protects them and supplies them with .... **[4 marks]**

G–E

2 Scarecrows are placed in fields to frighten birds away from the crops. The crows think the scarecrow is a real person. After being placed in the field for a while the birds are no longer scared.

a Name this type of behaviour.

.... **[1 mark]**

b Explain why this behaviour develops.

.... **[1 mark]**

3 20 small invertebrates called brine shrimps were added to a tank of water and left in a dark room for 5 minutes. Then, a light was shone at one end of the tank and the number of shrimp that swam to the light in a 5-minute period was recorded.

a Name this type of behaviour.

.... **[1 mark]**

b What is the stimulus the shrimps are responding to?

.... **[1 mark]**

D–C

c This experiment was repeated several times. The results are shown below:

Attempt	Number of shrimps that moved towards light
1	15
2	16
3	14
4	12
5	15

Do the shrimps show habituation? Explain your answer.

.... **[2 marks]**

4 Toby's dog reacts very excitedly and barks loudly when he hears the doorbell ringing because he knows that visitors are arriving. Explain how Toby can use habituation to train his dog not to react in this way.

....

....

....

.... **[3 marks]**

B–A*

Conditioning

1 Underline the examples of learned behaviour below. **[2 marks]**

  A A cat hissing when it meets another cat.

  B A dog sitting when told.

  C A lizard moving to the heat lamp when it is cold.

  D A rabbit moving towards its food bowl when it hears its owner opening the hutch door.

2 Dogs salivate when they smell or see food. Pavlov trained dogs to salivate when they heard a bell. No food had to be in the room for this to happen.

  a What do we call this type of conditioning?

  .... **[1 mark]**

  b What is the:

  i Primary stimulus?

  .... **[1 mark]**

  ii Secondary stimulus?

  .... **[1 mark]**

  c Outline how he could have trained the dogs to do this.

  ....

  .... **[2 marks]**

3 For each of these behaviours, state whether they are an example of classical or operant conditioning:

  a A sheep touches an electric fence and gets a shock. It does not touch the fence again.

  .... **[1 mark]**

  b A school class gets a reward when they are quiet for a whole lesson. They start to get quieter every lesson.

  .... **[1 mark]**

  c A dog who is afraid of thunder starts to get scared whenever grey clouds gather in the sky.

  .... **[1 mark]**

4 Describe how negative reinforcers can be used to train a police horse not to be startled by loud noises.

  ....

  ....

  ....

  .... **[4 marks]**

5 When training a dog it is best to use positive reinforcers. Give one example of what this could be.

  .... **[1 mark]**

Courtship and mating strategies

1 Define the term 'courtship behaviour'.

.... **[1 mark]**

2 Most species of animal have very distinct courtship behaviour that is only carried out by members of that species. Why is this important?

G–E

....

....

.... **[2 marks]**

3 Animals have different mating strategies. Puffins will breed with the same partner every year. Chimpanzees live in groups where the more dominant males will breed with many different females.

a Which animals mentioned above are polygamous?

.... **[1 mark]**

D–C

b How does this mating strategy ensure that only the 'best' genes get passed on to offspring?

....

....

.... **[3 marks]**

4 Robins will stay together during the breeding season after the eggs are hatched. The following year the male may breed with a different female.

a What do we call this bond between a male and a female during the breeding season?

.... **[1 mark]**

B–A*

b Explain how this strategy results in a high proportion of the offspring surviving to adulthood.

....

.... **[2 marks]**

c Are robins monogamous or polygamous? Explain your answer.

....

.... **[2 marks]**

5 Robins are very territorial. Explain why this is an evolutionary strategy.

....

....

.... **[3 marks]**

Parental care

1 Turtles and crocodiles are both reptiles but they display different parental care behaviour. A female green turtle will make a hole in the sand, lay her eggs into it, cover it and leave. Nile crocodiles will also bury their eggs in the sand but once the babies hatch the mother will open up the nest and help the young out of the eggs.

a Both animals cover the nests. Suggest the purpose of this parental care.

.... [1 mark]

b Which animal shows the lowest level of parental care? Explain your answer.

....

.... [2 marks]

c The female Nile crocodile will stay close to her young until they are bigger. State **two** ways that this helps them to reach adulthood.

....

.... [2 marks]

2 Parental care involves gathering food for the offspring and protecting them. Explain why this behaviour involves risks for the parent/s.

....

....

.... [2 marks]

3 Most species of fish lay hundreds of eggs at once, whereas most mammals will have only a few offspring at one time.

Explain, in terms of evolutionary strategy, why mammals show more parental care than fish.

....

....

....

.... [3 marks]

Animal communication

1 Animals communicate with one another. Study this image of a tiger.

a What emotion is the tiger showing?

.... [1 mark] G–E

b What event is most likely to cause the tiger to show this emotion?
Tick the correct box below: [1 mark]

He has spotted a potential mate ☐

Another male tiger has entered his territory ☐

Prey is nearby ☐

c What kind of communication is the tiger showing?

.... [1 mark]

d State another type of communication that the tiger may be giving at the same time.

.... [1 mark]

---

2 Chimpanzees live in groups. They use a variety of different sounds to communicate with each other.

a They use a loud, long 'wraa' call if they come across something dangerous. Explain why they make this sound.

.... [1 mark]

b They use a 'pant-hoot' to greet each other. Each chimp has its own distinct pant-hoot. Suggest why this is important.

.... [1 mark] D–C

c Explain why it is important that all chimps make the same sounds for each type of event.

....

.... [2 marks]

---

3 The female silk moth releases a chemical into the air which signals to males that she is ready to mate.

a What do we call this type of chemical?

.... [1 mark] B–A*

b The chemical diffuses away from the female moth. Explain how a male can accurately locate the position of the female.

....

.... [2 marks]

Plant communication and co-evolution

1 The flowers of some plants produce chemical scents which are attractive to bees. The chemical diffuses away from the plant into the air.

a What is the message sent as?

.... [1 mark]

b What is the sender?

.... [1 mark]

c What is the receiver?

.... [1 mark]

d Explain the advantage to the plant of this communication.

.... [2 marks]

2 When an acacia tree is being eaten by an animal it produces a gas which is released into the air. When another acacia tree detects this gas it produces toxic, bitter-tasting chemicals in its leaves.

a How does this communication help acacia trees?

....

.... [2 marks]

b The trees could just make the chemical all of the time. Explain why, in terms of the trees survival, they don't.

....

....

.... [3 marks]

3 Some species of plant are pollinated by hawkmoths. The moth hovers in front of the flower and inserts its long mouthpiece (proboscis) into a long tube on the flower, the bottom of which contains nectar. In doing so, pollen becomes attached to the moth's head.

a Describe how the moth and the plant both benefit from this.

....

.... [2 marks]

b Hawkmoths are nocturnal and are attracted by strong scents. Suggest **two** ways that flowers it pollinates are adapted to attract them.

....

.... [2 marks]

c Only the proboscis of the hawkmoth is able to reach the nectar at the bottom of the flower tube. Explain why this is an advantage to both plant and moth.

....

....

....

.... [4 marks]

4 The caterpillars of some species of hawkmoths are resistant to toxins found in the leaves of plants and are able to store them in their tissues. Explain how this adaptation is an advantage to the caterpillar.

....

....

....

.... [3 marks]

G–E

D–C

B–A*

Human evolution

1 Ethologist Jane Goodall was the first person to describe how chimpanzees used tools to find food.

How is this evidence that early humans probably also used tools?

.... [1 mark]

2 Describe how fossils provide evidence for how humans evolved.

....

.... [2 marks]

3 As our ancestors evolved, changes meant they became more human-like. Describe the changes seen in:

a Brain size

.... [1 mark]

b Stance when walking

.... [1 mark]

4 Brain tissue quickly decays after an organism dies.

a Explain why this means it rarely becomes fossilised.

....

.... [2 marks]

b Explain how scientists have evidence about the brain sizes of our ancestors.

....

.... [2 marks]

5 What does 'bipedalism' mean?

.... [1 mark]

6 Explain how climate change resulted in the evolution of bipedalism in our ancestors.

....

....

....

.... [4 marks]

Stone tool technology

1 State **one** way that our ancestors used simple stone tools.

.... [1 mark]

G–E

2 Describe why the stone tools our ancestors used got more complex over time.

....

.... [2 marks]

3 Match the description of the tool to the type of tool: [3 marks]

Description	Type
A pointed stone tool attached to a stick.	Acheulean
A small sharp flake of stone.	Mousterian
Large stone with many sharp edges.	Oldowan

4 Use the diagram to answer the following questions:

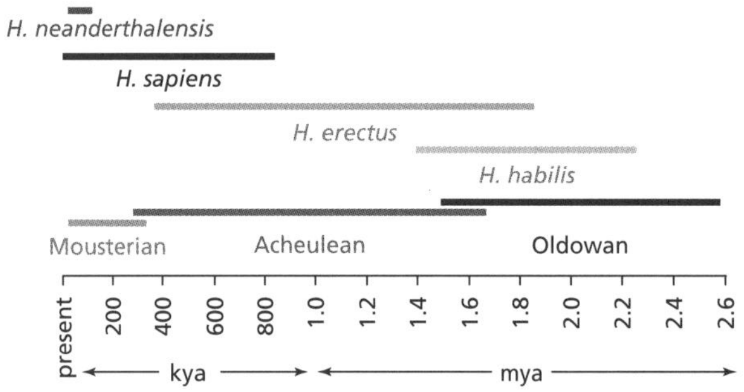

D–C

H. neanderthalensis

H. sapiens

H. erectus

H. habilis

Mousterian   Acheulean   Oldowan

present 200 400 600 800 1.0 1.2 1.4 1.6 1.8 2.0 2.2 2.4 2.6

←— kya —→ ←— mya —→

Which type of tool was used by:

a Early *Homo habilis* (2 mya)?

.... [1 mark]

b *Homo neanderthalensis*?

.... [1 mark]

c Both *Homo neanderthalensis* and *Homo sapiens*?

.... [1 mark]

5 The diagram below shows layers of rock found under the ground.

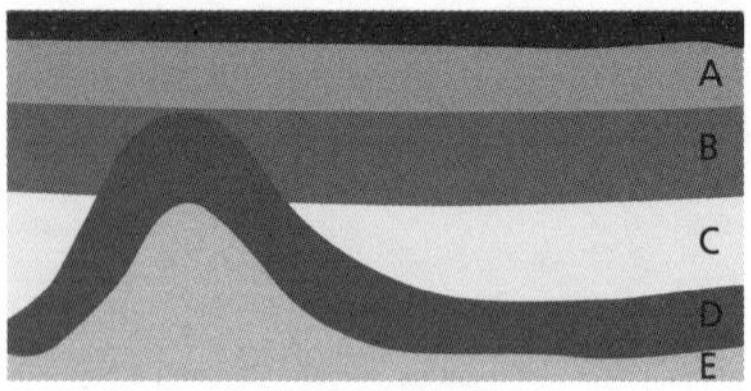

a Which layer holds the remains of the oldest tools? Explain your answer.

....

.... [2 marks]

B–A*

b The rock in layer B is cooled down lava. It has been dated to 20,000 years ago. What are the ages of the tools found in layer A?

.... [1 mark]

c What method is used to date rock?

.... [1 mark]

Human migration

1 Complete the sentence:

Around 85,000 years ago our ancestors started to migrate out of .... [1 mark] **G–E**

2 During an ice age sea water gets locked up as ice at the poles. Explain why human migration was more likely to happen during ice ages.

....

....

....

....

....
[3 marks]

3 Early humans spread out and migrated to different areas. Place these continents into order so they show places humans migrated to from earliest to most recent: **D–C**

Asia   Europe   South America   Africa

....
[1 mark]

4 Suggest **two** ways that humans had to adapt when they settled in new environments during migration.

....

....

....
[2 marks]

5 State **two** reasons why mitochondrial DNA is used instead of nuclear DNA to trace human ancestry.

....

....

....
[2 marks]

6 Explain how genetic markers in mtDNA have identified Africa as the place where *Homo sapiens* first lived.

....

....

....

....

....

....

....

....

....
[3 marks]

B–A*

Biotechnology

1 Biotechnology using living cells is used to make useful biomolecules.

a What is a biomolecule?

.... [1 mark]

b Circle the molecules below that are biomolecules:

Glucose   Polystyrene   Insulin   Nylon   [2 marks]

2 Microorganisms can be used to make foods.

Match the microorganism to the type of food it helps make.   [3 marks]

Microorganism	Food it helps to produce
Bacteria	Blue cheese
Yeast	Yogurt
Mould	Bread

3 For each description, state what plant-based drug is being described.

a Extracted from the bark of the Pacific yew tree, this drug is used to kill cancer cells.

.... [1 mark]

b A painkiller which contains salicylic acid, made from the liquid extracted from the leaves and bark of willow trees.

.... [1 mark]

c A drug used to treat malaria which is extracted from the *Cinchona* tree.

.... [1 mark]

4 Explain why producing artificial versions of plant-based drugs is important to biodiversity.

....

....

.... [3 marks]

5 Describe what is meant by 'side-effects' when discussing drugs.

.... [1 mark]

6 Many side-effects of cancer drugs are caused by the drug killing healthy cells. Explain one method that can be used to reduce this.

....

....

....

....

.... [3 marks]

Fermenters

1 Making wine at home is an example of small-scale fermentation. Read through the instructions on how to make wine and answer the questions below:

First, sterilise the demi-john and airlock using sterilising tablets and warm water. To the demi-john, add the grape juice and yeast. Put on the air lock and leave the demi-john in a warm place like near a radiator.

a Why is it important to sterilise the equipment used first?

....

.... [2 marks]

b Name the:

  i nutrient solution

  .... [1 mark]

  ii microorganism that carries out fermentation

  .... [1 mark]

  iii products of the fermentation reaction.

  .... [2 marks]

c Why should the mixture be kept in a warm place?

.... [1 mark]

G–E

2 Zenab investigated how temperature affected the rate of fermentation. She used the apparatus shown below:

a State **two** control factors she should use.

....

.... [2 marks]

b State her independent variable.

....

.... [1 mark]

liquid paraffin

yeast and glucose solution

limewater

c She decided to time how long it took for the limewater to go cloudy. Discuss how accurate her evidence would be.

....

.... [2 marks]

D–C

3 An industrial fermenter has a sparger. Explain its function.

....

....

.... [4 marks]

4 The fungus *Penicillium*, which produces the antibiotic penicillin, can be grown in a fermenter. The growth of one species of the fungi has an optimum pH of 2.8. Describe how this pH is maintained and why it is important to do so.

....

....

....

.... [4 marks]

B–A*

Eating microorganisms

1 For each underlined pair of words, cross out the incorrect word:

The commercial product Quorn is a good source of <u>protein/carbohydrate</u> made by the <u>bacteria/fungi</u> called <u>*Fusarium sp./Penicillium sp*</u>. **[3 marks]**

G–E

2 State **two** health benefits of eating mycoprotein.

....

....

.... **[2 marks]**

3 Discuss **two** advantages of using microorganisms for food rather than the farming of crops and animals.

....

....

....

....

.... **[2 marks]**

D–C

4 Explain how using continuous culture and pulp from fruit processing as a food source helps generate high profits when producing mycoprotein.

....

....

....

....

....

.... **[5 marks]**

B–A*

Making yogurt

1 What type of microorganism is used to make yogurt?

.... [1 mark]

2 This word equation shows the reaction involved in making yogurt. Write in the missing reactant:

.... → lactic acid [1 mark]

3 As milk turns into yogurt it gets thicker. Explain why this happens.

....

.... [2 marks]

4 Ashleigh carried out an investigation to see how the temperature milk was kept at affects yogurt production.

a Name two control variables she should use in this investigation.

....

.... [2 marks]

b She left each batch at different temperatures for 24 hours. Her results are shown below:

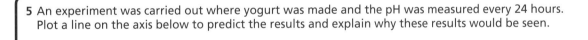

Temperature yogurt was left at (°C)	Time taken for ball to sink to the bottom of a measuring cylinder with 250 cm³ of yogurt (seconds)			
	1	2	3	Average
10	2	2	3	2
20	3	4	2	3
30	5	6	4	

i What is the dependent variable?

.... [1 mark]

ii Calculate the missing average time.

.... [1 mark]

iii Her teacher asks her to work out the optimum temperature for yogurt production.
Describe how she could improve her experiment to find the answer.

....

....

.... [3 marks]

5 An experiment was carried out where yogurt was made and the pH was measured every 24 hours. Plot a line on the axis below to predict the results and explain why these results would be seen.

....

.... [5 marks]

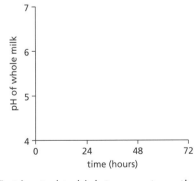

6 The milk used to make yogurt is first heated to high temperatures then left to cool, so it is warm when the starter culture is added. Explain the importance of these heating and cooling stages.

....

....

....

.... [4 marks]

G–E

D–C

B–A*

Using enzyme technology

G–E

1 Enzymes are a biological catalyst. What is a catalyst?

.... [1 mark]

2 Enzymes can be used in industry to allow reactions to happen at low temperatures. Why is this useful for manufacturers?

.... [2 marks]

D–C

3 Enzymes are used for a variety of industrial processes. Draw lines to match the name of the enzyme to its use in industry:

Enzyme	Use in industry
Invertase	Cheese making
Lipase	Added to biological washing powders
Chymosin	Making the soft centre in chocolates

[2 marks]

4 What is the difference between vegetarian and non-vegetarian cheese?

....

.... [2 marks]

B–A*

5 Why don't people who are lactose intolerant drink normal cow's milk?

....

....

....

.... [4 marks]

6 Describe how the process shown in the diagram produces lactose-free milk.

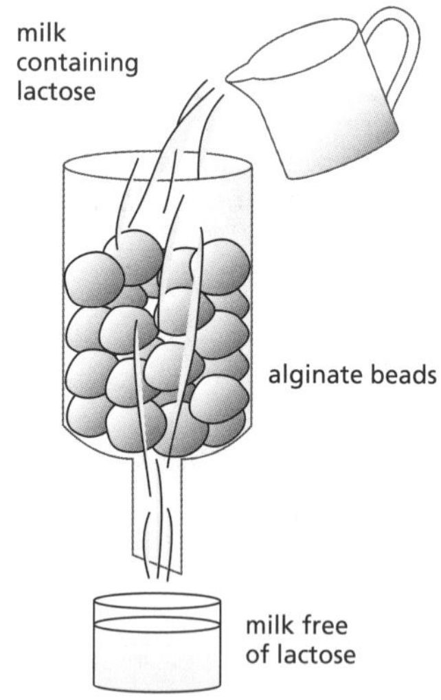

milk containing lactose

alginate beads

milk free of lactose

....

....

....

.... [3 marks]

Recombinant DNA technology

1 Choose suitable words to fill in the gaps in the following paragraph

.... are sections of .... which carry information enabling the cells

to synthesise ....

B–A*

[3 marks]

2 Bacteria can be genetically modified. Read through the information below about how this is done:
The human growth hormone gene is inserted into a bacterial plasmid. The plasmids are then
mixed with *E. coli* bacteria. Some take up the plasmid and are now able to make the human
growth hormone.

What is the:

a Vector?

.... [1 mark]

b Recombinant DNA?

.... [1 mark]

c Genetically engineered organism?

.... [1 mark]

3 Study the diagram below. It shows a plasmid being cut open ready for a human gene to be
inserted.

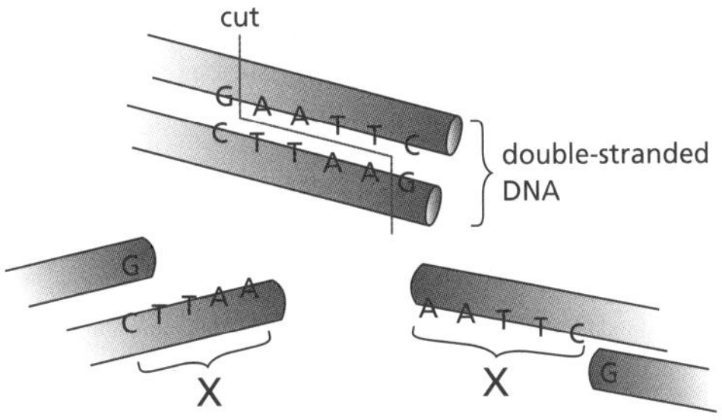

B–A*

Name:

a The type of enzyme used to make the cut in the DNA.

.... [1 mark]

b What we call the ends of the cut DNA, labelled X.

.... [1 mark]

4 Why is it important to use the same enzyme to cut out the human gene of interest?

....

....

.... [2 marks]

5 Outline the steps used to create genetically modified bacteria which can produce human insulin.

....

....

....

....

B–A*

....

....

....

.... [5 marks]

Producing transgenic plants

1 State **two** ways that crops can be genetically modified.

....

.... **[2 marks]**

2 Genetically modified crops are sometimes referred to as 'transgenic'.

What does this term mean?

....

.... **[1 mark]**

3 The gene for herbicide resistance is added to a Ti plasmid which is taken up by the bacteria *Agrobacterium tumefaciens*. Describe how this gene is transferred into the DNA of a plant.

....

....

....

....

....

.... **[5 marks]**

4 Transgenic corn can be produced which contains the gene for Bt insecticidal crystal protein (Bt ICP). Describe why farmers may choose to grow this corn rather than non-transgenic corn.

....

....

....

....

.... **[5 marks]**

5 State **one** disadvantage of growing Bt-modified crops.

....

....

.... **[1 mark]**

Food security and production

1 State **two** reasons why there might not be enough food for the world's human population in the future.

....

.... **[2 marks]**

G–E

2 Describe **one** advantage and one disadvantage of using chemical pesticides on crops.

....

....

.... **[3 marks]**

3 Choose **two** different varieties of wheat to breed together to produce a new variety with the highest yield and explain the reasoning behind your choice.

Wheat varieties:

A – Short, not much grain on each plant.

B – Tall, lots of grain on each plant.

C – Tall, not much grain on each plant.

D–C

....

....

....

....

....

.... **[4 marks]**

4 Study this graph, describe what it shows and state **one** explanation for this.

B–A*

....

....

....

....

....

....

....

.... **[3 marks]**

Biofuels

1 Define the terms:

a Biomass

....
[1 mark]

b Biofuel

....
[1 mark]

2 Identify **one** example of a biofuel made by fermentation and state the raw materials used in its manufacture.

....
[2 marks]

3 Compare and contrast the use of fossil fuels and biofuels in terms of:

a Pollution

....

....

....

....
[4 marks]

b Sustainability

....

....

....

....
[4 marks]

4 Explain why producing more biofuels could lead to a decrease in global food production.

....

....
[2 marks]

5 Study this diagram, which shows the production of ethanol-based fuel.

State events in the production of ethanol-based fuel which result in:

a An increase in atmospheric carbon dioxide.

....

....

....
[3 marks]

b A decrease in atmospheric carbon dioxide.

....
[1 mark]

6 Explain why some scientists are disputing the claim that ethanol-based fuels are carbon neutral.

....

....
[1 mark]

B3 Extended response question

*Evaluate the use of growing more genetically modified (transgenic) crops as a way of increasing global food production.

[6 marks]

Questions labelled with an **asterisk** (*) are ones where the quality of your written communication will be assessed. You should take particular care with your spelling, punctuation and grammar, as well as clarity of expression on these questions.

I can describe how organisms are classified into groups according to the characteristics they have in common.	
I know what the term 'species' means and can explain and state the limitations of this definition.	
I can construct keys that show how species can be identified.	
I know that Charles Darwin was the first (with Alfred Russel Wallace) to explain that natural selection is the mechanism of evolution.	
I understand that variation can be caused by genes or the environment.	
I know that the cell's nucleus contains chromosomes on which genes are located, and understand how forms of genes called alleles lead to differences in inherited characteristics.	
I know that genetic disorders can be caused by changes in genes (mutations).	
I know that homeostasis means maintenance of a stable internal environment, and that examples include maintaining the right body temperature and amount of water in the body.	
I know that the central nervous system consists of the brain and spinal cord, and that nervous responses can be voluntary or involuntary.	
I know that hormones are produced in endocrine glands and transported in the blood to their target organs.	
I know that lack of insulin causes Type 1 diabetes and resistance to insulin causes Type 2.	
I know that plants use hormones to respond to stimuli such as light and gravity.	
I know what a drug is and can describe how stimulants, depressants, painkillers and hallucinogens affect the brain.	
I know the effects of some chemicals in cigarette smoke.	
I know the harmful effects of alcohol abuse.	
I know that organs can be transplanted.	
I know that infectious diseases are caused by pathogens, including those in animal vectors.	
I know that antiseptics help to prevent the spread of infection.	
I know how energy is transferred along food chains and between trophic levels.	
I can describe the sources of pollution, including sulfur dioxide, and nitrates and phosphates.	
I know that decomposers recycle dead organic matter.	
I am working at grades G/F/E	

I can describe the characteristics of the five kingdoms and the hierarchy of classification, from kingdom to species.	
I can explain why scientists use the binomial system to name and identify species.	
I know that the individuals of a species vary, and this variation can be continuous or discontinuous.	
I can describe how and why organisms are adapted to their environment, including extreme environments such as polar regions.	
I can explain Darwin's theory of natural selection in terms of variation, overproduction, competition, survival, inheritance and gradual change.	
I can explain the meanings of different genetic terms, e.g. dominant, recessive, homozygous, heterozygous, phenotype, genotype.	
I can interpret monohybrid inheritance using Punnett squares, genetic diagrams and family pedigrees.	
I can describe the symptoms of sickle cell disease and cystic fibrosis.	
I can explain how body temperature and body water content are regulated.	
I can explain how blood glucose levels are regulated by insulin.	
I can explain how insulin injections control Type 1 diabetes and that diet and exercise help to control Type 2 diabetes.	
I can explain how hormones bring about plant responses and use data to support explanations.	
I can describe how drug abuse can lead to drug addiction.	
I can explain the effects of some chemicals in cigarette smoke.	
I can evaluate some of the harmful effects of alcohol abuse.	
I can describe how the demand for organs can be supplied.	
I can describe how different pathogens are spread.	
I can explain how animals and plants are able to defend themselves against pathogens by physical and chemical means.	
I understand that antibiotics are used to treat and control infections.	
I understand why living things are interdependent, giving mutualism and parasitism as examples.	
I can explain and apply understanding to the transfer of energy along food chains and between trophic levels in a pyramid of biomass.	
I can explain how the increase in human population has an impact on the environment and how the impact can be reduced by recycling.	
I can explain the processes of eutrophication and acid rain formation.	
I can explain how scientists can use indicator species to assess the impact of these phenomena.	
I understand how carbon is recycled.	
I am working at grades D/C	

I understand the issues surrounding the classification of viruses and vertebrates and can explain that most classifications reflect the relatedness.	
I can apply understanding of binomial classification to the conservation of species.	
I can explain how variations such as hybridisation and ring species complicate classification.	
I can apply understanding of adaptations to organisms near hydrothermal vents.	
I can explain how speciation occurs as a result of geographic isolation.	
I can explain how genetics, including DNA evidence and bacterial resistance, can be used to support Darwin's theory.	
I can analyse patterns of monohybrid inheritance, and calculate and analyse the outcomes of the crosses.	
I can evaluate pedigree analysis when screening for sickle cell disease and cystic fibrosis.	
I can explain how vasoconstriction and vasodilation are used in negative feedback during thermoregulation.	
I can describe the function of dendrons and axons, and explain how different components work together to bring about a reflex action.	
I can apply understanding of the effect of insulin to the role of glucagon regulating blood glucose levels.	
I can evaluate the correlation between obesity (including BMI calculations) and Type 2 diabetes.	
I understand the usefulness of plant hormones as weedkillers and substances that improve the growth of crop plants.	
I understand that drugs that affect the nervous system mostly have their effect at the synapse.	
I can evaluate data that establishes the correlation between smoking and ill-health.	
I can evaluate some of the harmful effects of alcohol abuse.	
I can discuss the ethical issues of organ transplants.	
I understand that antibacterials produced by plants may be useful to humans.	
I can evaluate evidence that resistant strains of pathogenic bacteria (including MRSA) can arise from the misuse of antibiotics.	
I can apply understanding to include mutualism in nitrogen-fixing bacteria in legumes and chemosynthetic bacteria in tube worms.	
I can explain and use data to show how the increase in human population has an impact on the environment and how the impact can be reduced by recycling.	
I can apply understanding of indicator species.	
I understand how nitrogen is recycled.	
I am working at grades B/A/A*.	

B2 Grade booster checklist

I know why light microscopes and electron microscopes are useful when studying cells.	
I can name the main components in plant and animal cells.	
I know what a gene is and can describe the basic structure of DNA.	
I know that the work of scientists Watson, Crick, Franklin and Wilkins helped discover the structure of DNA.	
I understand what we mean by genetic engineering.	
I can state some uses of genetically modified (GM) crops and know some issues associated with them.	
I know that mitosis results in two daughter cells identical to the parent cell, and that it is used for growth, repair and asexual reproduction.	
I can describe how plants are cloned by using cuttings and how embryo transplants are used.	
I know that stem cells in the embryo can differentiate into all other types of cell.	
I understand that each protein has its own specific sequence of amino acids, resulting in different-shaped molecules and that the order of bases in a gene decides the order of amino acids in a protein.	
I can explain what a mutation is.	
I know that enzymes are biological catalysts and can state what conditions affect their activity.	
I know the word equations for aerobic and anaerobic respiration.	
I know the meanings of the words diffusion and osmosis.	
I can explain why heart and breathing rate increase with exercise	
I know the word equation for photosynthesis and the conditions that affect its rate.	
I can describe how water, glucose and mineral salts are transported through a plant via the xylem, phloem and roots.	
I can describe how fieldwork techniques are used to investigate the distribution of organisms in an ecosystem.	
I understand that fossils are evidence for evolution.	
I know that growth is an increase in size, length and mass that occurs through cell division.	
I know the components in blood.	
I can name the four chambers of the heart and the four major blood vessels associated with it.	
I can name the parts of the digestive system and know the function of digestive enzymes.	
I know what a functional food is.	
I am working at grades G/F/E	

I can carry out simple magnification calculations.	
I can describe the functions of each cell component.	
I can describe the structure of DNA.	
I can evaluate the roles of Watson, Crick, Franklin and Wilkins in the discovery of the structure of DNA.	
I can describe the stages of the genetic-engineering technique.	
I can discuss the advantages and disadvantages of golden rice.	
I can describe simply how mitosis results in two diploid daughter cells and how meiosis results in four haploid daughter cells.	
I can describe how plants are cloned by using cuttings.	
I can discuss the advantages, disadvantages and risks of cloning mammals.	
I can describe how stem-cell therapy can be used.	
I can describe why the order of the bases in a gene decides the shape and function of a protein.	
I can describe how a mutation can be harmful, beneficial or neither.	
I can use the 'lock and key' hypothesis to describe how enzymes work.	
I can explain why a change in conditions will affect the activity of an enzyme.	
I can describe why muscles may start to respire anaerobically and state what EPOC is.	
I can describe how the movement of oxygen and glucose in the body is facilitated by diffusion.	
I can explain why heart and breathing rate increase with exercise.	
I can describe how the structure of a leaf is adapted for photosynthesis.	
I can describe how root hair cells are adapted to take up water by osmosis and explain why transpiration is important in the movement of water and mineral salts.	
I can describe simply the process of active transport.	
I can describe how fieldwork techniques are used to investigate the distribution of organisms in an ecosystem.	
I can explain why there are gaps in the fossil record.	
I can describe how growth and development happens in both plants and animals.	
I can describe the function of the components in blood.	
I can describe how the circulatory system transports substances around the body.	
I can describe how food is moved along the alimentary canal by peristalsis and evaluate Visking tubing as a model of the small intestine.	
I can describe some examples of functional foods.	
I am working at grades D/C	

I can explain why the development of modern microscopes has enabled us to see cells with more clarity and detail.	
I can explain the role of mitochondria and chloroplasts.	
I can explain what we mean by complementary base pairing.	
I can evaluate the implications of the Human Genome Project.	
I can evaluate the advantages and disadvantages of using bacteria to produce human insulin.	
I can evaluate the use of herbicide-resistant crops.	
I can explain in detail the process of mitosis and meiosis to include what happens to the chromosomes.	
I can describe how plants are cloned by using cuttings.	
I can explain each stage of the production of a cloned mammal.	
I can evaluate the use of stem-cell therapy.	
I can explain what happens in each stage of protein synthesis.	
I can explain the role of enzymes in DNA replication and protein synthesis.	
I can explain why a change in conditions will affect the activity of an enzyme.	
I can apply the term 'concentration gradient' to explain diffusion.	
I can calculate heart rate, stroke volume and cardiac output.	
I can explain how limiting factors affect the growth of a plant.	
I can explain why transpiration is important in the movement of water and mineral salts.	
I can explain how active transport is used in the absorption of mineral salts through the roots.	
I can explain how to reduce errors when using sampling techniques.	
I can explain how the pentadactyl limb provides evidence for evolution.	
I can interpret growth by using percentile charts.	
I can explain how the heart pumps blood.	
I can explain the role of the gall bladder in digestion and how the structure of villi allows efficient absorption of products from digestion into the blood.	
I can evaluate Visking tubing as a model of the small intestine.	
I can evaluate the evidence for the claimed benefits of the use of functional foods.	
I am working at grades B/A/A*.	

B3 Grade booster checklist

I can state that cells produce wastes including carbon dioxide and urea.	
I know that urea is produced from the breakdown of excess amino acids in the liver.	
I know that wastes are removed from the blood by the kidneys and released from the body as urine.	
I can describe what kidney failure is and identify its symptoms.	
I know that the menstrual cycle is controlled by the hormones oestrogen and progesterone.	
I can describe the stages in the menstrual cycle.	
I can explain how sperm and eggs are adapted to their functions.	
I know that the sex of a person is controlled by one pair of chromosomes, XX in a female and XY in a male.	
I can describe how the work of Edward Jenner contributed to the development of vaccines.	
I can describe the risks and advantages of immunisation.	
I know the role of antibodies.	
I can describe the growth of bacterial populations.	
I know that plants defend themselves from attack by pests and pathogens.	
I can describe how pests and pathogens impact on human food supply.	
I know that life's processes are often cyclical.	
I know what we mean by behaviour and can describe different types of behaviour: innate, courtship, habituation, imprinting, conditioning.	
I can describe types of parental care and identify a link between mating strategy and parental care.	
I can define the term 'communication' and describe the different signals used for communication.	
I know that plants can communicate with animals and other plants.	
I can describe the social behaviour of chimpanzees and gorillas as a basis for understanding human behaviour.	
I can describe the fossil evidence for human evolution.	
I can define the terms biotechnology, small-scale fermentation and mycoprotein.	
I can describe how yogurt is made.	
I know that enzymes are used as catalysts in several industries.	
I know that genes can be transferred from cells of one species into the cells of another.	
I understand the costs and benefits of GM crop plants to producing food.	
I can define food security.	
I can describe what biofuels are.	
I am working at grades G/F/E	

I can describe the structure of the urinary system.	
I can explain the possible treatments of kidney failure, including kidney transplants and dialysis.	
I can explain the events of the menstrual cycle, including ovulation and changes in the thickness of the uterus lining.	
I can explain that egg and sperm cells are haploid and that fertilisation restores the diploid state.	
I can explain how the sex of offspring is determined at fertilisation, using a genetic diagram.	
I can explain the process of immunisation and the function of antibodies.	
I can explain how microorganisms (bacteria) can be cultured in different growing media.	
I can explain that different factors affect the growth of bacterial populations.	
I can describe the ways in which plants use chemicals to defend themselves from attack.	
I can describe the importance of photoperiodicity in plants.	
I can explain different types of behaviour: innate, courtship, habituation, imprinting, conditioning.	
I can describe how the work of different ethologists helps to explain different types of behaviour.	
I can explain that animals have different mating strategies that may (or may not) include parental care.	
I can describe the costs and benefits of parental care.	
I can explain how animals use sound to communicate and how plants communicate with one another using chemicals.	
I can describe and explain the fossil evidence for human evolution.	
I can describe how stone tools developed over time and understand how stone tools can provide evidence for human evolution.	
I can explain the impact of climate change on human migration.	
I can describe how some biomolecules are useful as drugs to treat cancer and relieve pain.	
I can describe how mycoprotein is produced and understand the advantages of using microorganisms in food production and mycoprotein as a food source.	
I can describe and investigate the factors that affect the production of yogurt.	
I can describe how enzyme technology is used to produce cheese, soft-centred sweets and biological washing powders.	
I can explain how *Agrobacterium tumefaciens* is used as a vector to produce transgenic plants.	
I can explain how food production can be increased to improve food security.	
I can discuss why biofuels are being developed and used in some countries.	
I am working at grades D/C	

I can describe the structure of the nephron and how this relates to its functions of filtration and forming urine (osmoregulation).	
I can explain how antidiuretic hormone (ADH) regulates the water content of the blood.	
I understand that production of ADH is controlled by a negative feedback mechanism.	
I can explain how the menstrual cycle is controlled by the hormones oestrogen, progesterone, FSH and LH, and a negative feedback mechanism.	
I understand the advantages and disadvantages of infertility treatments.	
I can explain, using probabilities, percentages and ratios, how sex-linked disorders are inherited.	
I can describe the role of memory lymphocytes.	
I can explain the production of monoclonal antibodies and how they are used.	
I can describe the contributions of Louis Pasteur to the development of aseptic techniques.	
I can explain that some of the chemicals plants produce to defend themselves can be used to treat diseases or their symptoms.	
I can explain that some of the rhythmic processes in living organisms are circadian.	
I can explain a range of mating strategies and explain parental care as an evolutionary strategy.	
I can explain how animals use pheromones to communicate.	
I understand how plants and animals have co-evolved.	
I can analyse the link between bipedalism and brain size.	
I can explain how stone tools can be dated from the environment, including radiometric dating.	
I can explain how mitochondrial DNA provides evidence for African Eve and analyse the advantages of using mitochondrial DNA to track human migration and evolution.	
I can explain that producing biomolecules is an example of using science in the service of medicine.	
I can explain the conditions used in industrial fermenters.	
I can explain the bacterial fermentations that are the basis of yogurt making.	
I can explain the advantages of using immobilised enzymes on an industrial scale.	
I can explain recombinant DNA technology and its application in producing insulin and insect-resistant plants.	
I can evaluate the advantages and disadvantages of Bt-modified crops.	
I can evaluate evidence that continuing growth of the human population undermines strategies to achieve food security.	
I can evaluate the advantages and disadvantages of using biofuels.	
I am working at grades B/A/A*	

Answers

B1 Influences on life

Page 92 Classification and naming species

1 a i amphibian ii mammal iii fish iv bird v reptile

   b It is not a vertebrate/it is an invertebrate (it has no backbone)

2 They are cold-blooded (poikilotherms); so need the warmth of the Sun to keep their internal body at the right temperature

3 a They are able to make their food (by photosynthesis)

   b Chlorophyll; a cell wall made of cellulose

4 They are made up of both fungi and protoctists; so cannot be classified in one kingdom

5 It has a backbone so would be a vertebrate; but would be difficult to classify into a group because it has characteristics of both birds; and reptiles

6 a Organisms that are capable of breeding together to produce fertile offspring

   b Hybrids

7 a *Rattus*

   b *Rattus exulans*

8 They need to be sure that the spiders are of different species; as the biodiversity can only be reported as high if the area contains a number of different species

Page 93 Identification, variation and adaptation

1 To identify the types of organism they find

2 a Any two from: height; colour of leaves; length of roots; number of branches, etc.

   b i continuous

      ii discontinuous

      iii continuous

   c A line graph to display the hand-span data; because it is continuous; a bar chart to display the eye-colour data; because it is discontinuous

3 The birds live in a geographically close area; the birds in the ring will be able to interbreed but the two species at either end cannot

4 a Able to survive for long periods without food or water

   b Stops them sinking into the sand

   c Stops sand entering the nostrils

   d They have a small surface area relative to their mass; so they do not lose very much body heat from their surface

   e The hairs are full of air; which is a poor conductor of heat (good insulator); so prevents the heat energy from the caribou escaping

5 They would share some characteristics because they belong to the same phylum; but they would differ because they live in very different places; and would have different adaptations to survive in their environment

Page 94 Evolution

1 a Because they are adapted to live in different environments

   b i Food / shelter / mate

      ii They have died out / are no longer living

      iii They were not able to catch prey / they were killed by predators / died of disease

   c Those with dark skin are not well camouflaged; so they will not survive; because they will be spotted by their prey

   d Snakes showed variation – some had rattles and some didn't; the snakes that had rattles were able to scare off predators and not get eaten (better adapted) so they survived and reproduced; the genes for the rattle were passed on to their offspring; the snakes that did not have a rattle were eaten and so did not reproduce

2 a Any two from: there may be predators on Anguilla which they have no survival instincts against; there may not be suitable food on Anguilla; the climate may not be suitable

   b Variation will exist in the population; those with the advantageous characteristics will survive and reproduce; over time the changes in the iguana will be so great that they will become different enough to those on the Virgin Islands to be classed as a new species

Page 95 Genes and variation

1 a Inherited

   b Environmental

   c Inherited

2 a DNA

   b Genes

   c Chromosomes

3 He has probably inherited the tallness gene; from both parents

4 As their DNA is so similar; they must have a common ancestor; which shows that they both evolved over time from this animal

5 a She inherited one from her mother and one from her father

   b Heterozygous

6 a Grey fur

   b Grey

   c Because the babies have inherited alleles from each parent, each baby must carry the allele for white fur; but its effect is hidden by the allele for grey

7 a They are brother and sister

   b The father (Chris) inherited the allele from his father (Robert); Holly inherited the allele from Chris; as the allele is hidden in Chris it is probably recessive

Page 96 Monohybrid inheritance

1 a The allele for red flowers

   b A mixture of red and white flowers

2 He was not a scientist (he was a priest) / he did not publish his findings

3 a Any two upper-case letters, e.g. AA

   b Any two lower-case letters, e.g. aa

   c Any upper-case letter and its corresponding lower-case letter, e.g. Aa

4

Cross: Rr × rr		
Parental gametes	R	r
r	Rr	rr
r	Rr	rr

5 a 1 in 2 (50%)

  b 1 in 2 (50%)

  c 1 in 2 (50%)

  d 0 (0%)

  e 1 in 2 (50%)

6 a

Cross: Rr × Rr		
Parental gametes	R	r
R	RR	Rr
r	Rr	rr

  b 1 in 4 (25%)

Page 97 Genetic disorders

1 a A change in the DNA/a gene

  b The mutation will be passed to the children during fertilisation (mutated sperm fuses with an egg)

2 a An illness that is inherited

  b Any two from: blocked airways of the lungs, which makes breathing difficult; lung infections because of bacteria becoming trapped in the mucus; problems digesting food, which can lead to malnutrition

  c The sickle-shaped cells cause a blockage in a blood vessel; that leads to an organ; which starves the organ of oxygen (and nutrients)

3 a To predict the risk of someone inheriting a particular disorder

  b I-1, I-2, II-1, II-2

  c

Cross: Aa × Aa		
Parental gametes	A	a
A	AA	Aa
a	Aa	aa

  d 1 in 2 (50%)

Page 98 Homeostasis and body temperature

1 Any two from: temperature; water content of blood; glucose content of blood; ion (salt) content in blood

2 a There will be an increased amount of water in the blood

  b They will produce more urine

  c Her brain detects an increase in water in blood and sends a message via hormones to the kidneys; the kidneys produce more urine

  d Because the body does it automatically

  e The kidneys would have produced less urine; her blood water content would have increased

3 a 37 °C

  b Muscles under the skin start moving (contracting and relaxing) and produce heat

  c The thermoregulatory centre in the brain; detects when his temperature has risen back up to 37 °C; and sends responses to the muscles to stop contracting and relaxing

  d Any four from: the thermoregulatory centre in the brain; detects when his temperature has fallen below 37 °C; sends responses to the walls of blood vessels under the skin; stimulating contraction of the muscles so they narrow (constrict); this results in the flow of blood through the skin being reduced; therefore less heat is lost through the surface of the skin

Page 99 Senses and the nervous system

1 a Brain; spinal cord

  b Any two from: skin; eye; ear; tongue; nose

  c As electrical impulses; along nerves (neurons)

2 a **i** Skin **ii** Eye **iii** Ear **iv** Nose / tongue

  b They contain more touch receptors than any other part

3 a Retina

  b Impulses; travel along the optic nerve

4 a Diagram A **b** Motor neurone

Page 100 Responses and coordination

1 a Involuntary **b** Involuntary **c** Voluntary

2 Blinking stops the eye being damaged / pulling hand away from hot pan stops skin being burnt

3 Chemicals (neurotransmitters) are released into the gap; they travel across it and stimulate an impulse in the next neurone

4 a Nerve impulses have less distance to travel

  b To bring about a quick response; and minimise damage to the body

5 Receptors in the skin detect pain and an impulse is sent along a sensory neurone to the spinal cord; the impulse travels across the synapse to the relay neurone; the impulse travels across the synapse to the motor neurone; the impulse travels along the motor neurone to the arm muscle; the muscle contracts, pulling hand away

Page 101 Hormones and diabetes

1 a Testosterone

  b Testes

  c In the bloodstream

2 a Insulin

  b To bring the amount of glucose in the blood back down to normal

3 a 30 minutes / 360 minutes

  b Between 210 minutes; and 300 minutes

  c The contracting muscles took glucose from the blood; to provide energy

  d Insulin; was released by the pancreas into the bloodstream; which converted glucose into glycogen

  e Glucagon

Answers

4 a Insulin

  b Type 1 diabetes

  c Daily insulin injections

  d Her blood glucose levels would become high; which can result in serious health problems

  e She inherited a mutated gene; from one of her parents

Page 102 Plant hormones

1 a Positive

  b Negative

2 a Maximises the rate of photosynthesis in the leaves

  b To firmly anchor the plant into the ground so it doesn't fall over / to enable roots to absorb water

3 a Side A

  b Phototropism

  c Side B

  d The high concentration of auxin on side B; will cause the cells here to elongate more than the cells on side A; which makes the shoot bend towards the light

4 a To stimulate the growth of roots on the cuttings

  b To produce large numbers of new plants quickly; because the new plants are identical to the parent plants, growers can make sure that desirable qualities of the parent are kept in the new plants

5 a It affects the growth of plants

  b The higher the concentration, the taller the plant

Page 103 Drugs, smoking and alcohol abuse

1 a Depressant

  b Stimulant

  c Painkiller

  d Hallucinogen

  e Stimulant

2 a They crave the short-term effects of the drug (a sense of well-being); their body becomes used to the changes so they become dependent on the drug

  b Heroin is an illegal drug so is only available through drug dealers, who charge a lot of money for the drug; addicts may turn to crime to get money to pay for it

3 a They got quicker

  b Caffeine is a stimulant; so it increases the activity of the brain by enhancing the release of neurotransmitters

4 a Tar

  b Nicotine

5 They have tar in their lungs; they are coughing to try and remove it

6 a Any one from: lowered inhibitions; slowed reaction times; blurred vision; difficulty controlling the arms and legs

  b Eight units

  c The safe daily amount of alcohol to drink per day is four units; Paul has drunk more than this and so if he does it often he is at risk of developing an illness (e.g. liver cirrhosis, brain damage, heart disease, cancer, raised blood pressure)

7 a Any one from: treatment became better; living conditions improved; disease transmission slowed; better diagnosis

  b More people were smoking tobacco

  c They could have been another reason why cases of lung cancer rose (e.g. more pollution from cars) so the data does not directly link smoking with lung cancer

Page 104 Ethics of transplants

1 a She needs a kidney from a donor to be put into her body

  b As she is related to Maria, there is less chance of Maria rejecting her kidney

2 Because lungs can only be donated by someone who is dead

3 Any two from: there is an increased risk of transplanting diseased organs into recipients because poor donors do not receive regular health care; the deal exploits poor people and violates their human rights; it encourages people to enter into an illegal activity

4 a They are about the same size

  b The animal organ will probably be rejected by the human body

  c Genetic modification

  d Animal cruelty

5 There is a lack of organs available for transplant

6 Answer should include a discussion of the following: the age of the recipient; the cause of their illness; how healthy their lifestyle is

Page 105 Infectious diseases

1 a Pathogen

  b It can be spread from person to person

  c The lungs have ideal conditions for bacteria growth / lungs are warm and moist

2 a Cold / flu

  b *Salmonella*

  c Cholera

3 The bacteria produce endotoxins (poisons); which stimulate the small intestine wall to contract violently and more frequently than normal; absorption of digested food and water is prevented; as a result, the victim quickly dehydrates

4 a An animal that spreads pathogens

  b An (*Anopheles*) mosquito bites the infected person and sucks up the pathogen that causes malaria; before biting another person and transferring the pathogen into their blood; which then causes them to develop malaria

5 The cream will stop any microbes around the cut from multiplying; to stop the cut becoming infected

6 Colds are caused by viruses; antibiotics only control infection by bacteria

7 a MRSA cannot be treated with most antibiotics; so the patients could get an infection which cannot be treated and this could lead to health problems

  b Some bacteria contain resistance genes; these individuals survive antibiotic treatments; they reproduce and spread quickly

Answers

Page 106 Defences and interdependency

1 To stop blood loss; to prevent pathogens from entering the body

2 a Eyes (tears)

b (Glands in the) skin

c (Glands in the) stomach

3 They do not have as many white blood cells to destroy pathogens; so the pathogens will be able to multiply in the body

4 Plants may be found that have antibacterial properties; we need new antibacterial chemicals because many of the ones we are using today are no longer effective against bacteria

5 a Parasitism; because the aphids are removing the plants' food, which damages them and the plant gets nothing in return

b Mutualism; because both the ants and aphids get something useful out of the relationship

6 a The nitrogen-fixing bacteria live in its root nodules and convert nitrogen in the air into nitrogen-containing compounds; that the bean plant uses to make proteins; the plant produces sugars, which the bacteria need as a food source

b The bean plant uses the corn plant to grow up so it can reach the light; the leaves of the bean plant are prickly, which deters animals from eating the bean and the corn plant / the squash leaves cover the ground to stop weeds growing around the bean/corn plant and competing for water/minerals

Page 107 Energy, biomass and population pressures

1 a i Seaweed

ii Limpet / octopus / seal

b It only eats plants

c Predator; octopus

d Scavenger

2 a Consumers usually eat more than one type of food; only food webs represent this, as in a food chain consumers just eat one type of food

b Energy is lost at each stage in the food chain, so eventually the food energy available dwindles to zero; no energy available means no further links in the food chain

3 Pyramid should have levels labelled with the name of the organism, starting with the seaweed at the bottom; each level should get progressively smaller

4 a There are more adults than children

b It will decrease; because there are fewer children to replace the adults that will die

5 a Demand will increase; because the population is increasing

b Oil is non-renewable so it will run out if we keep using it to make plastics

6 a Landfill; incinerator

b Recycling saves energy as it removes the need to make a new items from raw materials; this process uses up vast quantities of energy – more than is required to collect and sort the items in the recycling process

Page 108 Water and air pollution

1 a Chemicals that are harmful to human health and to wildlife

b Nitrates / phosphates

c The pollutants are not absorbed by the plants; so they enter groundwater, which is a source of drinking water, in the run-off from the fields

2 a The pollutants cause plants and algae to grow at a fast rate; there is an increase in dead plant material; as bacteria decompose the plant material, the amount of bacteria rises

b The bacteria use up the oxygen in the water; and create toxic chemicals

3 The oxygen concentration is low; which means that the water is highly polluted

4 a Sulfur in the fossil fuel reacts with oxygen to release sulfur dioxide; this dissolves in water vapour, which falls as acid rain or snow

b **Either**: acid rain falls into water and causes the gills of fish to overproduce mucus; this clogs the gills and the fish die of oxygen starvation; **or**: acid rain washes substances important for healthy tree growth out of the soil; poisons are released from the soil and the trees die

5 a As the distance increases, so does the number of different species of lichen

b They show that as you get further away from the city the level of pollution decreases; because many species of lichen are very sensitive to sulfur dioxide; so the higher the levels, the less variety of species of lichen there are growing

6 Car engines burn petrol and release sulfur dioxide; the sulfur dioxide gets carried in the wind to Sweden; where it dissolves in water vapour and falls as acid rain

Page 109 Recycling carbon and nitrogen

1 a Bacteria / fungi

b Decomposers break down the dead plants and animals; to form nutrients that the plants need to build new tissue

2 a Combustion/burning

b Photosynthesis

3 a From eating plants or other animals

b The animal will die; its tissue will be decomposed by decomposers; the decomposers carry out respiration, releasing carbon into the atmosphere

4 a They convert the ammonia from the decomposition of dead organic matter; to nitrates which plants can absorb

b They convert nitrates into nitrogen gas

c The water has forced oxygen out of the soil so the oxygen levels are low; this means that nitrifying bacteria die so the levels of nitrate in the soil decrease; the grass cannot make protein so cannot grow; also, as oxygen levels are low denitrifying bacteria can thrive; removing nitrates further from the soil